THE LAKE COUNTIES

Self-portrait of W. G. Collingwood, 1886

The Lake Counties

W. G. Collingwood

Edited and Revised by William Rollinson

J. M. Dent and Sons Ltd
London

THIS EDITION IS DEDICATED TO MELVYN AND CATE BRAGG

First published in this edition 1988
First published 1902
Revised 1932
Reprinted 1938, 1939, 1942 (reset)
New edition 1949

Revisions © J M Dent & Sons Ltd 1988

This book is set in Monophoto Ehrhardt and
Printed and bound in Great Britain by
Butler & Tanner Ltd, Frome and London
for J. M. Dent & Sons Ltd
91 Clapham High Street, London SW4 7TA

British Library Cataloguing in Publication Data

Collingwood, W. G.
    The Lake Counties.—[New ed] edited
    and revised by William Rollinson
    1. Lake District. Visitors guides
    I. Title   II. Rollinson, William 1937
    914.27′804858

    ISBN 0–460–04758–2

CONTENTS

I KENT AND LUNE   1

Greater Lakeland—The Kent valley—Figures in the landscape—
The port of Westmorland—A cluster of peles—Brigsteer woods—
The skalds of Crosthwaite—The Vikings' farms—Castles on the
Kent—'The terrible knitters of Dent'—Kendal church—Robin
the Devil—The Romans in Westmorland—The Lune valley—
Kentmere—The Apostle of the North

II WINDERMERE AND GRASMERE   14

The forgotten battlefield—Nabs and neuks—Bowness church—
The Finsthwaite princess—Backbarrow iron—The skulls of Cal-
garth—Low-wood—The Romans at Ambleside—High Street—
The Brigg o' Dread—Cumbrian poets—Wordsworth—Ruskin at
Dungeon Gill—Mickleden and the Stake—The home of the Soli-
tary—The Thing-mount

III FURNESS AND CARTMEL   29

Furness, the lands of the Flemings and the monks—Outlaws and
'fellows fierce'— Ancient industries—Conishead Priory and Chapel
Island—Cartmel Priory—Humphrey Head Spa and caves—
Atterpile Castle—Furness Abbey, history and ruins—Piel Castle—
Barrow—Dalton Castle and St Helen's chapel—The Giant's
Grave—Coniston Water—Ancient Bloomeries—Ruskin's home
and grave—The worthies of Coniston—The Old Man—Wonderful
Walker.

VIII FROM HELVELLYN TO STAINMOOR   125

Catstycam—Gough and his dog—Striding Edge—Mountain
names—Patterdale, its saint and its king—Lyulph and his tower—
British forts—Roman road and red deer—Dacre Castle—The four
Bears—Mayburgh and King Arthur's Round Table—The bishop
as general—Giants' caves and holy-wells—The Countess of Pem-
broke—Swindale stories—Bolton and Bewley Castle—Appleby
Castle and town—The Kaber Rigg Plot—The Bound Devil of
Kirkby Stephen—Lammerside and Pendragon.

GAZETTEER   147

WILLIAM GERSHOM COLLINGWOOD, 1854–1932

I suppose most people, at some time in their lives, have wished they could have met a much respected hero—perhaps a sportsman, writer, artist or scientist. My personal choice would be the author of this book, William Gershom Collingwood. Born in Liverpool in 1854, W. G. Collingwood was the son of William Collingwood, a noted artist, and his Swiss wife, Marie Imhoff. The site of the family home, 87 Chatham Street, is now part of the campus of the University of Liverpool. Although a Lancastrian by birth, W.G.C. was introduced to the fells and mountains of the Lake District at an early age; he visited the area on sketching tours with his father and later spent many holidays on the shores of Windermere. After a brilliant academic career at Oxford, he married and settled at Gillhead, Windermere, and in 1884 published his first book, a scientific study of the limestone Alps of Savoy. At the same time he established himself as a painter and an authoritative art historian. Influenced by Ruskin and William Morris, from whom he derived his life-long interest in Norse settlement, art and language, W.G.C. began his investigations into local dialect and place names and some of his earliest papers in the Transactions of the Cumberland and Westmorland Antiquarian and Archaeological Society are concerned with these topics. His interest in art and Scandinavian scholarship prompted his research into the pre-Norman crosses and carved stones of Cumbria and the North of England; in 1899 he edited the painstaking work of the late Rev. W. S. Calverley and the publication of this book established him as the major authority on pre-Conquest carved monuments. His work in this field culminated in the publication in 1927 of *Northumbrian Crosses of the Pre-Norman Age*, illustrated by his own distinctive line drawings which are still a source of information for modern researchers. The activities of the German miners of the Company of the Mines Royal also attracted his attention. After examining the original account books of the Augsburg company he produced *Elizabethan Keswick* (First edition, 1912, reprint, 1987), a fascinating book that brings to life these illuminating sixteenth-century documents.

Yet Collingwood was no pedantic academic; he was an accomplished musician, a great climber and swimmer and he remained a tireless walker even in old age. He was essentially a man of action who delighted in physical activity; indeed, it was said of him that one of his proudest moments was when he was returning from a visit to Iceland, bronzed and bearded, the pilot mistook him for the captain of the ship! At the end of the last century he was inexorably drawn to Iceland and with Jón Stefánsson wrote *A Pilgrimage to the Saga Steads of Iceland*, a book which even today is recognized as one of the finest ever written about the country. But he was not content merely to write about Iceland—he recorded the landscape and the local architecture in a series of evocative water colours which hold pride of place today in the National Museum in Reykjavik. Justifiably, W. G. Collingwood is acknow-ledged as one of Iceland's foremost historians.

For several years, W.G.C. acted as secretary to the ageing and infirm John Ruskin at Coniston. Following his death in 1900, Collingwood became Professor of Fine Art at University College, Reading, now the University of Reading. By this time he had established another career—that of novelist. Of his three best known historical romances, *Thorstein of the Mere, A Saga of the Northmen in Lakeland*, is arguably his finest. It was described to me by a distinguished Icelander as 'the only English saga'—W.G.C. would have been delighted by such praise. As Editor of the Transactions of the Cumberland and Westmorland Antiquarian and Archaeological Society for 32 years, he was always ready to encourage aspiring writers and researchers and fire them with his own enthusiasm. One such was the young Arthur Ransome for whom W.G.C. became an avuncular mentor and guide; Ransome ultimately became a member of the Collingwood family circle and was a close friend of W.G.C's son, Robin, who was later to become one of Britain's most respected philo-sophers and Roman historians.

Of all W.G.C.'s many accomplishments, he was, above all, a communicator. His beautifully rounded, elegant prose and lyrical descriptions of his beloved fells, lakes and dales are masterly and the clarity of his writing ensured that his work was read by the academic and the holidaymaker alike. Almost his last task was the revision of *The Lake Counties* for the printer; though he was dogged by ill health, his optimism for the future of the Lake District shone through the new preface in which he noted the changes which had taken place in the thirty years since the book was first published in 1902. Not for him the fears and apprehensions often found in old age; instead, a refreshing confidence in change:

> ... let me confess that I could never have believed our Lake Counties had changed so greatly in thirty years, and that under my very eyes. It is like looking at a kaleidoscope. But in such a toy the changes are never for the worse: always into something rich and strange.

Since his death in 1932, even greater changes have taken place, some of which would not have pleased him. He would have deplored the construction of multilane highways, the creation of further reservoirs and the insistent, ruler-straight lines of some of the forestry plantations, but at the same time he would have welcomed the establishment in 1951 of the Lake District National Park, the marking of long-distance footpaths and the opening of the Brockhole Visitors Centre which encourages visitors to appreciate and conserve the landscape which he himself loved so much.

WILLIAM ROLLINSON,
Ulverston, Cumbria.
October, 1987

Editor's Preface

In 1902 when this book was first published, the Lake District was rather different from the landscape we see today. Cumbria did not exist and the three Lakeland counties, Cumberland, Westmorland and Lancashire met at the Three Shires Stone on Wrynose Pass as they had for centuries. There was no National Park and the Forestry Commission had not yet been created; the heads of valleys such as Ennerdale and Dunnerdale were still free from the monotonous blanket of coniferous plantations. Mardale slumbered in its valley, unaware of its fate, and it was necessary to search the map carefully to find the name Sellafield, just south of the farmhouse at Yottenfews. The National Trust was in its infancy—indeed, the stripling organization acquired its first Lake District property, Brandlehow Park, in the very year *The Lake Counties* was printed. Yet even at the beginning of the century, it was clear that the tourist industry was growing; ever since those intrepid Victorians realized that they could actually ascend the mountains without a fainting fit and the need for blood-letting half way up, the Lake District has become one of Britain's major tourist areas. In 1902 most of those visitors arrived at Windermere, Keswick and Coniston by train and were conveyed by horse-drawn coaches and waggonettes to their hotels and inns, where they stayed to enjoy a week or a fortnight exploring the district. This book was written for those visitors but in many ways it is timeless; like Wordsworth's *Guide To The Lakes*, first published in 1810, it can still be read with pleasure by some of the twelve million visitors who annually flock to the Lake District National Park. In editing and revising this latest edition of W. G. Collingwood's classic book, I have tried to retain, as far as possible, his intimate style and quiet enthusiasm for this area which meant so much to him. I hope he would have approved.

Acknowledgments

PHOTOGRAPHS Norman Duerden: Sizergh Castle, Coniston Water, Elterwater, Kentmere Hall, Scafell and Wastwater, Langdale Pikes, Haweswater, Troutbeck, Tarn Hows

Simon Crouch: Pack Horse Bridge, Slate Quarry, River Eden and viaduct, Wastwater, Newlands Valley, Kirkstone Pass, Crummock Water

Landscape Only: Milburn, Brough Castle, Great Salkeld, Lowther Castle—Val Corbett; Boot Chapel—David Ward; Farm near Threlkeld—Andrew Butler

William Rollinson: Furness Abbey, Cartmel Priory

BLACK AND WHITE LINE DRAWINGS A. Reginald Smith, R.W.S.

SELF-PORTRAIT OF W. G. COLLINGWOOD by permission of Miss Janet Gnosspelius

Conversion Tables

500 feet = c. 152 metres
1,000 feet = c. 305 metres
2,000 feet = c. 610 metres
3,000 feet = c. 914 metres

Scafell Pike, the highest mountain in England, is 3,206 feet or c. 978 metres.

1 mile = 1.609 kilometres
5 miles = 8.047 kilometres
10 miles = 16.093 kilometres
20 miles = 32.187 kilometres
50 miles = 80.467 kilometres

I

KENT AND LUNE

Greater Lakeland—The Kent valley—Figures in the landscape—
The port of Westmorland—A cluster of peles—Brigsteer woods—
The skalds of Crosthwaite—The Vikings' farms—Castles on the
Kent—'The terrible knitters of Dent'—Kendal church—Robin
the Devil—The Romans in Westmorland—The Lune valley—
Kentmere—The Apostle of the North.

A FINE passage of Ruskin's on a pine-forest in the Jura tells how he took a
walk among some lower hills on the outskirts of the Alps—little seen or
known nowadays when the railway runs you straight through to Lausanne or
Lucerne—but full of a beauty of their own. He walked, he says, among the
flowers—'the wood anemone, star after star; the oxalis, troop by troop; a blue
gush of violets,' and so forth—until he came to the edge of a cliff overlooking
a deep limestone valley, with the river glittering beneath, and a hawk sailing
slowly off the opposite brows of crag: a lovely scene, charmingly painted in
words. And then he goes on to say how he tried to fancy that this was in
some new continent, uninhabited and without history, without any romantic
associations; and for the moment 'a sudden blankness and chill were cast upon
it; the flowers in an instant lost their light, the river its music; the hills became
oppressively desolate; a heaviness in the boughs of the darkened forest showed
how much of their former power had been dependent upon a life which was
not theirs; how much of the glory of the imperishable or continually renewed
creation is reflected from things more precious in their memories than it in its
renewing.'

Perhaps he overstated his case. There are splendid views in the Selkirks
and New Zealand, Norway and elsewhere. But I take it that he merely meant
what we all feel—story alone and scenery alone may interest specialists, but
the thing that appeals to us all, and charms us, and carries us out of ourselves,
is the union of story and scenery. Then you get poetry and romance, and it
need not be very ancient or momentous history to light up the landscape with
'the consecration and the poet's dream.' For most of us to have met with the
place in literature is enough.

The Lake scenery is wonderfully rich in these associations. It is no use for
us nowadays to pretend that it can impress by the height of its crags and the
breadth of its panoramas, though there are some hints of grandeur and

Low tide, Morcambe Bay

moments of mountain gloom and glory as fine as anything in the world. But it is all very tiny. A new house or a new road will dwarf a view that Gray the poet found stupendous. Coming home from Switzerland, I wonder where the tops of the mountains have gone, and the trees are so stunted and the rocks so tame that I am ready to sulk. Then follows a spell of autumn sunshine, hazy, opalescent, magical; faint blue above and below; 'an unsubstantial fairy place'; and Wordsworth's runecraft bewitches me 'till I do beget that golden time again.' Or on the cloud-swept moor the cairn-dwellers come out, clad in skins of wolf and bear; or by the lake shore at twilight the ashes of the ancient furnace flame up, and the men from the hall ride past with hawk and hound. The scene is so peopled, what does it matter how large the canvas is—so rich in detail and variety, why trouble about the smallness of the picture-frame? And, if I could put the figures into the landscape for you as I see them for myself, I think even a new book on the Lakes would be worth writing.

Another reason for the attempt is on this wise. Our tiny Lake District, properly and strictly so called, lies within a circle of about thirty miles across. A good walker can go right through it in a day. But all round this inner circle lies a fringe of hill country, full of charming scenery, full of interesting story, which is far less known than it deserves. Of course, who goes to Lakeland goes to view the lakes, and is disappointed if there is not a sheet of water in the picture. But some of the finest dales have no lakes, like Eskdale and the Duddon valley. Some of the prettiest have no great mountains overhanging, like the Winster and the Rusland valleys, the Kent, the Lune, and Edenside. The guide-books say there is nothing to detain the traveller, and so the traveller drives through Windermere or Keswick, rushes from height to height, and tires out 'admiration, hope, and love.' In old times they lingered on the journey; posted quietly through the outer dales, and found them charming; crossed the sands for a little excitement, and slowly made their way towards the Delectable Mountains in the distance: wise feasters, who refused not the soup and the fish, and so were not gluttons of the turkey and plum pudding. In these times also there are many who have discovered the outer dales, not less attractive than the fashionable centres, more genuine in their yet unspoilt rusticity; where you see the ancient pastoral life of Wordsworth's days, clean gone from Grasmere and Ambleside; the old-world cottages and manor halls; the real Dales-folk, not the new-come population of 'resorts.' I should like to take you with me into such places too, as well as up Skiddaw and down Windermere; and so to widen out the boundaries of our district from the Lakes of the guide-books to the whole of the Lake counties, all Cumberland, Westmorland, and North Lancashire, every mile of which is worth exploring.

I shall not be able to describe every turn in the path or every point of view; fortunately, signposts are plentiful; unfortunately, when one is really lost in a mist on the mountains or on the moors, no guide-book is of much use.[1] For many details I must refer to a map or the gazetteer at the end of the volume; for much of the further information which is sure to be wanted, to the local literature of each neighbourhood. But I think it is possible to perambulate the counties, omitting no really important place, and pointing out by the way most of the things which a resident would show to his friend from a distance.

.   .   .   .

For many people, the first sight of the distant blue Lakeland fells comes just north of Lancaster as they speed northward along the M6 motorway. For the exile, this is the moment when he knows that he is home, but let us turn aside from the noise and frenzy of the traffic and follow the old road to Burton, a little village that stands at the foot of the rising limestone fell. Eight or nine hundred years ago this was called Bortun in Kent-dale; it is down in Domesday book. Under Charles II it was made a market-town, and then became a centre for the corn trade of the neighbourhood; the old-fashioned, comfortable-looking houses round the market-place, with its cross, give it a Cranford-like air of retired respectability, clean and tidy, though they are irregular and picturesque. If one were an artist who painted nostalgic rustic scenes, here would be the backgrounds ready made; and the clean limestone of the neighbourhood, which goes so well with green leaves and grass, makes one say: 'I have seen this in a picture somewhere!' And yet I never heard of any one painting Burton. Through the long street and out of the town at the north end stands the church.

It is nearly always worth while looking into a church, even if you have to ask for the key and spend a few pence on the guide; there are very few churches in all this district without some bit of interest, even when they seem rebuilt or hopelessly restored. Very often the restoration or rebuilding has brought to light fragments of ancient times quite as valuable as all that has been destroyed by the process; and here it was the case. In a corner there are some dusty stones; one is the shaft of a grave-cross set up over some thane or lady

1 Unless it is a 'Wainright' [Editor's note].

of the place even earlier than Domesday. See the elaborate interlacing of knots on one edge and the maze-pattern on the other, the ornament like that of a Viking brooch on the back, and these rude reliefs on the face. The carver knew little of anatomy, but no doubt he meant that figure under the crooked arch for Christ rising from out of the cave tomb, with the glory round His head, and the palm branch and cross in His hands, while He tramples underfoot the old serpent, writhing round to attack Him in vain. Overhead there are Mary and John by the untenanted Cross: 'He is not here; He is risen!' And now, is this not something of a story for us at the outset of our journey? That this church is indeed a very old church, here for nearly a thousand years; that in 'Bortun' before the Norman Conquest there were English folk worshipping the same Christ and dying in the same faith, and that we to-day can see and touch the very stone they carved—does not this put figures into the landscape?

Northward, through Holme, it is an easy run to Milnthorpe. This was the port of Westmorland once upon a time, though the Lancaster and Kendal Canal, opened 1819, and the railway in 1846, put an end to any chance of traffic at so tiny a harbour. But formerly it must have been of real importance, and there is very curious evidence of the fact in a group of pele-towers and a group of early churches clustering round. In the fourteenth and fifteenth centuries, wherever there was a possibility of invasion, they built a small square pele-tower, with very thick walls, a vaulted store-room below, a narrow-windowed chamber above, and higher still a more airy room for the ladies. When danger threatened, they retreated from their wooden or wattle-built houses and crowded into the tower, driving the cattle into a little walled yard beside it, or into some hiding-place in the wood. The roof of the tower, battlemented and turreted, was their fighting deck, from which they shot and threw at the enemy beneath, who usually tried to burn them out. But these raiders were not come to stay; they rarely had provisions or material for a siege; they wanted the cattle and anything they could carry off, without killing the goose that laid the golden eggs. And so the folk in the fort were pretty safe; and when the last trooper had ridden away, they set to work rebuilding the wattle-and-daub homestead, collecting the strayed cattle, and saving what could be saved; and life went on as before.

Now in the north of our district towers are at the fords of rivers and at the passes through the mountains. But ordinary raids never came so far south as this. One or two great invasions swept over the country, against which peles were no more defence than a sand-castle against the tide. Why are these six or seven ancient towers close around this spot—Sizergh and Levens, Dallam and Beetham, and Hazelslack, Arnside and Wraysholme—except for defence against visitors by sea? We have no definite records that I know of describing attacks by pirates or a hostile fleet at this particular spot, but all along the coast it was possible, and not infrequent. Here, too, if boats—and the ancient boats were small and shallow—could come up to trade, they could come to raid.

If we take a run from Milnthorpe round by Arnside and Silverdale, we shall pass Dallam Tower, once a pele but rebuilt 1722, and Hazelslack Tower and the ruined tower at Arnside, visible against the sky from the railway. It is pretty scenery too. The estuary of the Kent, when the tide is up, is quite as good as the Lakes, and in some ways even more picturesque: for while there are mountains not far away, close at hand the limestone breaks into white crags at the water's edge, and dark trees crown the rocks with more than a touch of romance.

Silverdale also has its woodland walks, clean limestone cottages, and bold rocky shore. It has a lake of its own, deep and clear, being in line with the curious chasm of Troughbarrow, where, they say, folk used to hide their cattle in times of trouble. And at Beetham Hall or Castle we come to another site of a pele; near it, in the church, are the defaced effigies of the lord and lady who once lived there, the last Thomas de Betham, Knight of the Shire for Westmorland in 1425, and his wife.

The church—apart from its pretty site near the little river, which, close at hand, breaks into a waterfall by the mill and the bridge—is interesting as one of our earliest foundations. At the base of a pillar in the north aisle a hoard of coins was discovered, which must have been put there in the reign of William Rufus, and collected from the middle of the eleventh century onwards. This place is called Biedun in Domesday, that is, Beda-holm (on the analogy of Ergune, Arkholm), and whoever in those times had a hundred coins must have been rich. The mere fact of this fine stone church being built in early Norman days means wealth and population; another result of the sea-trade, and at a much earlier time than the age of pele-building. So when we pass through Milnthorpe again we shall look on it with more respect. We may picture to ourselves the Frisian chapmen in their barge-like vessels floating up with the tide, and chaffering on the shore with Anglo-Saxon or Norse-speaking thanes and churls from Kent-dale and Lunes-dale and all round about; come to barter wool for wine and so forth. Even three or four hundred years before Domesday there were merchants and their ships here. I will show you what seems to me evidence of the fact.

Little more than a mile north of Milnthorpe is Heversham—Evres-haim in Domesday—on the hillside looking over the rock-set Kent, and out to the sea and the mountains. There is a fine old church, finely placed, and in the porch a most precious monument. You need to see it with a discerning eye, for it is as battered as a Parthenon slab, but no less classic in its art. You can tell at once that the sculptor knew his business; no rude stone-cutter like him of Burton; the grapebunches among their graceful stems, the 'little foxes that spoil the vines,' with bushy tails and pricked ears, are work of that first great

English school of art taught by Italian masters in the eighth and ninth centuries. We shall travel far before we see the like of it again; but when we do, it will be near the chief early ports of Cumberland—Ravenglass and Workington. I think the inference is plain; where trade was, wealth came and art followed, even in those ancient days before King Alfred.

The neighbouring halls invite us less than Brigsteer woods, where the lily of the valley grows wild, and the damson orchards of the nestling cottages along Scout Scar, and along the Lyth that answers to it across the peat-flats and fields of the Gilpin valley. It is a pleasant ride past Helsington to Underbarrow, or by Cunswick Hall, once 'Connyswick,' perhaps in the twelfth century, like Coniston and Cunsey, meaning 'King's Village,' the seat of the old Catholic and Tory Layburnes until they lost it in the Jacobite rising of 'the Fifteen'; and by Crook Hall, the seventeenth-century seat of the Philipsons, and the old tower of their church, all that was left at the rebuilding, and then by the Wild Boar Inn turning down the dainty little dale of Gilpin to Crosthwaite, where those rustic skalds of the century before last rhymed and rhapsodized in their cups—John Audland and Jamie Muckelt. They, and many more up and down the country, had a trick of talking in verse, exactly like the heroes of the Viking age, and sometimes they made neat rhymes which were remembered. Audland, once falling foul of some lawyer, Ulverston way, vented his wrath in these terms:

> God meäd men, and men meäd money;
> God meäd bees, and bees meäd honey.
> Bit the Divil himself meäd lawyers and 'tornies,
> And pleäced them i' U'ston and Dalton i' Forness.

The first couplet no doubt he had heard before; the later lines we have often heard since, quoted as a household word. Once, turning out of the 'Dog' in Dalton with empty pockets, he gave his IOU in this way:

> I, John Audland, afore I gang hence,
> Owe thee, Betty Woodburn, just six and twea pence!
> And coom Thorsda' sennit I'll pay off t' scoore,
> And wha knas bit I may spend twice as mich moore?

Even yet Crosthwaite and the Lyth (*Hlídh* is the Icelandic or Norse for a long hillside; *Leath* ward in Cumberland is the district on the *Hlídh* of the Pennines) are primitive and rustic. Whoever has read Mrs Humphry Ward's *Helbeck of Bannisdale* knows what the mountain chapel and the fellside farm are like, and Brigsteer woods in spring. The old hall of the story seems to have been studied from the next two places we have to visit, after riding over Gilpin bridge and back to the Kent.

Levens and Sizergh are both examples of pele-towers gradually enlarged into Elizabethan and Jacobean mansions and enriched by the continued inhabitance of wealthy familes.[1] Levens appears in Domesday, and Sizergh not long after as 'Sigaritherge,' i.e. the dairy farm of Sigrid, I suppose, lady or dairymaid of Sedgwick or Beethwaite, or some great house in the valley, who sent her cattle up to pasture among the woods in summer. In 1208 one Sigrid, daughter of Uchtred, had land hereabouts, though one cannot say that she was the person in question. The Anglian or Norse farmers held large tracts of ground only partially cleared, and not at all drained. They sent their various flocks and herds to graze wherever there was a bite to be got. On the swampy mire the calves or horses were turned out, and the custom has left us such names as Calf-mire and Hest-mire; or the horses roamed on the Hest-fell or the Capplerigg; and the calves up the Calf-dale. Calder in a Norse district of Scotland is, in a saga, written Kálfa-dals-á, calf dale-water; Grisedale must be where the pigs (*griss*) fed, and Swinside was where the swine were pastured. But in time the chalet or sæter on the summer hill, used at first only for shepherds or herdsmen in the summer, grew into a homestead, whence Satter-thwaite and Seathwaite; and the great early estates were broken up into smaller holdings. Thwaite, as in Iceland, seems usually in these parts to mean *a field sloping down to a mire or mere*; not simply a clearing or 'ridding.' Round the house was a garth. We shall see old dykes which probably enclosed the *tún* or home-field of early farmers, the one bit of grassland which was manured, and after hay-making kept the few cattle which were not killed in autumn. In the bigg-land and haver-thwaite were the acres of barley or oats, and so forth. Most of the local names refer to ancient farming usages, with here and there the owner's personal name fossilized, as it were, in a stratum of old nouns and adjectives, worn out of shape like pebbles in a rock. But they tell us much of their history, and not the least interesting point is the traceable growth of a proud castle like Sizergh from the shieling where Sigrid's cows were grazed in summer.

Under the third Edward, after the Scots had been stirred up to active hostility by the high hand of the first and the weak hand of the second, pele-building began: we have seen why there was need hereabouts. The Redmaynes of Levens and the Stricklands of Sizergh built their peles[2] and enclosed their parks, and, somewhat later, added stone-built halls and kitchens, to make the dwelling-house, formerly wooden, as proud and permanent as the fortress, and to imitate the grander lords who lived in castles all of stone. In Elizabeth's time another fit of building ran through the district like an epidemic: it was

---

1 Both houses are open to the public [Editor's note].

2 'Pele' for 'pele-tower' is not correct, say the purists, but it has long been used, and by writers of some authority. (See p. 92)

an imitation of new fashions, first adopted by the wealthiest, then followed by the greater squires, and filtering down, later on, to the smaller folk.[1] The Stricklands built wings to their old house, surrounding a court; and Sir James Bellingham, whose ancestor, Alan, in 1489, had bought Levens, did the same for his mansion. Rich carved wainscots and staircases were added, plaster-work ceilings, handsome fireplaces; and the collection of family portraits and heirlooms gradually filled the rooms with beautiful things. In 1689 Levens passed to Colonel James Grahme,[2] who had been Privy Purse to James II, and remained a Jacobite. King James's gardener, Monsieur Beaumont, had lost his place at the Revolution and came to Levens. It was he who laid out the gardens, with their quaint bowling green and clipped trees, which set the fashion throughout the neighbourhood. You see clipped yews at most of the farmhouses dating back to the eighteenth century. Later still, there have been restorations and additions to both houses, or they could not be as they are now—beautiful private mansions; all the more beautiful because still cared for, and not left, like some, to the owls, or like others, degraded into barns and byres.

Kendal is, of course, the name of the valley, Kent-dale. The church town therein was Kirkby-in-Kendal. In the days when Sigrid's *erg* was a shieling, I suppose the lord and master of the Kirk-by lived in a wooden house on the top of that moated mound up All Hallows Lane—the Castle How or Castle Law—where an obelisk was erected in 1788. These moated mounds were the usual 'castles' of the gentry before the age of pele towers, and we shall find them in many parts of the district. Often they have a square garth or base-court somewhere near, as a fold for cattle, and perhaps as an enclosure for the wattle-and daub cots of the peasants who kept the herds. In some cases this moated mound—mote-hill, castle-how, or burg—grew into a medieval castle, as the tower grew into an Elizabethan mansion, and so its original form is almost lost in later building. Sometimes the site was deserted for a stronger or more convenient one. Here at Kendal, across the river, is another castle, which is best known as the birthplace of Catherine Parr, the last and cleverest of the queens of Henry VIII. The earliest part of the walls now in ruins may be as old as the time of Henry III, and the earthworks, great trenches, and ramparts around the curtain-wall may be earlier; but perhaps the Norman lord of Kendal, whose predecessors had lived on the castle-how, chose this as a better site for his fortress and moved there in the late twelfth century. It is hardly likely that there were ever two rival castles so close together,

---

1 The so-called 'Great Rebuilding in stone', when the timber-framed farmhouses were demol-ished and re-built in stone, seems to have occurred between approximately 1640 and 1750 [Editor's note].

2 Or Graham, of the family of Netherby.

Kendal was a market-town under Richard Cœur-de-Lion,[1] and when Edward III was king, certain Flemings, headed by John Kemp, are said, but not with any authority, to have settled there, and introduced the woollen manufacture, which soon became famous. We have all heard of 'Kendal Green,' which was a rough drugget dyed with woad and the dyer's broom (*Genista tinctoria*). Kendal coatings, woollen goods, though the name gives us our familiar word 'cotton,' were mostly white, or coloured in spots by hand, and thence called 'ermines' or 'spotted cottons.' The town was also headquarters of the great country industry of hand-knitted stockings. What that industry (well named) was like is told in the famous dialect story preserved by Southey from the lips of Betty Yewdale, who was sent from Langdale as a child, somewhere in the eighteenth century, to learn knitting at Dent.

'We o' knit,' she said, 'as hard as we cud drive, striving whilk cud knit t' hardest yan again anudder: we hed our darracks [dayworks] set afore we com fra heam [to school] in t' mworning, and if we dudn't get them dun we warrant to gang to our dinners. They hed o' macks o' contrivances to larn us to knit swift; t' maister wad wind three or four clues togedder, for three or four barns [it is always *barns*[2] not *bairns*, in the Lake District] to knit off—*that* at knit slawest raffled tudders' yarn, and then she gat weel thumpt. Then we ust at sing a mack of a sang, whilk we were at git at t'en on [which we were to get to the end of] at every needle, ca'ing ower t' neames of o' t'fwoak in t' daal; but Sally and me wud never ca' Dent fwoak, sea we ca'ed Langdon [Langdale] fwoak. T' sang wos:

> Sally an' I, Sally an' I,
> For a good pudding pye;
> Taa hoaf wheat, an' tudder hoaf rye,
> Sally an' I for a good pudding pye.

We sang this, altering t' neames at every needle; and when we com at t' end, cried "Off," an' began again; and sea we streave on o' t' day through.' In 1795 Joseph Budworth, writing of the Kendal area, claimed that 'both men and women were knitting stockings as they drove their peat carts into the town,' and by 1801 2,400 pairs of stockings was the average weekly supply sent to Kendal market.

This knitting-trade went out when knee-breeches were no longer worn; but the leather and tobacco trades[3] of Kendal, important in the seventeenth century, still continue. The ancient guilds are described in the quaint 'Boke

---

1 The charter was granted in 1189 [Editor's note].

2 *Barn* is the Norwegian word for child [Editor's note].

3 Kendal is the home of 'K' shoes and the snuff industry still continues [Editor's note].

off Recorde,' giving all the details of the medieval town. In the eighteenth century, before turnpike roads were made hereabouts, some three hundred and fifty pack-horses, carrying the manufactures of the neighbourhood, passed through Kendal weekly; some of the old saddles and bells, relics of this curious traffic, are to be seen in the Kendal Museum in Station Road, with many other local antiquities and specimens of natural history. It was not until 1786 that the first mail-coach to London began to run; in 1846 the railway was opened, and Kendal became a modern town.

But there are many pleasant reminders of the past in its two long streets and riverside buildings; not a little picturesqueness in spite of the prevailing grey. Abbot Hall is a fine old house[1] and there are others worth stopping to look at as you walk down to the parish church by the Kent. The church has been rebuilt over and over again, in one part or another, but never so modernized as to spoil its interest. The four rows of pillars, the carved oak screens, ancient monuments, and tattered banners, make you feel that you are in a real old church, not in an architect's imitation. The Strickland Tomb is of the fourteenth or fifteenth century, and the alabaster monument of a boy under a black marble canopy dates from 1656. The Parr Tomb is probably fifteenth century. The Bellingham Tomb is ancient, but with modern brasses; several ancient brasses, however, are in that chapel. Quaint verses on 'Mr Ravlph Tirer,' vicar, who died in 1627, are on a brass within the altar rails. The painter Romney's cenotaph is there,[2] and Thomas West, the Furness antiquary, is buried just outside the Strickland Chapel. The helmet called the 'Rebel's Cap' is said to have fallen from the head of Robert Philipson, 'Robin the Devil,' when he rode into church one Sunday during the Civil Wars to challenge the Parliament Colonel Briggs, who had besieged him on the island in Windermere: a local legend which has been put into many a book and ballad, and used by Scott in *Rokeby*, 'dressed up,' as he said of his incidents, 'in a cocked hat and feathers.' I do not know that the story has ever been disproved: of course it has been doubted.

A mile south of the church there is a loop in the river, the Watercrook, and in the peninsula so formed is the site of a Roman fort—Roman Kendal, seven hundred years older than the burg on the castle-how. Early antiquaries, misled by what seemed like a resemblance in the name, thought this to be the Concangium which was somewhere in the north of Britain, and the Ordnance Survey unfortunately perpetuated the error. But the Roman name was almost certainly Alauna and we know that this was a place of some importance, for various relics have been dug up. Most interesting among them is the tombstone

---

1 Abbot Hall now houses a splendid art gallery and the outstanding Museum of Lakeland Life and Industry [Editor's note].

2 But Romney is buried in the churchyard at Dalton-in-Furness [Editor's note].

(now in the British Museum) for an officer of the 20th Legion, with an inscription that goes on to say: 'Any one putting another corpse into this grave will be fined.'[1]

Hence a Roman road crossing the Kent ran up the Scar and over the hills to Windermere and Ambleside, where we shall meet it again; southward it ran to Lancaster with a branch to Overburrow, near Kirkby Lonsdale. This was probably the first great road through the district; as it is very unlikely that any regular Roman route crossed the sands of Morecambe Bay, we may take it that this was the main line of traffic to their harbour at Ravenglass, and thence round the coast to Carlisle and the Great Wall. Another main military road ran north and south from Manchester to Carlisle, though the trough of the Lune, near Tebay. At Low Borrow Bridge close to the M6 motorway, the platform of the Roman fort is clearly seen in the narrow, deep valley of the foaming Lune. It housed an infantry battalion of 500 men within its three acres. The fort is, of course, the burg or *borrow* from which the bridge and tributary valley get their names. The fort was first explored in 1883, and the gateways, hypocausts, and remains of a Roman bridge were found.

Returning southward, we might follow the Lune down its beautiful dale. Sedbergh, the home of a famous school, lies to the left, and at Middleton, where there is an interesting fifteenth-century hall, with Elizabethan woodwork, you can see a Roman milestone, re-erected in 1836 near the spot where it was disinterred. It bears the numerals 53, being the distance from here to Roman Carlisle. Half-way between Barbon and Casterton there is a curious old cross, set up in the field where it was found, and near the Roman road; perhaps the gravestone of some one slain in battle, because it was on these roads, used for centuries after the Romans had left, that hostile armies travelled and encountered. And a mile south of Kirkby Lonsdale there is the site of a very great and important Roman fort at Burrow, the Borch (burg) of Domesday book. About two miles from Burrow at Cowan Bridge was the school at which Charlotte Brontë and her sisters had such bitter experiences.

Kirkby in Lonsdale is the twin sister of Kirkby in Kent-dale. It has not grown so populous, but its origin and early history are much the same. Near a Roman fort, and a Roman road, some early lord held his burg—the moated mound in the vicarage garden. Under Henry III the place grew into a market-town: even before 1275 there was a bridge over the river, of course not the present 'Devil's Bridge,' though this is ancient. The church was a fine one in Norman days, and some Norman work is still to be seen in it; most part was rebuilt in the thirteenth century, and in 1486 was founded the Middleton Chapel, containing an effigy, which, though mutilated, seems to be of about that date.

1 Recent excavation of the site suggests that the fort could not be earlier than late Flavian (A.D. 69–A.D. 96) [Editor's note].

The Devil's Bridge, Kirkby Lonsdale

Returning to Kendal over the green hills of Westmorland, we might look for the traces of a Roman road between High Biggins and Sealford, passing a prehistoric earthwork half-way on the left; and then through Lupton to Preston Patrick, where an abbey of Premonstratensians was founded in 1119 and afterwards removed to Shap. The church has some bits of early grotesque built into it inside, and the old hall is a pele with Jacobean wings added. But there are so many such remains between Lune and Kent that no single itinerary can take them in: most of them will be found noted in the gazetteer at the end of this volume. We must hasten on to Kendal again, which might be headquarters for many an expedition—to Hilton, and Firbank, and Killington, or to the ancient forts on Helmfell and Hayfell, or by Selside Hall to lonely Bannisdale, and up Long Sleddale or to the ancient tower and modern papermills of Burneside. Note that Burneside is not short for Burn-side but for Bronolf's Head, and is therefore pronounced Burn-e-side. There are no burns in the Lake District in the sense of brooks, though some with other meanings, which deceive the unwary. I will leave to the gazetteer even the mention of many interesting scenes round about, and make for Kentmere.

Staveley is at the gate of the dale. There are pretty lanes, slowly ascending the valley on either side of the stream, and mountains ahead, within reach at last. Three miles up the road on the right hand of the stream is Millrigg, above which there is one of those curious sites of heaps and holes, with a prehistoric rampart enclosing them, once known as British villages. Another, very similar, may be found about two miles to the south-west, near the Borrans in Hugill. From this ancient homestead one looks down on the fields which used to be the mere of the Kent, now drained and formerly exploited for a deposit of diatomite. During dredging operations in 1955 a wooden boat, thought to date from the tenth century, was uncovered; it is now in the

National Maritime Museum at Greenwich. Although the valley has lost its original 'mere', modern hands have created a tarn at the head of the dale. Kentmere Reservoir was dammed in the nineteenth century to provide a constant head of water for the mills further down the valley; here the scenery is impressive, with Rainsborrow and Ill Bell, Froswick and the Gavel, precipitous above, and the winding path up Nan Bield pass and over to Mardale and Haweswater.

When Kentmere Hall, the old ruin half hidden among the trees beneath the mountain flank, was a fine new castlet, the Gilpins lived there, lords of Kentmere-dale.[1] Richard Gilpin it was who killed the last wild boar, and took for motto 'Dictis factisque simplex.' John, of comic memory, you will certainly recall; and he may have been some far-away scion of the family, not wholly degenerate, for he stuck to his saddle! But in the early days of Henry VIII there was a lad born here and christened Bernard. His uncle, the head of the family, had fallen on Bosworth field, one of King Richard's captains of horse; and so Bernard's father had come to the estate, married Margaret Layton of Dalemain, and brought up six sons, of whom one became ambassador to Holland for Queen Elizabeth, and another was this Bernard. One Sunday at the church, that same little church besides its old yew tree on the hill, a travelling friar preached. The boy listened, and, turning up to his mother said: 'Mother, how dare he preach against drinking? He was drunk in our hall last night!'

There spoke the little Reformer, who became the Apostle of the North; by mere sincerity and straightforwardness the one most powerful for good throughout the turbulent Northern lands in that troubled age. It was his horse that the robbers brought back, 'for they knew that any who robbed Master Gilpin would go straight into hell.' It was he who took down the glove, hung in church for a challenge, and made it his text against violence. Ordered to London for the stake, 'It is well,' he said; 'I had looked for this.' His horse fell, and his leg was broken.

'Is it well now?' asked his captors.

But before they could move him, Queen Mary, the persecutor, was dead. Elizabeth I restored him to his position as Archdeacon of Durham.

---

1 There is some evidence that the Hall was occupied for some time by the Stapleton family [Editor's note].

II

WINDERMERE AND GRASMERE

The forgotten battlefield—Nabs and neuks—Bowness church—
The Finsthwaite princess—Backbarrow iron—The skulls of Cal-
garth—Low-wood—The Romans at Ambleside—High Street—
The Brigg o' Dread—Cumbrian poets—Wordsworth—Ruskin at
Dungeon Gill—Mickleden and the Stake—The home of the Soli-
tary—The Thing-mount.

'IF you go down into Cumberland by the railroad, live in some frequented hotel, and explore the hills with merry companions, however much you may enjoy your tour or their conversation, depend upon it you will never choose so much as one pictorial subject rightly; you will not see into the depth of any. But take knapsack and stick, walk towards the hills by short day's journeys—ten or twelve miles a day—taking a week from some starting-place sixty or seventy miles away; sleep at the pretty little wayside inns or the rough village ones; then take the hills as they tempt you, following glen or shore as your eye glances or your heart guides, wholly scornful of local fame or fashion, and of everything which it is the ordinary traveller's duty to see or pride to do. Never force yourself to admire anything when you are not in the humour; but never force yourself away from what you feel to be lovely in search of anything better; and gradually the deeper scenes of the natural world will unfold themselves to you in still increasing fulness of passionate power....'

That is as true as it ever was. We have not found our journey to Windermere dull, though it has been longer than sixty or seventy miles; and I think the view, at last, of lake and mountain from Orrest Head will be all the more delightful after the pastoral overture that has led up to it. On a clear summer evening it is best; or when the snow is half-way down the hills, and the woods are a brown glow in the level winter sunshine. Coniston fells, to the left; the Scafell group in front and Langdale Pikes with sharp-set, rocky outlines; and to the right, the softer, though still massive, forms of the Grasmere mountains, and Ill Bell rising above Troutbeck. Below this last, from Ings church towards Troutbeck Bridge and the lake ran the Roman road. The name Orrest is that of a farm close to it, on the flattish bit of ground between us and the Troutbeck stream, and this name is one of the few which are not merely pastoral, for *Orrest* is a late Anglo-Saxon word derived from Norse *orrosta*, 'battle.' It was on the old roads, we saw, that armies encountered, and here must once have been a fight of more than ordinary moment, in the days when such Scandinavian words were in use.

The long lake is spread out like a map; you see that it is not really one lake, but two at least, joined by narrow channels at the group of islands which nearly cut the two great basins apart. Between the largest island (Belle Isle, or more properly Longholme) and the Ferry there is another shallow basin; and the lower reach has two successive deeps. Windermere is really a chain of lakes, and one of its greatest charms is the variety you find in following its river-like course. 'It's a' nabs and neuks, is Windermer-watter,' but you cannot see the nabs and neuks from the steamer; only from a small boat and at leisure. Some of them are gone for ever, filled up with fancy boat-houses and landscape-gardening; many are still unspoilt, sweet little rocky coves, wooded above and fringed with ferns, where the fishermen in old days used to draw their nets and boil their gipsy kettles for breakfast in the sunrise. That is Windermere; not the skyline, for it has no great mountains near; but the shore-line.

Modern Windermere and Bowness are well able to speak for themselves; the wayfaring man cannot err therein. The fame of Professor Wilson, the once-renowned Christopher North, who lived at Elleray, is almost as forgotten as his house, which was pulled down many years ago. There is one beautiful heirloom of antiquity left, the east window in Bowness church, originally in Cartmel Priory (not Furness Abbey); and though restored, so well restored that there is no cause to complain.

If you wish to see what the villages were like at the time when the old writers praised them, come to Winster and Cartmel Fell. The valley is one which has no lake, and so it has been let alone. Narrower and more scenic than the Gilpin valley, it is more domestic and populous than Kentmere or Long Sleddale; and for any one who likes the true picturesque it is a perfect feast. The old post office with its typical northern porch and door; Bowland Bridge where Jonas Barber made 'grandfather clocks' in the early eighteenth century;[1] the ford and rustic footbridge at Wood farm; the hanging woods, with here and there a bit of crag jutting out, and the tumbled fields, beset with bare rock, but blossoming in early summer with damson and apple-bloom, and flowering all the season through: this is like what Wordsworth saw. A friend of his, naturalist and poet, lived hereabouts—William Pearson of Borderside, one who roamed and returned to the dear little native vale.

South of Bowland Bridge one can follow the lanes on both sides of the Winster. On the east side there are two interesting old houses, Cowmire Hall, a pele tower with a seventeenth-century mansion built about it, and Poolbank, with quaint balcony and plaster-work mantelpiece in the old parlour. Farther down the lane, fringed with coppice and orchard, beneath the scar of the long

---

1 See Brian Loomes, *Westmorland Clocks and Clockmakers*, 1974.

limestone height of Whitbarrow, lies Witherslack; the hall, a seat of Lord
Derby; the church built 1671, among beautiful surroundings, by the bequest
of John Barwick (1618–1669) who became Dean of St Paul's. Somewhere near
here Sir Thomas Broughton, who joined the rebellion of Lambert Simnel in
1487, took refuge in the woods and lived long in hiding; faithful tenants carried
food to his cave, and buried him at last in the forest. About two hundred years
ago the grave was known, but now it is not to be found.

West of the Winster is the rustic parish of Cartmel Fell, with many a pretty
and ancient farm: the inn at Strawberrybank and Hodge Close with its balcony
like Poolbank, and the chapel of St Anthony, beautifully and intelligently
restored, with its most romantic garth, all daffodils in spring beneath the yew
trees, and curious old box pews and fifteenth-century glass from Cartmel
Priory. Rising behind the homesteads—for there is no regular village, but only
scattered farms on the steep hillside—the moors and woods go up to reach
their highest point in Gummer's How, over a thousand feet above sea. Hence
you view Windermere in all its length, the whole panorama of mountains, the
Leven valley winding seaward, Newby Bridge below your feet, the Lakeside
station with trains and steamers like toys, and Finsthwaite hill over against
you with its tower on the top, monument of naval victories of Nelson's day—
itself now something of an antiquity. Finsthwaite village lies in a little dell
behind the hill; in the churchyard is buried a princess, the villagers say, with
wonderful fair hair; she came to live in seclusion at the Waterside house in
1745, and was buried in 1771 by the name of 'Clementina Johannes Sobiesky
Douglas,' arguably the illegitimate daughter of Charles Edward Stuart 'the
Young Pretender,' by Clementina Walkinshaw.

Down the Leven—a beautiful river every yard of it from Newby Bridge to
Greenodd—is Backbarrow, once famous for its ancient ironfoundry, the last
place where charcoal was used in smelting; the old furnace with its date 1711
is still to be seen.[1] I have known a Coniston quarryman walk there to get a
Backbarrow 'gavelock' (crowbar), for a quarryman's life hangs, literally, on
his gavelock, and 'Backbarrow iron will never give.' Here, early in the eighteenth-
century, John Wilkinson helped his father to make flat irons; then invented
iron ships, discovered the secret of the blast furnace, and became one of the
pioneers of our great English industry. However, there was an unhappy chapter
in the industrial history of this small village. In the eighteenth century the
falls of the Leven spawned another industry—cotton. The mill at Backbarrow
earned an unenviable reputation for the ill-treatment of its child labourers
some of whom were 7 years old. In the early nineteenth century the working
day began at 5 a.m. and finished at 8 p.m. and on Sundays the children cleaned
the machinery from 6 a.m. until noon. By 1890 the site was used for the

1 Sadly now in a very poor state of repair [Editor's note].

manufacture of ultramarine dye and this continued until 1981. The mill is now a luxury hotel.

There are sites along the margin of Windermere not without story. There is a high bluff, just below Blakeholme, which the fishers used to call Cornelius, from an outlaw who harboured there; when or why I know not. At Silverholme I used to be told there was a 'kist o' silver ligging under t' watter,' and of course turned treasure seeker in the days of my youth. At Graythwaite there is the Elizabethan hall of the Rawlinsons, and hidden behind its jealous wall the ancient home of the Sandys. Basswick, just above Catcrag and its pretty little island, was famous for an awful 'boggle' that met Graythwaite folk coming home from the Ferry of a Saturday night; and opposite, at Beech Hill, was a wraith no less terrible of renown. Hammerhole, south of Rawlinson Nab, was the landing spot for Cunsey forge in the old days of smelting by charcoal, and up through the coppice, by the beck, you still find the slag and ashes blackening the ground. Storrs was the grand Italian hall where Scott and Canning and all the Lake poets were entertained with a regatta and high feasting by Mr Bolton in 1825; later, the home of the first 'stroke' of the first Oxford boat that rowed against Cambridge, in top hats and in the year 'twenty-nine, and won the race. He was the Rev. Thomas Staniforth, who died at an advanced age, late in the last century, and his fine old house was turned into an hotel.

The Ferry—one of the most pleasant spots on Windermere—has its history too. Here, time out of mind, has been the natural crossing-place. Here in 1635, on the 19th October at sunset, the great boat sank and forty-seven persons, some of them said to be of a wedding-party returning from Hawkshead church, were drowned. The legend of the Crier of Claife, the ghostly passenger who calls for a boat and haunts the ferryman to his death, seems to be hardly a genuine folk-tale in the form usually given, although it is very likely some such tale was current; I remember also a vague story of a phantom boat with terrible sights aboard, as told me when I was a boy. In the beginning of the nineteenth century the Ferry Inn became the scene of annual wrestling, under Professor Wilson's patronage, and it was kept up until about 1861, after which the sports were held at Grasmere. Then the long, low cottage inn gave place to the big hotel,[1] and the old romance of clogs and pewter was succeeded by the romance of boating flannels and tea in the garden. But Claife heights are so noble above, and the wooded islands are so sweet around, that the Ferry is still and always must be an enjoyable spot for a summer day.

The 'tea-caddy' on the Long Island was built by Mr English, sadly belying his name, in or soon after 1774; he found the remains of pavements, which some have supposed to indicate a Roman villa. The Philipsons had a tower

---

1 Now the headquarters of the Freshwater Biological Association [Editor's note].

here, besieged by Colonel Briggs in the Civil Wars, and pulled down by Mr English. Before then, and as early as 1272, the de Lindeseys had their manor house here, which came to de Coucy through the famous Lady Christiana. On Lady Holme there used to be a medieval chapel, which has entirely disappeared. The whole of the lake and its shores up to high-water mark are reckoned in the township of Applethwaite and in the county of Westmoreland, as formerly belonging to the barons of Kendal, though more than two-thirds of the shore above high-water is in Lancashire; so that anywhere south of Storrs on the one side and of Brathay on the other the boat-houses are in two counties.[1] Windermere or Wynander-mere is certainly not the 'winding mere,' nor is it the Wonwaldremere of the chronicles, where in A.D. 791 two princes of Northumbria were slain. As Ullswater is Ulf's-water, and Thurston-water (Coniston lake) in old records is Thorstan's water, this must have been the mere of Winund, as Professor Ekwall thinks—a Norse settler who may have owned the place in the tenth century; witness his name, with the Scandinavian possessive case ending in -r like Amounder-ness and Asmunder-law (Osmotherley).

Calgarth Hall, near the mouth of the Troutbeck, is the Elizabethan mansion of these same island Philipsons; and it is of them that romancers tell the gruesome tale of the Calgarth skulls; how—do what folk would—the skulls of the wicked squire's victims always came back. The same story is told of other old halls, and one is tempted to ask, were they toadstools? The old name Calygarth, connected with the Latin name for skull that appears in Calvary, may have helped to fix the legend; but it means merely the calf-yard, one of the old farm names like Sizergh. We have enough true romance in Lakeland, both ancient and modern, to afford the loss of one or two tales like this, and of one or two bogus castles like that of Wray opposite.

Low-wood has real and pleasant associations. It was the usual stopping-place in the old post-chaise times for Lake tourists after their drive from Kendal; and many a happy face has looked out of the windows at the Langdale Pikes, while the ham and eggs were frying. I always wish Elizabeth in *Pride and Prejudice* had come to the Lakes, as she planned; perhaps, on the whole, 'twas better for her; but we have missed a treat.

In old days the 'Salutation' was the favourite inn at Ambleside. Earlier than that there was the 'Cock.' Bishop Watson bought it, and out of compliment to the new owner the name was changed to 'The Bishop,' with a rough sign-board portrait, wig and all. Meanwhile a rival innkeeper mounted the sign of the 'Cock,' and got the custom. To prevent this lamentable falling-away, Boniface No. 1 added to his new sign, 'This is the "Old Cock."'

Although the Roman fort at Borrans Field at Waterhead is not as impressive

1 Since 1974 the whole of Windermere has been within the new county of Cumbria [Editor's note].

as Hardknott, it is nevertheless worth a visit. The visible remains at Galava
include a stoutly-buttressed granary, a Principia or headquarters, and a house
for the commandant. The auxiliary fort was probably built during the reign
of Hadrian and occupied for almost three hundred years, but below the site,
the excavators encountered traces of an earlier turf and timber fort which
seemed to date from the first century A.D. This fort was almost certainly liable
to flooding and was therefore abandoned but later covered with a deposit of
clay and sand to heighten the site and on this platform the Hadrianic fort was
constructed. There appears to have been a civil settlement close by and in
1963 a tombstone was found bearing the dramatic inscription:

> To the good gods of the Underworld
> Flavius Romanus Record Clerk
> Lived for 35 years
> Killed in the Fort by the Enemy.

From Galava, Roman military roads ran north and south; Ambleside is on
the route which led from Manchester and Ribchester to Ravenglass and the
north-west coast. Near Ambleside, between the fort and Rothay Bridge, a
corduroy road was found in 1900, with Roman remains proving its age and
origin, and thence the Roman road can be traced up Little Langdale towards
the coast. Another route is not so plain to see hereabouts, but it starts from
the Roman road that crosses Troutbeck, and once started, is very distinctly
marked on the hills of Westmorland.

This High Street is a most fascinating road, and well worth the rather long
walk needed to trace it. From the rustic homesteads of Upper Troutbeck[1] you
go up to the Tongue, a long low hill which splits the main dale into two. All
this part was the park, that is to say the deer preserve, of medieval owners;
and earlier still the home of prehistoric Cumbrians who have left foundations
of their dwellings in the cove at the head of the valley. From here a green path
goes up the steep side of Ill Bell in one leap—never a carriage road, of course,
but practicable enough for pack-horses and the slave-borne litter of the
travelling Roman. This way also may have come occasional raiders from the
north; it is the 'Scots' Rake,' i.e. path. Aloft, the view is superb; the graceful
foreshortened curve of Windermere, broken across by its islands; Morecambe
Bay, a long stripe of silver, thrown into distance by the dark pyramid of Ill
Bell that towers in front of it, and falls away to the left, down and down in a
succession of precipices, blacker and deeper as they plunge towards the tarn
below. Then on the broad back of High Street top the track is lost for a while;
two great stones, prostrate on the ground, seem once to have stood as way-
marks. Then comes the Brigg o' Dread (to adapt an old mythical name to a

---

1 For a survey of the history of Troutbeck, see S. H. Scott, *A Westmorland Village*, 1904.

real place). Bleawater and Hayeswater, to the right and left, more than a thousand feet beneath, and Riggindale, another pit of black crag, narrow up the footway, encroaching bit by bit. The road stoops to the dangerous edge, and swerves at it, and climbs again; and you are on Kidsty Pike, looking back. An army could pass in safety; but there is something in the whirl and heave of the mountain lines that makes the place much more impressive than many where the danger is real. Hence by Loadpot to Moor-divock and its cluster of burial cairns, and so on to Pooley Bridge and Penrith, is easy walking.

The valley of Ambleside, with its wooded knolls of rock standing among the grass, and Loughrigg looking down, shadowy and solemn; and the sudden turn to new scenery when you come to Rydalwater, very dainty with its fringy shores and islets—to use the old word, 'smiling' under the frown of Nab Scar; and then the new surprise, swiftly following, of Grasmere, whether you take the low road by the lake shore, or the old road over the hill, or the middle road by the spot where the Wishing Gate used to be, Grasmere under Silver How, as shadowy as Loughrigg, and still more solemn, and the water's face untroubled, and the island-hillock severe in outline, pensive and lonely; then in a few minutes again another scene—the opening dale, and the great masses of the mountains lifting up their lines from it in one huge heave together, shoulder to shoulder, and the splintered crest of Helm Crag and the multitudinous heights behind it, over against Helvellyn—it is rarely that so much beauty is crowded into so little ground. And if you take the well-known walks—Greenhead Gill where 'Michael' built his sheep-fold, Tongue Gill and its waterfall, or up to Grisedale Tarn—Greenburn behind the Helm, or Easedale with its tarn and force, or any of the gills along the breast of wooded Silver How—'custom cannot stale their infinite variety.' Wordsworth chose well.

But long before Wordsworth, Rydal was the home of a man who was not unworthy to be his predecessor; one who like Wordsworth cared for the place and the people, practised the plain living of a frugal, farming squire, and the high thinking of a student and a scholar; wrote also books of no little interest on Cumberland and Westmorland folk and their history. Sir Daniel Fleming

Rydalwater

Sizergh Castle near Kendal is the ancient home of the Strickland family. Built around a 14th century pele tower, it is certainly one of the most impressive houses in the Lake Counties.

was born of the Coniston family in 1633, went to Queen's College, Oxford, and to Gray's Inn, followed his father in the cause of King Charles, and suffered heavily in pocket and prospects. So he left the hall at Coniston to others of the family and settled at Rydal Hall, which had been the second house of the Flemings since 1484 or 1485; living in retirement and economy until he should repair his broken fortunes. Not only that, but he was fond of history and research, corresponded with many of the learned men of the age, and became distinguished for his antiquarian knowledge, among other things for an interest, then very uncommon, in the Northern languages and in runic inscriptions, of which several were known at his time in Cumberland. It was at Grasmere, one hundred and fifty years later, that De Quincey struck out the line of thought which led to the recognition of the Viking element in the Lake District dialect and place-names. Daniel Fleming at the Restoration became an important person; he took a great share in county business, was knighted, became M.P. for Cockermouth, and died in 1701, nearly a hundred years before the time when Wordsworth—a native of Cockermouth—settled in Grasmere, and a century and half before he died at Rydal.

Rydal Mount, Wordsworth's home from 1813 to 1850, is not his shrine of pilgrimage; nor is Allan Bank at Grasmere, where he lived from 1808 to 1813. All the associations are with Dove Cottage, or, as he knew it, Townend. There he did his best work; there he was most characteristically the Wordsworth of history, the one out of many local poets who could speak to the world at large of his rustic home, and give it the touch of artistic idealization that made a fairyland of it. There have been many Cumbrian poets, most of them, like Wordsworth at Grasmere, cottage folk, and, like him, at their best when they wrote of cottages and rural life and the more familiar aspects of nature around them. He was the representative man of the group, as Shakespeare among the London playwrights or Dante among the early Italian sonneteers; surpassed in certain qualities by some—in humour and realism of portrayal; rivalled by others in lyrical effect; unequal to himself and often wandering from his true vocation; but still the one who rose head and shoulders above the crowd and compelled attention.

We are proud in these parts of our native local poets; that Cumbria should have bred such a nest of singing birds, though so many of them are unknown abroad. Before Wordsworth we had Relph and Clark, old Hoggarth and blind Stagg, Lonsdale, and Miss Blamire and Miss Gilpin. Contemporary with him were Anderson and Sanderson, Rayson and Graves; a little later Gibson and Richardson, all in their measure true poets.[1] Before the eighteenth century there were the ballads; some of the finest Northern ballads and songs were from our side of the border. Before the Middle Ages, we are told, Cumbria was the birthplace of many Welsh bardic poems, and possibly of Norse Edda lays and drapas of the skalds. All this long line of poetic tradition led up to Wordsworth. In him the homely native muse at last found her instrument— unwilling at times, it seemed, and unresponsive, but when truly touched, how perfect!

1 The Rev. Josiah Relph of Sebergham, born about 1700, died 1743, and Ewan Clark of Wigton (1734–1811), wrote dialect pastorals modelled on Virgil and Theocritus. J. Stagg of Burgh-by-Sands, died 1823, author of *The Bridewain* and *Rosley Hill Fair*, was a blind fiddler, a Wandering Willie in real life. Mark Lonsdale, author of *The Upshot*, died 1789. Miss Blamire of Thackwood died 1794, and Miss Gilpin of Scaleby died 1811. Robert Anderson, the Burns of Cumberland, a Carlisle man, lived from about 1770 to 1833. Old Sanderson died 1829 on hearing that his box of poems was burnt in the fire that made him homeless. John Rayson, a schoolmaster, lived 1803–59. John Woodcock Graves, who wrote *John Peel*, emigrated to Tasmania in 1833. Dr Alex. Craig Gibson, born at Harrington 1813, died 1874, lived at Coniston, and wrote many fine dialect songs like *Lal Dinah Grayson* and *Mappen I may*. John Richardson of St John's Vale, 1817–86, was the author of *Cumberland Talk*, and William Dickinson (died 1882) wrote good dialect prose and verse. Of the twentieth-century poets, Norman Nicholson (1914–1987) is pre-eminent; his imagery and appeal are unsurpassed.

Any one who lives at the Lakes can hardly shake off Wordsworth. He haunts the place.[1] It is not the 'Maister Wudsworth' of the peasantry that one remembers, humming his lines along the road, nor the somewhat uncongenial neighbour of country gentry who were hardly able to discern greatness. Hartley Coleridge and Christopher North could take the ear of their contemporaries; Southey was an ornament to Keswick; but Wordsworth lived, and still lives, only in his work, in the glamour he has thrown around every scene and every season. When 'the first mild day of March' comes, what else takes us to the woods? When the celandine peeps through dead oak leaves by the wayside, why do we make holiday? Who taught us to watch at Easter for the daffodils and in the east-wind haze of April for the cuckoo? To find the 'beauty born of murmuring sound' in the cottage-child's face, and 'old age serene and bright' in the quiet country home? Who has so painted our sunsets, 'vivid as fire, clouds separately poised, innumerable multitude of forms,' or our twilights, 'breathless with adoration'; or in autumn, 'when not a leaf seems faded,' who but Wordsworth brings us on our way to 'nobler cares than listless summer knew'?

We go, of course, in duty bound to Grasmere sports. It is a noble game, the wrestling, and the fell-race is a fine show of pluck, and the hound-trail of sagacity: moreover, there are sure to be friends among the thousands at the gathering. But this is only an episode. To the wider world Grasmere means the hills he loved, and Dove Cottage where he wrote, and his grave beside the Rothay.

Red Bank, Loughrigg's northern slope overlooking Grasmere, and the road past it to High Close, and Loughrigg Tarn, and Elterwater, a true lake of the Lakes, though tiniest of all; the village of powder-mills[2] and quarries, church and hamlet perched on the spur of Silver How, Baisbrown nestling under Lingmoor, the filled-up lake-basin, flat beneath loftier and loftier heights: these are stages in our approach to the Pikes which appear and reappear, continually dominating Langdale—the main feature of the scenery. 'Those lusty twins,' exclaimed Wordsworth's Solitary, 'if here it were your lot to dwell, would soon become your prized companions.' It is a fine passage which follows, wonderfully in tune with the exact chord of feeling struck by the actual scene:

> A harmony
> So do I call it, though it be the hand
> Of silence, though there be no voice. The clouds,
> The mist, the shadows, light of golden suns,
> Motions of moonlight, all come thither—touch,

1 See Norman Nicholson's poem *To the River Duddon* [Editor's note].

2 Now a time-share complex [Editor's note].

And have an answer; thither come and shape
A language not unwelcome to sick hearts
And idle spirits. There the sun himself,
At the calm close of summer's longest day,
Rests his substantial orb. Between those heights
And on the top of either pinnacle
More keenly than elsewhere in night's blue vault
Sparkle the stars, as of their station proud.
Thoughts are not busier in the mind of man
Than the mute agents stirring there.

This busy fairy-life or gnome-life of the mountains here, where they are not mere grassy slopes, but chiselled rocks, tenanted by water in all its forms; where they are great enough to give the sense of power and steep enough to give some notion of sublimity, and yet lovable and companionable in their comparative smallness: all this was felt by Ruskin too, and prettily expressed in one of his letters, not written for publication, as a 'purple patch' of eloquence, but mere after-supper gossip to his mother at home. It is dated 13th August 1867, and continues: 'It is perfectly calm to-night, not painfully hot, and the full moon shining over the mountains opposite my window, which are the scene of Wordsworth's *Excursion*. It was terribly hot in the earlier day, and I did not leave the house till five o'clock. Then I went out, and in the heart of Langdale Pikes found the loveliest rock-scenery, chased with silver waterfalls, that I ever set foot or heart upon. The Swiss torrent-beds are always more or less savage and ruinous, with a terrible sense of overpowering strength and danger, lulled. But here, the sweet heather and ferns and star mosses nestled in close to the dashing of the narrow streams; while every cranny or crag held its own little placid lake of amber, trembling with falling drops, but quietly trembling, not troubled into ridgy wave or foam; the rocks themselves *ideal* rock, as hard as iron—no, not quite that, but *so* hard that, after breaking some of it, breaking solid white quartz seemed like smashing brittle loaf-sugar, in comparison—and cloven into the most noble masses; not grotesque, but

Wrynose Pass

*The wooded shores of Coniston Water once rang with the voices of iron smelters
and charcoal burners; today the tranquillity of these woods is disturbed merely
by the sounds of picnickers and sail-boat enthusiasts.*

majestic and full of harmony with the larger mountain mass of which they
formed a part. Fancy what a place for a hot afternoon after five, with no wind,
and absolute solitude; no creature, except a lamb or two, to mix any ruder
sound or voice with the plash of the innumerable streamlets!'

The higher crags of the Pikes, above Dungeon Gill, and of Pavey Ark above

Stickle Tarn, afford some fine rock-climbing.[1] On the way up there are splendid outlooks. The tops, when you reach them, are disappointing, for all the excitement is in the broken edge that overhangs Langdale—behind the summits it is moorland and waste, up and down, by High White Stones and Ullscarth and Blea Tarn and Armboth Fells, all the way to Keswick. But such a walk in cloudy weather has its effects of wildness and mystery, with sudden peeps into valleys and vistas of mountain summits, and the continually chang-ing grotesques of the desolate hummocks and boulders among turf and peat and heather. It is a grand walk, too, up Mickleden, past the mounds and pits of a long-forgotten 'British settlement,' and up the zigzags of the Stake, over into lonely Langstrath, once filled with wood, but disafforested by the iron-smelters of old times, who brought the ore from Eskdale by the arduous path of the Ure Gap (Ore Gap) west of Bowfell. On leaving Mickleden by the track to the left, along the brink of Rossett Gill, there is a famous route by Angle Tarn and Sprinkling Tarn to Styhead and Scafell. Or for some of the biggest cliffs and darkest chasms we can show, there is Oxendale with Brownie Gill, Crinkle Gill, and Hell Gill converging on the combe, and towering heights all round against the sky.[2] The heights are all accessible, and almost any route, path or no path, will lead in fair weather and with ordinary caution to the top of Bowfell or Shelter Crags or Crinkle Crags or the Pike of Blisco; but the finest views are not the panoramas from the summits, and they are hardly found or enjoyed when you try ascents against time. A week's rambling and scrambling round Dungeon Gill as a centre, and never crossing the water-shed, would not exhaust the variety and interest of Upper Langdale.

The road from Little Langdale by Blea Tarn is the usual car route, nearly always taken from south to north in order to get the surprise of the Langdale Pikes, suddenly breaking into grandeur over the little sharp tooth of Side Pike by the tarn. But going from Dungeon Gill you meet Wetherlam, hardly less fine, and rising nobly over the valley. Wordsworth's excursionists climbed Lingmoor from Little Langdale village and dropped upon Blea Tarn, 'the little lowly vale,' from the wild table-land of the 'savage region' which he 'paced dispirited'; much the best way for an epicure in fell-scenery who wants to taste the contrast. But scores of permutations and combinations are possible on these hills, and one of their greatest delights is the freedom to wander with 'no enemy but winter and rough weather,' and the certainty that towards evening one can't be far from supper and bed.

1 In 1947 the screes on the Pikes were found to be the site of a Neolithic stone axe factory [Editor's note].

2 Crinkle (Norse *Kringla*, circle) may have once been the name of the whole ring of crags, of which various points are now separately named. 'Hell' is a dialect word for to pour, gush (Norse *hella*), seen again in Hellbeck. As a noun the word *hella* in Norse meant slate-rock or slab.

Approaching Skelwith Bridge

At Fell Foot, where the Blea Tarn road joins the valley of Little Langdale, is one of those old houses which stud the map; arms of Fletcher Fleming, son of Sir Daniel, are over the door; stories of old pack-horse and smuggling days are told about this isolated spot, the last house on what was the main road over Wrynose toward the old port of Ravenglass. This was the Roman road too;[1] and no doubt the chief pass from east to west all through the Middle Ages. Behind the farm there is a curious knoll with terraces round it. If it was meant for a terraced garden, one asks why were some of the terraces made to look north, out of the sun? But any one who has seen Tynwald Hill in the Isle of Man will recognize a certain likeness here to the Thing-mount of the Vikings; there was another, known from old prints, in Dublin. And as this is on the high road east and west, and at the meeting-place of passes to north and south, it has been suggested that the Viking settlers met here for their annual parliament. I do not know that the theory can be considered as proved, but nothing so far has disproved it.[2]

Little Langdale Tarn, Slater's Bridge, and the pretty dale of the Brathay that leads rapidly down to Colwith Force, and then round the corner to Elterwater and Skelwith, are too familiar in pictures and photographs to need many words here. The Langdales have four fine waterfalls. Dungeon Gill for Wordsworth's sake, and for the real curiosity of its vertical spout in the black cleft under a natural rock-bridge—Hell Gill Force for downright wildness—Colwith for confusion of foam and rocks and foliage—Skelwith for the perfect picture it makes—all are distinct in character and each finished in every detail. And so, by Brathay and Clappersgate, we find our way back to Ambleside.

---

1 Still traceable on the fell side above the present road [Editor's note].

2 In 1896 Collingwood wrote: 'This thingmount in Little Langdale may be regarded as the Lakeland Tynwald' [Editor's note].

*Sheep gathering at Kentmere. The Hall is a 14th century pele tower built as a
refuge against the marauding Scots.*

III

FURNESS AND CARTMEL

Furness, the lands of the Flemings and the monks—Outlaws and 'fellows fierce'—Ancient industries—Conishead Priory and Chapel Island—Cartmel Priory—Humphrey Head Spa and caves—Atterpile Castle—Furness Abbey, history and ruins—Piel Castle—Barrow—Dalton Castle and St Helen's chapel—The Giant's Grave—Coniston Water—Ancient Bloomeries—Ruskin's home and grave—The worthies of Coniston—The Old Man—Wonderful Walker.

Until 1974 much of what is now south Cumbria was part of the County Palatine of Lancaster; Barrow, of course, had industrial affinities with the towns of central and south Lancashire, but it was always a source of surprise to our visitors that villages such as Cartmel, Coniston and Hawkshead were part of Lancashire rather than Westmorland or Cumberland. The reason was largely historical; Furness and Cartmel, or Lonsdale North of the Sands as it was known, seemed to be a detached part of the county, but in effect the sands of Morecambe Bay formed a link with Lancashire rather than a divide. The ancient cross-sands route at low water across the shimmering wastes tied Furness and Cartmel to Lancaster. Even to-day old loyalties die hard; there are still those who would agree with the old Furness saying that 'Nowt good ever comes round Black Combe,' and the loyal toast remains as it always has: The Queen, Duke of Lancaster.

All that lies between the Duddon and Windermere is Furness, given in the twelfth century to the great abbey; all that lies between Windermere and the Winster is Cartmel, given at the end of the same century to the priory. The grant of King Stephen to Furness Abbey was not quite clear and conclusive; others claimed rights in the same territory. The family of Fleming had already gone to settle there; the Baron of Kendal thought he had rights in the fells—a vaguely-known 'hinterland' of boors and backwoods; but these differences were composed, and the monks remained paramount, though parts of Furness were practically in other hands. In somewhat later times even the monks dealt direct with Lancaster where the king's sheriff held court; and when the county of Lancashire was carved out of Yorkshire and Cheshire, and given a definite status and boundary, Furness and Cartmel remained within it.

Hawkshead was the Furness monks' hunting-ground and timber forest,

From the churchyard, Hawkshead

with a few descendants of old Viking settlers farming in their primitive way, and greatly resenting the new rule. King John gave Furness a charter permitting them to use force against refractory 'tenants,' which shows what society was like hereabouts in the early Middle Ages. Then, I infer, as the woods near the abbey were used up, the ore from the mines, which was a chief source of revenue to the monks, was carried up into the fells to be smelted with the charcoal made on the spot, and so the land was gradually brought under new management. Hawkshead church was granted the rights of a parish church in 1219, as the centre of all the hill country between Coniston, Brathay, Windermere, and the Leven; and the manor-house of the monks was fixed at Hawkshead Hall, where you still see some of their building in the traceried window of the gatehouse, dating from about 1410.

Hawkshead church, as we see it, has no part earlier than the fifteenth century; the apparently Norman arches are not real Norman building. The earlier Sandys effigies are Elizabethan, and of the same date as the foundation of the Grammar School, which Hawkshead owed to Archbishop Sandys, born

Tablet in Hawkshead church

at Esthwaite Hall farther down the lake. At this school Wordsworth was educated from 1779 to 1787; like any schoolboy he cut his name, still to be seen in the schoolroom, and lodged at Ann Tyson's, the cottage to the right, beyond the archway opposite the 'Red Lion.'[1] *The Prelude* contains many true pictures of old Hawkshead, 'that beloved vale'; how he snared woodcocks, boated, skated, fished, and nutted; how he noted the first changes in the building of a 'smart Assembly-room,' how he came back to see, from the Windermere road:

> The snow-white church upon her hill
> Sit like a thronèd lady, sending out
> A gracious look all over her domain.
> —Yon azure smoke betrays the lurking town.

Still true to the scene that last touch, though modern restoration has stripped the homely roughcast from the church and coarsely pointed it over. Wordsworth's yew is gone. The flags or slate slabs which gave the name to Flag street, are no more and the syke which once ran down the middle of the lane has been channelled into a culvert, considered by the authorities to be more sanitary. Perhaps we are not yet quite clever enough in these matters to do the needful cleansing and restoration without destroying the old landmarks and the old rustic charm; Hawkshead has been modernized and sanitized.[2]

Hawkshead

But off the beaten track there is plenty of the old country left. Down the lake by Esthwaite Hall and over the fell there is Dale Park, famous for its daffodils, and once the deer park of the bad Abbot Bankes, who turned out

1 Recent research suggests that Wordsworth lodged with Ann Tyson at the nearby hamlet of Colthouse from 1783–7 [Editor's note].

2 One can only guess at Collingwood's reaction to the huge car and coach park and 'The Norseman Restaurant' [Editor's note].

*The crags and gullies of the Scafell range, the highest land in England, offered
the early climbers challenges to test both strength and agility. Here and on
neighbouring rock faces, the sport of English rock-climbing was born in the late
19th century.*

The Langdale Piles present one of the most familiar and best-loved mountain profiles in Cumbria, instantly recognized by the fell-walker and the car-confined visitor alike. Yet four and a half thousand years ago this fellside was the site of the Lake District's first export industry—the manufacture of stone axes from the local fine-grained volcanic rock.

Esthwaite Water

his tenants—descendants of the free Norse settlers—to make a hunting-ground. At Satterthwaite the sister valley of Grizedale joins Dale Park to make the lakeless but most charming Rusland Vale—Role's Land, in old documents, and perhaps once the possession of some forgotten Rolf. Hereabouts from 1346 to 1363, a gang of outlaws under Adam of Beaumont (near Leeds) resorted, 'boasting of their misdeeds' as the old ballad says; and the ballad of Flodden Field speaks of the natives of the neighbourhood in one alliterative line as 'fellows fierce from Furness Fells.'

It has always been woodland, and a place of woodland industries. In the thirteenth century there were already the beginnings of the charcoal-burning business; by the time of the dissolution of the monasteries under Henry VIII the great timber was gone, used for building, but 'Byrk, Holey, Asshe, Ellers [alder], Lyng, lytell short Okes and Hasells' are mentioned, and the 'yerely profytte comming and growing of the said woods, called Grenehewe, Bastyng, Blecking, bynding [making of bast-mats, bleaching, cooper's work], making of Sadeltrees, cartwheles, cuppes, disshes, and many other things wrought by Cowpers [coopers] and Turners, with making of Coles [charcoal] and pannage of Hoggs' (whence the name of Grizedale).

The once-important woodland industries are now no more; smoke from charcoal pitsteads no longer hangs over the still waters of Coniston, the small circular huts made of withies which once sheltered the colliers have decayed and fallen in, bark peeling and swill-basket making are virtually extinct and most of the bobbin mills have been converted to other uses though the Stott Park Mill near Newby Bridge has been opened as an imaginative museum which keeps alive some of the traditional skills. That other mainstay of the High Furness economy, the smelting of iron, has also become extinct but here and there, in the prettiest places by romantic gills or tranquil coves of the lake shore, one finds the heaps of black slag where the furnaces used to be. It is difficult to fix a date, but roughly speaking there must have been iron-smelting always going on in the Lake District since the times when they were settled by folk civilized enough to need tools and weapons. The smaller bloomeries, as they are called, may be of very various dates, mostly from Norman times until the seventeenth century, when a larger type of furnace came into use. That at Force Forge, by the waterfall in Rusland, was established before 1680, and other important furnaces were built in the neighbouring Crake Valley at Nibthwaite, Penny Bridge, and Spark Bridge about the same time. It is curious to note these evidences of disappeared industries and the relapse of the countryside to nature. Maybe some day other parts, now hideous with smoke and flame, or scarred with quarrying and mining, may become another Words-worth's favourite walk.[1]

Colton church on its green hill must not be forgotten, nor the old Baptist chapel at Tottlebank, founded 1669, nor the Quakers' Meeting at Rook How, founded 1725. Colton Old Hall was a home of the Sandys family in the seventeenth century; Oxenpark has its cockpit—not many of the old style are left, though he would be a bold man who should say that cock-fighting is extinct; and at Greenodd (the Norse *græn-oddi*, the green point), where the Crake from Coniston and the Leven from Windermere meet among delightful wooded hills, one can trace the old seaport where Coniston slate and ore were once shipped.

Hawkshead Hill

Ulverston, though Dalton was its rival in medieval times, and Barrow have shot ahead in very modern times—still Ulverston is one of the most attractive towns in Furness. It was a market-town in 1280.[2] Its parish church has a

---

1 Collingwood's words were prophetic to a degree he could scarcely have imagined. Many abandoned quarries have been landscaped and turned into car parks, others have become unofficial nature reserves while at least one, Hodge Close, Tilberthwaite, provides local mountain rescue teams with a splendid training ground. In Furness, the waste tips of long-closed iron works have been converted to playing fields and recreation areas while at Hodbarrow near Millom, the great lake created when the haematite mines were closed has become the haunt of wildfowl. Collingwood would have approved [Editor's note].

2 Sadly it has lost its market cross and 'fish-stones' but these have been replaced by the town's war memorial—designed by W. G. Collingwood [Editor's note].

Haweswater is one of the most silent and poignant of all the lakes. Following the construction of a dam in 1929, the former lake was converted into a reservoir for Manchester with the consequent destruction of the community at Mardale.

twelfth-century doorway, which is a kind of guarantee of respectability and old establishment, like family pictures and plate. There is within it an effigy of Myles Dodding, 1629; the larger effigy of William Sandys, who died 1558, is a modern antique. There is also a brass of the Doddings of Conishead (1606), and a not less interesting tablet to Sir John Barrow (1764–1848), who, born in a cottage at Dragley Beck, travelled widely in China and South Africa, became Secretary to the Admiralty, encouraged Arctic exploration and was one of the founding members of the Royal Geographical Society. The lightless lighthouse on Hoad Hill above the town was built as a monument to him. Half a mile south of the town is the Elizabethan hall of Swarthmoor, home of George Fox, the first Quaker, who married the widow of Thomas Fell, the owner, and built a meeting-house close by in 1688. On Swarthmoor, Lambert Simnel's foreign troops encamped in 1487 under Martin Schwartz, their German commander; it used to be said that the moor was named after him, but the name occurs earlier, and simply means Black Moor.

Near Ulverston there are several ancient sites in pretty surroundings, for though this is Low Furness, all the country is hilly, and the peeps of fiord and farther hills over wooded dells and homesteads are full of beauty. At Pennington is the Ellabarrow, reputed to be the mound where 'Lord Ella sleeps with his golden sword,' and near it, at Conynger Hurst, an interment of perhaps the Iron Age was found some years since; when the railway was made, querns and stone weapons were discovered. Higher up the road is Castle Hill, with great ramparts overhanging a ravine; the place was a seat of the Pennington family down to the fourteenth century, and many of these old ramparts appear to have enclosed early medieval houses, built of wood, or wood and clay, which might have been quite large and comfortable in their time, but when once ruined leave no trace behind.

Urswick is famous for the legend of its tarn, which covers, they say, 'lile U'ston' (little Ulverston), sunk beneath the waters. A similar tale is told at Kirksanton and elsewhere, and suggests to any one who knows of the lake-dwellings in Switzerland, Ireland, and Galloway that there might have been a crannoge, or group of huts built on an artificial platform, which, when once deserted, would soon sink beneath the surface. But no such remains have yet been found in the Lakes. There are island dwellings, and there may yet be discoveries of crannoges; meanwhile close to Urswick there is a very curious enclosure with foundations of huts, like those in Kentmere and elsewhere, and adjoining it a square rampart; the site is known as the Stone Walls, and is dated by exploration to the Iron Age. Another such ancient garth is at Foula (one mile and a half south-east of this), and on the north side of Birkrigg, the hill east of Urswick, is a third such rampart at Appleby Slack. At Skelmore Heads, a hill overlooking Urswick Tarn, a small hill fort, thought to be Iron Age in date, was excavated in the late 1950s and on the east of Birkrigg, between Bardsea and Sunbrick (written Swenebrec in the thirteenth century, and evidently meaning the breck or slope where swine were fed, like Swinside), is a double ring of boulders, almost certainly a Bronze Age cremation site. Farther south, on the brink of the shore, is Aldingham Mote-hill, another of those burgs we have seen at Kendal and Kirkby Lonsdale. This is remarkably complete, with the basecourt at its foot, and, though some have given an earlier date, may be taken to be the first house and farmstead of the Flemings, who settled here under William Rufus. They held Gleaston too, and lived there; St Michael's Well at Gleaston is thought to be a corruption from *Sir* Michael (le Fleming), but Gleaston Castle was built by their successors, the Harringtons, in the fourteenth century. There are still considerable ruins, ivy-grown and picturesque.

Bardsea (not named from Welsh bards, but in Domesday written Berretseige), and Conishead (Conyngshead, king's estate) were sites of religious houses: at the first was a Hospital of St John of Jerusalem, and at the second a priory of Austin canons. Foundations of the priory church underlie part of the grounds of Conishead, now a Buddhist college. Out in the Firth of Leven is a little rocky islet called Chapel Island, formerly Harlesyde, where, it is said, 'divine service was performed at a convenient hour for such as crossed the sands with the morning tide.' I do not know what authority Father West (writing in 1774) had for the statement, but the chapel and its occupant must often have been a welcome sight to wayfarers over this rather dangerous route.[1] Wordsworth gives a picture of the spot in pre-railroad days, paraphrasing West, and ending with a dramatic incident. You remember he was something of a revolutionary himself at first, until the Reign of Terror opened his eyes.

> Upon a small
> And rocky island near, a fragment stood
> (Itself like a sea-rock), the low remains,
> With shells encrusted, dark with briny weeds,
> Of a dilapidated structure, once
> A Romish chapel, where the vested priest
> Said matins at the hour that suited those
> Who crossed the sands at ebb of morning tide.
> Not far from that still ruin all the plain
> Lay spotted with a variegated crowd
> Of vehicles and travellers, horse and foot,
> Wading beneath the conduct of their guide
> In loose procession through the shallow stream
> Of inland waters; the great sea meanwhile
> Heaved at safe distance, far retired. I paused,
> Longing for skill to paint a scene so bright

1 The present 'ruined chapel' is a folly [Editor's note].

And cheerful, but the foremost of the band
As he approached, no salutation given,
In the familiar language of the day,
Cried, 'Robespierre is dead!'

Cartmel is the name of the district between the Leven and the Winster, just as Furness is of the larger division between Duddon and Leven. The name is very ancient; as Cartmel the land was given to St Cuthbert by King Ecgfrith of Northumbria, A.D. 678, 'with all the Britons therein,' the Cumbrian Welsh of the day. About 1189 William Mareschal, Earl of Pembroke, gave lands here to the Austin canons, and a priory was founded, an important place, though Furness Abbey had the start and overshadowed Cartmel in power and fame.

The outskirts of Cartmel

And yet, while Furness is all a ruin, we still have the church of the priory at Cartmel—not intact, but fairly well preserved, and bringing down the tradition of the Middle Ages into the usage of the present. At the dissolution under Henry VIII the country-folk begged that the church—their only one—might remain; it was dilapidated, and new-roofed in 1618 by George Preston of Holker; the Parliament troops damaged it in 1643, but the fine window had already been removed to Bowness. Between 1830 and 1867 it was 'restored,' but you can still see the twelfth-century pillars, and the tower set curiously askew, the monks' seats carved beneath, and various tombs of priors. The

Cartmel Priory

Harrington tomb seems to be a patchwork of several monuments, inserted after the Reformation, and there are many curious mementoes of the seventeenth century. The effigy, by Thomas Woolner, R.A., of Lord Frederick Cavendish, assassinated in Dublin, 1882, is interesting both for its art and its associations. The old gatehouse of the priory is also to be seen, now restored. It is owned by the National Trust.

Round about Cartmel are many bits of historic building, set in charming landscape. Holker Hall, the seat of the Cavendishes, is practically a modern mansion, largely rebuilt after the fire of 1871; but Hampsfield Hall was built before 1636, and Cark Hall has a seventeenth-century interior, with a front perhaps added by the once famous Anglo-Saxon scholar, Christopher Rawlinson (d. 1733). Flookburgh boasts itself a market-town, having charters from Edward I and Charles II, and regalia, sword, and halbert, still preserved in the church.

A little to the east of this is Wraysholme Tower, a ruined pele, once a seat of the Harringtons, the family of Gleaston Castle. They forfeited their possessions after the battle of Bosworth Field, and this place was granted to the Stanleys, whose crest long remained in a bit of stained glass preserved at the farm. South of this is Humphrey Head with its holy well, once popular as a spa and much visited by lead miners from Alston. Here, it is said, the last wolf in the county was killed. There is a long ballad, of doubtful origin, quoted in Stockdale's *Annales Caermoelenses*, the standard old collection of Cartmel lore, and giving a romantic turn to the story, but nothing by which date or circumstances can be fixed. The headland is now a Country Park. There is more to dream about in the Kirkhead and Capeshead caves, where real prehistoric and Roman age remains have been found. In a cave near Merlewood Anglian coins (among other things) have been discovered; and on Castle Head beyond Grange—that high cone rising solitary from the flats, once tidal sands—a very curious collection of antiquities was found when John Wilkinson, the Backbarrow boy who became a great iron-master and inventor, built his house and laid out his garden there in 1765. They found a large deposit of human, buffalo, deer, and other bones and flint implements, with Roman and Northumbrian coins, showing that the rough Welsh folk, both before and after St Cuthbert's time, had made use of these caves and this Atterpile Castle, as it used to be called, as their retreats. 'Attercop' is the dialect word, pure Anglo-Saxon, for a spider; *attor* in Anglo-Saxon is 'poison'; upon which one might romance about the spider's den of these robber natives; but possibly it is the matter-of-fact Scandinavian that comes in here, *attar* or *ættar*, 'of the family', the old folk's pele, the stronghold of the ancient stock. There are no records whatever concerning it, for it belongs to the time before the Norman scribe arrived here.

We must leave the sunny, rocky shores of Grange and Kentsbank, still delightful, though houses and hotels have filled up the undercliff and the railway blocks out the beach, and return into Furness to the abbey.

In 1123 Stephen, afterwards King of England, gave land at Tulketh near Preston in Lancashire to the Norman-French abbey of Savigny. A colony of monks was sent over, but stayed there only three years, for in 1127 Stephen gave them a much larger grant, namely, the whole of Furness except the lands of Michael le Fleming.

We look round, in the richly wooded, luxuriantly green dale, and say: 'What a charming spot the monks chose! How well they knew the way to make themselves comfortable!' But when they first arrived Furness was a wild and dismal region, thinly populated with a few rough Norse-speaking farmers, the borderland against hostile Scots. That was why Fleming was sent to Aldingham as a buffer colonist; these monks were planted out one step farther into the wilds; it was a move in the game of the Norman settlement. The poor, plucky monks do not seem to have turned out any of their new subjects from their strongholds or established farms; they did not plant their home conspicuously on the shore to invite sea-rovers, who still haunted these coasts; they hid themselves in the deepest central valley, Bekansgill, then no doubt a mere tangle of wild wood, and there they built themselves wattle huts, and soon began to raise a tiny stone church, the foundations of whose apse, in the style of earliest Norman buildings, have been unearthed and are there to see.

In 1148 the parent abbey of Savigny joined the great Cistercian Order. This little distant colony had already caught the conservatism and independence of the North and refused to join in the movement. Its abbot, Peter of York, actually went to Rome, and got the Pope to sanction its freedom; but on his way home he was seized by the Savigny monks, and, as the official record calmly says, 'he resigned his office as abbot, and became a most worthy monk in the same place [Savigny] learning the Cistercian Order.' Savigny sent a

Cartmel village

Frenchman to Furness, 'by whose diligence and counsel' the independent North-countrymen were coerced—after what heart-searchings and heart-breakings we are left to imagine—into the tight and hard rule of the great organization. Ultimately Furness became the second most affluent Cistercian monastery in England.

It would be very far from the truth to suppose that these early monks were a party of beggars and impostors. They were a college of gentlemen, the upper class of their district; a firm of business men who carried on a great land-agency, managing the estates given—not to them personally, but to their Order; developing the uncleared, untilled wilderness, digging and smelting iron, farming sheep and exporting the wool, and gradually bringing their countryside into so high a state of wealth and civilization that their fall meant its ruin for many a long generation. They were the missionaries of religion and culture and all the arts of life; they established, in effect, a medieval welfare state, caring for the sick, the needy and the infirm.

In 1537 came 'the Great Northern Tragedy'—Furness Abbey was dissolved by Henry VIII's agent, Thomas Cromwell. Each monk was given forty shillings and sent out into the world. The beautiful house, the work of centuries, was, as King Henry's commissioners reported, diligently plucked down. Just enough was left standing for a farmer or caretaker to live in, with the comfortable reflection that even this might be 'myche easyere at any tyme pluckyde downe then sett upp.'

Near to the new Information Centre built by English Heritage was the great gatehouse which opened into the outer court of the abbey: in this were found traces of two guest-houses where travelling laymen used to be lodged. In the green between the Information Centre and the main ruins is a small isolated building; this was the porch leading into the cemetery of the monks, between the church and the little beck that flows through the dale. The church is the great building to which you come first, approaching from the entrance: the archway by which you enter was the north door, at the end of the north transept.

Entering the north transept, you find three chapels on the left; then, from the crossing, or space under the central tower, the presbytery, with its still beautiful *sedilia* and the place of the high altar. From the south transept there opens (on the left) the sacristy and two more small chapels; opposite are the steps by which the monks came down from their dormitory, and on one of the brackets facing the steps there would have been a figure of St Christopher, for whoso gazed on St Christopher in the morning would come to no harm through the day.

Standing at the crossing, one looks down the nave. In the monks' day this was not one great vista of a church open from end to end; it was blocked across by a screen at the third pair of pillars, counting from where you stand. In front of that screen was the *pulpitum* (a raised gallery), and in front of that was the monks' quire. Behind the screen, and occupying the western half of the church, was, in earlier times, the chapel of the *Conversi*, or lay brothers, and when they ceased to exist as a separate class, that part of the church, but not the east end, was free to the public of the day. The tower at the west end was a late addition; it was against Cistercian rule to build lofty towers, and the rule was only broken or evaded in the degenerate fifteenth century.

From the south transept you reach the cloisters, the green inner court, once surrounded on all four sides with buildings, now on two sides only. The church forms its north side; on the east the first and third round-arched doors led to book-rooms, the second to the chapter-house, beautiful in its decay. Farther south you find the parlour, and then a long arcaded ruin which contained the monks' dormitory in the upper story and a range of offices and workshops beneath.

On the south of the cloisters a few stones in the grass mark where used to be, next to the dormitory, the calefactory, in which monks coming from prayers or work could warm themselves at fireplaces. Next to that was the frater, or ordinary dining-hall, above a room called the misericord. It was a rule of the Order that meat was not to be eaten in the dining-hall, but as time went on this rule was found to be too stringent, and by the 'misericordia,' sufferance of the authorities, meat was allowed to be eaten on certain days, but not in the frater—only in this lower room. The kitchen was to the west of this, and all along the last of the four sides of the cloister the lay brothers had their dormitory on the upper floor and their frater and offices below. Their infirmary was at the south-west corner of the block, behind the kitchen; but after the middle of the fourteenth century lay brothers ceased to exist; the buildings formerly theirs were used as store-rooms and offices, and their infirmary was probably pulled down.

The detached vaulted building was the chapel of the monks' infirmary; the octagonal building close by was the monks' kitchen. Farther east and apart was the abbot's hall, at first the infirmary, and after the dissolution the one part spared. It is impossible in this brief sketch to go into the age of the various parts, but enough has perhaps been said to suggest the real use and meaning of the ruins.

Connected with Furness Abbey there are several medieval remains at a little distance; the monks' hall at Hawkshead has been already noticed. On Piel Island is Piel Castle, sometimes called the Pile (pele) of Foudrey, a barrack-like fort built by the Abbey in 1327 on the site of an earlier work, to guard the harbour—for much of their revenue came from the export of wool, and in the fourteenth and fifteenth centuries a fair-sized port flourished, the forerunner of the nineteenth-century docks at Barrow-in-Furness.

Barrow is a town more sinned against than sinning; it is unashamedly a nineteenth-century no-nonsense red brick boom town, the creation of the Furness Railway, slate, iron and ships. In 1801 it had a population of approximately 65 and was described by one writer as '... a place to which invalids often repair to bathe in the summer season.' In 1846 a mineral line linked the slate quarries at Kirkby and the iron mines near Dalton with four wooden piers jutting out into Barrow Channel; in 1852 the first ship was launched, in 1859 the great haematite iron furnaces were lit for the first time and Barrow was well on the way to becoming the 'English Chicago.' Although the population never quite reached the projected 100,000, Barrow earned its place as one of the most brash, burgeoning towns in Victorian England. Today things are different; the iron and steel works, once the largest in the world, have been closed, the iron-mines are overgrown and derelict, but the shipyard continues to launch vessels—not the splendid passenger liners of the 50s but the more sinister nuclear submarines of the 80s.

Although it is often pilloried by television comics and jocular journalists, the town has much to be proud of; within its present boundaries are two nature reserves, a National Trust 'wilderness' area, two medieval castles and the ruins of one of Britain's most magnificent Cistercian monasteries—how many 'industrial' towns in England can boast as much?

Returning northward past the abbey, we see at Dalton the pele-tower built by the monks. It has four quaint stone figures at the four corners of the battlements, and it contains ancient armour and part of a cannon dating from 1340 or thereabouts.[1] The church is modern on a commanding site where earthworks formerly existed, considered by the older antiquaries to be Roman; but they were probably the rampart of the Daltune of Domesday book. At Tytup Hall lived Father West, the eighteenth-century antiquary, near the mines of Orgrave, the Ouregraue of Domesday, a name which seems to show that even in the eleventh century, before the Normans, the iron-mines were known. On Highhaume Hill close by, where 'every mack of stone that God Almighty ever made is ligging'—such was a local description of its geology—there are the remains of a beacon; for this way, once or twice, came Scots invasions, and perhaps oftener came alarms of strange vessels, threatening the peace of Furness.

Askam, a former industrial village, and Ireleth in its ravine looking over the firth of Duddon to Black Combe are passed on the way to Kirkby-in-Furness, very prettily placed and famous for its Norman church and quaint bodiless effigy. A mile up the Broomsgill is a ring embankment called the Kirk, where games used to be held at Easter, and near it a great cairn in which an interment was found. Kirkby Hall is a manor-house of the time of Henry VIII, with curious frescoes in the chamber which was once the chapel. Still northward

1 Only one of the original fourteenth-century stone figures now survives. The Castle is owned by the National Trust [Editor's note].

is another great ring embankment beneath enormous and not uninteresting slate-quarries. Above Heathwaite farm is a site somewhat resembling the 'British settlements' we have seen elsewhere;[1] in the Giant's Grave at its north end an interment was found.

Crossing the hilly country of rocks and moors and pretty little surprises of dips and dells, we rejoin the Crake which we left at Greenodd, and through Blawith and the picturesque hamlet of Wateryeat[2] we reach the foot of Coniston lake, the view from which is one of the finest in the Lake District. The name of this lake in 1196 was Thorstanes Watter, in medieval Latin 'Turstini Watra,' evidently from some early owner with the Scandinavian name of Thorstein. Like Windermere, it is not one single rock-basin though the bar that breaks it into two deeps is not so apparent. The greatest basin is that which sinks to a depth of 184 feet a little above the rocky Peel Island, conspicuous from the waterfoot. On the right is the once wooded slope of Heald Brow: on the left is heathery Beacon Hill with Torver Moor beyond, and a background of peaks rising in a concert of tossed and tumbled breakers, varied in form but harmonious in the swing of their lines—Dow Crag, the Old Man, Wetherlam, Helvellyn, Fairfield. Down below 'neuks and nabs' vary the shore, and beyond, the lake spreads into breadth with Peel Island, steep-sided and crowned with trees, 'ornate and gay like some stately ship of Tarshish,' lifted above the surface. When you come nearer, the resemblance to a ship of old times is increased by the little 'calf-rock' like a boat in tow at its stern, joined to the main rock at low water by a narrow ridge, beside which there is a pretty little cove for harbour, and a well-blackened fire-spot where many a picnic kettle has boiled. The name, and some appearance of artificial surface, led me to dig some years ago, and curious remains of building were found, medieval pottery, and an old smithy-hearth on the western side, from which a stairway over the ridge led to the houses between the sheltering rock-walls of its central gap; but there are no records to give the least clue to the ancient folk who made this their home, unless it was the stronghold of Adam of Beaumont and his outlaws (see p. 34), with whose date the finds agree. In May the island is a mass of bluebells; later in the summer bell-heather and fern blend their colours; in autumn the varied foliage is singularly rich against the background of distant blue. Many readers of the books by Arthur Ransome, *Swallows and Amazons* and *Swallowdale*, will no doubt recognize this place, altered a little by the usual literary camouflage, but with all its charm preserved. It is also described in the story of *Thorstein of the Mere* as it may have been one thousand years ago.[3]

1 Thought by some archaeologists to be medieval [Editor's note].

2 Water-yeat, i.e. water-gate [Editor's note].

3 Written by W. G. Collingwood [Editor's note].

But Coniston Water is a singular instance of nature's *vis medicatrix*, the way she heals old sores. Along the beach and in every little dell where an unfailing streamlet runs down, there used to be iron furnaces (bloomeries), where small charges of ore, brought on pack-horses and boats from Low Furness, were smelted with charcoal. At one time the woods were nearly destroyed, and we can imagine a period when the barren hills were only varied by smoking 'pitsteads,' where charcoal was made, and flaming 'hearths' where grimy workers toiled at the bellows, or shovelled the red ore and black coals, with shouts and rattling, and the thud of the little waterwheels that worked the hammers and drove the blast. Perhaps not all the scene was at any one time so filled, but that was the character of the place. And now there is no such dainty frondage and foliage, no such utter peace and stillness, as in the coves and crannies of the water's edge, where softly rowing you may start the kingfisher, and hear no noise but the splash of the leaping trout, and the distinguishable call of many streams—this one tinkling, that one gurgling, and one beyond belling through the woods, and another across half a mile of water chattering over the stones or roaring down its coppice-hidden ravine.

As we sail up the lake, we pass Land's Point on the left, Wordsworth's 'grove, whose boughs stretch from the western marge of Thurston Mere.' Behind it is Coniston Hall, the seat of the Flemings from about 1250 to some

Near Coniston Bridge

time after 1700, when they deserted it finally for Rydal, and left it to ruin. Mrs Radcliffe, author of *The Mysteries of Udolpho*, came here a little before 1794, and confused Coniston Hall with Conishead Priory, like several later writers. In 1871 Ruskin bought the cottage and a bit of ground which had been the home of the wood-engraver and poet, W. J. Linton, and Mrs Lynn Linton, the novelist. For nearly twenty years he worked here at Brantwood— it was the period of his Oxford lectures, *Fors Clavigera*, and autobiography— and for ten years more waited there as a worn-out invalid, until death released him (20th January 1900). He was buried in Coniston churchyard, where the tall greenstone cross marks his grave. Behind the village institute, close to the church, is a museum where many drawings, engravings, manuscripts, and other Ruskin relics are on view, with other things illustrating the neighbourhood.[1]

On the east side of the lake is Tent Lodge, where Tennyson spent his honeymoon; and behind it is Tent Cottage, the home of Elizabeth Smith (*b.* 1776, *d.* 1806) a remarkable and precocious girl, who taught herself a dozen languages while she was still in her 'teens, and wrote poetry and translations which scholars and critics of the day commended highly. At Monk Coniston lived Mr James Garth Marshall, M.P. for Leeds, who was one of the first scientific students of the metamorphic rocks of these mountains, and made some valuable contributions to geology.[2] Coniston, from its position between the volcanic ash formation of the higher fells and the Lower Silurian blue slates and flags, with the narrow band of Coniston limestone dividing the two great series of strata, and from the curious evidences of ice action (e.g. up the copper-mines valley), and the problems connected with its lake basins, has always been interesting to geologists; and much of the pioneer work of Professor Adam Sedgwick was done here. There is a comic story in dialect by Dr Gibson, the Coniston poet, in which Joe, the local bumpkin, saves himself a good deal of trouble by 'teeming' out the specimens from the geologist's bag, and refilling it from a handy stone-heap nearer home. Dr Gibson said it was *not* Sedgwick on whom the trick was played; probably not, or there would have been a sequel to the story. A. C. Gibson lived from 1844 for seven years at Yewdale Bridge, and wrote *The Old Man, or Ravings and Ramblings around Coniston*, and *The Folk-speech of Cumberland*, with rollicking humour and capital dialect; but his antiquarian legends are not to be taken too seriously, and his antipathy to Wordsworth strikes one nowadays as doing him more harm than it ever did to the dying lion.

One of the most visited places in the Coniston area—indeed, within the Lake District—is Tarn Hows, though it is essentially a man-made beauty spot. The Marshalls of Monk Coniston were responsible for the dam which

1 Brantwood is now open to the public. It contains many items associated with Ruskin [Editor's note].

2 Monk Coniston is now a Holiday Fellowship centre [Editor's note].

created a single sheet of water from three small, reed-fringed tarns. Today the property is part of the National Trust and is visited annually by more than three-quarters of a million people. Most visitors are content to stroll around the tarn but there are more demanding paths; the route down Tom Gill from the dam is rewarding since the small ravine has a tiny waterfall, beautifully set in rocks and trees. Farther down those who find an interest in the old industries may notice the slag and ashes of an ancient bloomery, for the old folk hereabouts were no respecters of scenery. In this their descendants worthily sustain the ancestral character, for in Tilberthwaite, the deep valley opposite, entered between Raven Crag on the right and Yewdale Crag on the left, when once you have penetrated its recesses you hardly know which to wonder at more—the romantic natural beauty of the dale or the enormous and undisguised masses of quarry rubbish. It is the best slate in the world that they find here; the industry once made Coniston prosperous; the working of the quarries is most interesting, but the rubbish heaps are an eyesore.

The Coniston 'Old Man,' in spite of various guesses as to the meaning of the name, is probably nothing more nor less than the old cairn on the highest of Coniston fells. The present cairn was made by the Ordnance Surveyors; before that there were three ancient stone heaps—'the old man, his wife, and his son.' Wordsworth readers do not need to be told that 'a man on the peak of the crag' means a pile of stones. Under the Old Man and its cliffs, nearly one thousand feet beneath the cairn, is Low Water, from which a cascade falls down a cleft in a precipice five hundred feet high; beneath it is the Pudding Stone, a large block nearly rivalling the Borrowdale Bowder Stone. In spite of mines and quarries and watercourses, this labyrinth of coves and crags is impressive mountain scenery. The rocks are so bold that in winter the snow breaks upon them into real Alpine forms. The ravine of Red Dell, the bluff of Kernel Crag, the wild corrie of Levers Water, the peak of Raven Tor, have all the power of much larger and more inaccessible ranges; and at the back of the Old Man there are Seathwaite Tarn among huge descents of desolate grass and stones, Blind Tarn, perched in its seat under Brown Pike, and Goat's Water, deep and mysterious, beneath nearly five hundred feet of scree slopes and a giant's castle wall of sheer precipice five hundred feet higher, with couloirs worth an Alpine climber's notice. I often wish Gray, of the *Elegy in a Country Churchyard*, had been dragged up here: he found the Jaws of Borrowdale so terrible that it would have been pleasant to watch him accumulating adjectives half-way up Dow Crags, one of the finest climbing grounds in the Lake District. Most fine weekends the crags are festooned with brightly coloured ropes and 'tigers' and 'crag rats' in garish anoraks.

Walna Scar is the continuation of the ridge southward. The old pack-horse road went from Coniston over this pass, joined by another road from Torver ('Torfi's *ergh*' or shieling in Norse times). There are burial cairns, ancient dykes, and ring embankments on these moors also, as well as curious ancient dwellings traceable on the Duddon side of the watershed. All these fells must once have been the happy hunting-grounds of primitive races, children of the mist, perhaps surviving long after the outskirts were settled by civilized folk.

Coniston

At the foot of the pass lies Seathwaite, where the tributary stream from the tarn meets the Duddon. This was the scene of the life and labours of 'Wonderful Walker'—the Rev. Robert Walker, born here 1709, became curate 1735 or '36, died here 1802—'That lowly, great, good man,' Wordsworth called him in *The Excursion*; in the Duddon sonnets:

> Such as the Heaven-taught skill of Herbert drew,
> And tender Goldsmith crowned with deathless praise.

As a picture of life in the dales over two hundred years ago, a letter dated 'Coniston, July 26, 1754,' and describing the Walker household, is as good as any Wilkie or Faed:

'I found him sitting at the head of a long square table, such as is commonly used in this country by the lower class of people, dressed in a coarse blue frock, trimmed with black horn buttons, a checked shirt, a leathern strap about his neck for a stock, a coarse apron, and a pair of great wooden-soled shoes plated with iron to preserve them (which we call clogs in these parts), with a child upon his knee, eating his breakfast; his wife and the remainder of his children were some of them employed in waiting upon each other, the rest in teasing and spinning wool, at which trade he is a great proficient; and moreover, when it is ready for sale, will lay it, by sixteen or thirty-two pounds' weight upon his back, and on foot, seven or eight miles, will carry it to the market, even in the depth of winter. I was not surprised at all this ... but I must confess myself astonished with the alacrity and the good-humour that appeared

both in the clergyman and in his wife, and more so at the sense and ingenuity
of the clergyman himself.'

The church was rebuilt in 1874, but the homesteads and general aspect of
the dale are much as they were in those days, or when Wordsworth wrote his
sonnets on the Duddon.[1] 'Still glides the stream, and shall for ever glide,' he
said, in all the fallacy of hope.

Duddon was, until 1974, the boundary of Lancashire and Cumberland. It
rises near the Three Shires Stone on Wrynose, runs by the line of the old
Roman road to Cockley Beck, turns south among wild and bare mountains,
Hardknott, Greyfriar, and Harter Fell; and then the dainty contrast begins
between the sternness of the background and the sweetness of homestead and
garden and flowery garth.

At Birks Bridge, where the rowans hang over grey rocks and green foaming
pools; at the Stepping Stones, where it broadens under the wooded heights of
Grassguards; at the great ravine below and the gate of Dunnerdale under
Wallabarrow, and then through the valley bottom to Ulpha, it is more poetical
in the reality than Wordsworth's often-quoted but still inadequate sequence:
The kirk of Ulpha on its hill, and Ulpha old hall, a ruined pele on the brink
of a tributary gorge, with its legend of the lady who was lost in the chasm as
she fled from the wolf, and Stonestar with its bloomery mound and more
venerable, mysterious cairns: these give us hints of ancient story. And then
the river flows on through its woods and down by shelving banks all massed
with daffodils in spring, till it slides under Duddon Bridge and out into the
sands. Not far from Duddon Bridge on the west side of the river are the
remains of the Duddon Iron Furnace, one of the finest eighteenth-century
furnaces in Britain. From 1736 until 1867 the rich, red haematite ore from
Furness was smelted here with charcoal produced locally in the woodlands
bordering the river. The 40-foot high furnace and the great barns where the
ore and charcoal were once kept have recently been conserved as a memorial
to an important phase of the Industrial Revolution in this now tranquil corner
of the Duddon valley. Up on the hill to the west is the circle of huge stones
at Swinside—the Sunkenkirk, that gives no answer to the antiquary exploring
it with spade and measuring line. In the dale to the east is little Broughton,
with its quaint market-square and cross, and its old hall masking the pele of
earlier days. Farther down, past Ladyhall, perched on its headland, and the
whitewashed, flowery cottages of Thwaites, Millom Castle stands in ruin, with
the grim record of the gallowshill beside it. And beyond the castle lies Millom,
a town which, like so many in West Cumbria, enjoyed a period of nineteenth-
century industrial prosperity based on haematite iron ore; in the late 1960s
both the iron works and the mines closed within a year of each other.

1 Though many of the cottages are now holiday homes [Editor's note].

The hum
And blare that for a hundred years
Drummed at the town's deaf ears
Now fills the air with the roar of silence.
They'll need no more to swill the slag-dust off the windows;
The curtains will be cleaner
And the grass plots greener
Round the Old Folk's council flats.

Norman Nicholson
On the Closing of Millom Ironworks, 1968
Selected Poems 1940–1982, Faber & Faber Ltd

IV

ESKDALE AND WASTWATER

Cairns and circles of South Cumbria—Waberthwaite crosses—
The ancient port of Ravenglass—The Luck of Muncaster—The
runes of Irton—Unspoilt Eskdale—The heart of Cumbria—Gosforth and its Norse sculptures—The torment of Loki—Thor's
fishing—The hall and the holy well—Dane's camp and King's
camp—Calder Abbey—The Flemings' mote—The puzzle of St
Bridget's—The Boy of Egremont—St Bees: the story of snow in
summer.

THE large triangle of country between the Duddon, the Esk, and the sea, is
much less known, even to its neighbours, than it deserves. It may claim in a
way to be Lake District; for has it not Devoke Water, greatest of the moorland
tarns, with fine and varied scenery at hand and the grandest of our summits
in the background? It may claim to be mountain country, for there is no
ruggeder top than Harter Fell, no more wonderful group of rocks than
Buckbarrow—the heights which look like some enormous prehistoric fortification as you see them, rising over the moors, from any point near Foxfield
or Broughton; and there is no other height in all the fells which lifts itself like
Black Combe right up from the coastline, and figures massive and distinct far
out to sea. This upland region is a peculiarly wild and impressive tract of
country, not unlike some parts of Iceland in its effect—huge form and sombre
colour contrasting with the level gleam of sea-line continually reappearing;
and it is singularly rich in very curious 'remains' which are well worth hunting
up and dreaming over, if one cannot do more.

The great circle at Swinside has already been named; south of that, at Lacra,
there are the remains of four stone circles. At Standing Stones farm is the
Giant's Grave of Kirksanton, and in a cliff near is the Giant's Chair; the
legend is that the giant was killed in battle and buried in the tumulus, and the
last two upright stones seem to be survivors of a circle, which suggests a
prehistoric interment. There were three great circles on the other side of Black
Combe, at Gutterby, Annaside, and Hall Foss, all now destroyed; but on the
moor behind Bootle are many cairns, and two interesting ancient homesteads,
foundations of small dwellings, with garths enclosed by dykes, very like the
old type of Icelandic farm, and no doubt the deserted homes of early settlers.
Behind Corney, towards Stoneside Fell, is another garth, formerly called

Near Drigg

Roman, of perhaps the same age. This upland country was all wooded formerly, and before the middle of the twelfth century it was quite a no-man's-land—neither England nor Scotland nor Cumbria proper; and so it would have been just the place for a sort of Adullam, a haunt of outlaws and sea-rovers, refugees and Viking squatters. In almost every part there are traces of ancient huts, round or square—for instance, on Thwaites Fell on the moor near Fenwick (where stone implements have been found, as at many other sites in South Cumbria), up Crosby Gill, under Worm Crag, around Devoke Water, and south of it on both sides of Stainton Beck, and west of it at Barnscar. This last has been locally called 'a Danish city' populated by the 'lads of Drigg and the lasses of Beckermet'; but the finding of urns in the cairns suggests that it was a prehistoric settlement and cemetery.[1] Some of the many small ruins with which the upland is dotted may be as old; others are of various dates, down to ruined shepherds' bields and sheepfolds of comparatively modern times.

The mountain region at which we have been looking is surrounded by a fringe of deep little wooded dales, and old, picturesque farmhouses among rocks and ravines. North and east are the two great valleys of Esk and Duddon; south is the charming Whicham valley, and west is a narrow shelf of land between the hill-slopes and the sea, on which are planted several interesting villages and churches. Bootle, indeed, claims to be a market-town, with a charter dating from 1346, but it is one of the smallest market-towns in England. At Seaton Hall there is the traceried east window and some ruins of the Benedictine nunnery founded in the thirteenth century. At Waberthwaite, on the Esk, in the churchyard of the quaint little cottage-church, has been erected the shaft of a pre-Norman cross. There is also a still more ancient fragment with Anglian work something like that on the stone at Heversham with fox and grapes: this dates back perhaps to the ninth century, and records the otherwise forgotten Anglian settlers from Northumbria, who after King Ecg-frith's conquest of Cumbria gradually crept round the coast from the north, and took the harbours and the more fertile land between firth and fell, until the Northmen in their turn became the dominant race.[2]

1 Between Black Combe, the Duddon valley and Eskdale, there are thousands of cairns, making this one of the best preserved prehistoric landscapes in England [Editor's note].

2 Dr Richard N. Bailey has advanced an alternative theory. He suggests that the patterns at Waberthwaite are Anglian ornament set in a Viking-period context [Editor's note].

Ravenglass

Ravenglass was the great seaport for which the races contended. The name is a puzzle; its early form is Reinglas, which ought to mean the plough-land of Glas, or Grey-man, with a Celtic (Viking) name.[1] Here three rivers, Esk, Irt, and Mite, join to make a large and almost landlocked harbour with one narrow entrance between long spits of sandhills that shelter the port and ancient town. On the north side of the estuary is the Ravenglass Gullery and Nature Reserve owned by Muncaster Castle but managed by Cumbria County Council; here black-headed gulls, terns, shelduck, and merganser nest in their tens of thousands. Straight through the estuary you see the Isle of Man, forty miles across the sea. The bar now prevents any but small craft from entering, and at all times it must have been impossible for big ships to get into this harbour. But in ancient times up to the last century most of the trade was done in vessels which drew very little water. If Milnthorpe was a port, how much more would Ravenglass have suited the needs of early commerce!

The Romans occupied the place, and made a fort south of the present little town; however, little remains today for in 1850 the railway line was constructed through the centre of the site and later the eastern side of the line was planted with coniferous trees. Nevertheless, the remains of the former bathhouse still stand outside the perimeter of the fort. Curiously named 'Walls Castle' (? Wallis i.e. Welsh), the walls are high enough for you to pass through the doors and see the skeleton of the original house.[2] Excavation has proved that there was the usual hypocaust. There is a curious door-sill with square furrows at the sides, and bevelled furrow in the middle, and hard rose-coloured plaster in the still-undefaced niche. The preservation of the building is said to be accounted for by its use in the early Middle Ages as the dwelling-place of the

1 That is to say, in these parts such Gaelic names came in with the Vikings, who had lived in Ireland or the Isles before coming here.

2 In 1928 Professor Robin G. Collingwood suggested that 'Walls Castle' was 'the best preserved Roman building in the north of England. Nowhere else in the north—perhaps nowhere else in the whole country—is there a Roman house still standing to the full height of its walls' [Editor's note].

Penningtons, who seem to have occupied this old house before building Muncaster Castle. Hence, the Roman road went past Muncaster, and past a Roman pottery by the Esk (north of Croppel How) to Hardknott and Wrynose, where we have seen it before, leading from Ambleside and Kendal. The great jars of Italian wine and other foreign wares, of which fragments are found in the inland sites, must have been landed here. In those days Ravenglass was an important place. Later on, it was still important; it got its market charter in 1209, and flourished through the Middle Ages, to decay at last when new routes took away its traffic. So late as 1825 the beacon on the hill was built as a lighthouse for the coasting trade; but of course the railway superseded all that.

Just as we found near the port of Milnthorpe evidences of medieval fortifications and the still earlier remains of pre-Norman wealth, so it is near Ravenglass. Muncaster Castle was originally a pele-tower serving as refuge from raiders at the harbour: the Penningtons gradually enlarged their tower into a castle about 1325, and about 1800 it was rebuilt as a great mansion, the seat of the Lords Muncaster while that ancient family lasted. When King Henry VI took refuge there after one of his defeats, in 1461, it is said he gave his host a curious bowl, of greenish glass, enamelled and gilt, which is still preserved and known as 'The Luck of Muncaster.' The king's bedstead and a portrait of him with the Luck in his hand are among the treasures of the place.[1] Another curiosity is the portrait of Tom Skelton, the Muncaster fool, said to have flourished in the time of the Civil Wars. In the pretty churchyard near the castle an old cross has been re-erected, dating perhaps from the eleventh century—a relic of the Norse lords of that period.

At Irton, again, we find both a pele and a cross. The pele-tower has grown into Irton Hall, now a special school, and the cross in the churchyard is one

Walls Castle

1 The Castle is open to the public [Editor's note].

of our finest, for it still carries its head and stands about ten feet high. The panel on the front once had runes, which read, 'Gebidaeth forae—'—pray for some lord or lady unknown. This, and the scrolls, and symmetrical ornament, show that it is Anglian work, earlier than the Muncaster cross; and with the fragment at Waberthwaite it is evidence of Anglo-Saxon settlement near the harbour—certainly of wealth, probably of trade, more than a thousand years ago.

If Eskdale owned a lake—for the two large and many smaller tarns on the hills enclosing it do not make up for the want of a real lake in the valley—it would long since have been one of the favourite parts of the district. The bright, clean granite that breaks into such fine forms; the dale closed in at the foot by lofty and rugged Muncaster Fell, and so having no tame end, but growing in grandeur at every step up the stream to Harter Fell and Hardknott and thence to Bowfell and Scafell Pike; the wealth of vegetation, these and many other points of natural scene or ancient story combine towards the appeal this valley makes to those who know it. But it has no lake, and, what is more curious, it never could have had more in all its length than a very small basin holding water. At the elbow, near Butterilket,[1] there are flat fields which may represent an old lake surface, but there is nothing to compare with the deep and broad hollows in other valleys. And so Eskdale has been saved from being a 'resort.' A little village of villas has grown up at the point where the miniature railway enters it from Miterdale,[2] but above this the old farms are still picturesque; and above Butterilket there is the completest wildness and solitude that the wearied townsman can desire. Real countryfolk often fail to understand this delight in 'unspoilt' neighbourhoods and tracts of ground where you can walk all day without meeting a soul: they think of the land as something to make money out of, or at least to be farmed or mined for a living. But there is many a farmer who pays his rent from his summer visitors, and they come to see the old-fashioned country, not third-rate imitations of town— the wild hills, not roads and signposts—a clean sky, not the smoke of the big cities. Here, in Eskdale, there still is country, and hills, and sunshine; the little railway is so quaint and so leisurely and so inconspicuous that one forgives it—though I have smelt it from the top of Hardknott; and the mines it was built to serve have been closed for many years.

At Beckfoot station you alight for Dalegarth Force, or Stanley Gill as it is called, from the Stanleys who lived at the old hall among the trees and under the crags. Like most of our cascades, this has no great volume of water, but plenty of white and black and green, and all the finish that Nature's daintiest miniature-painting can give. Passing the church, you follow the lanes hedged with wild rose and the granite river-banks to the Woolpack Inn; thence up

1 Brotherilkeld [Editor's note].

2 The Norse genitive in -r, from the name of the river Mite: not 'Mitredale.'

Dalegarth Force, Eskdale

the valley, taking the Kendal road—Kendal is a far cry, but this was the old pack-horse route and the Roman road before that—towards Hardknott Hause. Crossing the river, on your left is the ancient farm of Butterilket, or, as the Furness monks wrote it in the thirteenth century, Brotherilkeld. The name, variously spelt, might be the 'booths of Ulfkell' or the 'bubbling spring of the booths' or 'of the road'; no one can dogmatize in this case. And then, after twenty minutes' easy walking up the road you get upon the ridge and find:

> That lone camp on Hardknot's height,
> Whose guardians bent the knee to Jove and Mars.

There are not many places where story and scenery are tuned together to such a high pitch. There are Chillon and Tell's Chapel, but the story is apocryphal in both places. There is the field of Sempach, but the scenery is naught. But here is a wonderfully complete relic of that marvellous Roman power which threw all the savage North into fetters of roads with locks of fortress, and held it so for three centuries of civilization; their walls you see, their gates, their dwelling-houses, their baths, the very plot of rugged moor levelled by their engineers for the daily drill and sport of their troops—'Law,

On the railway between Boot and Ravenglass

order, duty and restraint, obedience, discipline,' visibly stamped upon the
wildest, proudest heart of the intractable mountainland.

It is a green ridge with a wall of precipice five hundred feet high to the
north, and a deep ravine to the south; behind are the crags with one narrow
gap leading out to the eastward; there the road came in, and passed along the
edge of the green and down to the valley and out to the sea: the sea visible in
the distance, and far over it the Isle of Man. Around are the greatest mountains
of Cumbria—Scafell and the Pikes, Great End and Bowfell rise peaked above
the crags of the valley, and to the south Harter Fell stands over the pass with
its dark masses of rock and down-rushing streams. As a mere landscape there
is nothing more magnificent; unless it is this when the tops are white among
the snow clouds, or as I have seen it at sunrise when the mist, all aflame in
the first red light, breaks from one rock and another, and moves and melts
away beneath the cloudless summits.

Formerly it was by no means certain what was the meaning of these ruins:
many hesitated at believing that the Romans would have planted a fort on
such a spot, though its form was regular, unlike the rudely planned ramparts
of the Britons. So in 1889 it was determined by the local Antiquarian Society
to explore. In the north tower we found a gem-ring, spear-head, and key,
showing that the site was Roman and worth more attention, and digging was
carried on until 1894. Indeed, the fort was one of the first in Britain to be
systematically examined; in 1949 the site was acquired by the Ministry of
Works and a conservation and partial reconstruction programme was under-
taken, not without criticism from some academics. The last major excavation
took place in the 1960s.

The fort was about three hundred and sixty feet square, with stone walls,
and a deep ditch partly enclosing them; rounded corners and a tower in each,
with glass windows; a gate in each side, even in that which almost overhangs

the cliff, though this gate was only half the width of the others, and probably would serve merely for carrying out rubbish and throwing it overboard. In the middle are three buildings; the headquarters in the centre, with open court and small rooms all round; the granary on the east, with buttresses indicating that it was tall; and on the west a long room with a smaller one at the end, quarters for the commandant. The rest of the space was filled with wooden barracks and offices. From the east gate a road led to the levelled area, locally called the bowling-green, where no doubt the men drilled and took exercise, as they could hardly have done in the broken ground in the neighbourhood. A water supply was brought from the hill behind and led under the bowling-green to the camp—which of course was drained, wet as it now is with the rainwater that collects in the earth choked with stones and rubbish. Between the fort and the road, to the south-east, are the remains of a long building, west of which was a furnace, and in the easternmost of the three rooms there was a large tank; the building was a Roman bath, with the hottest room next to the furnace and the cold plunge at the other end. Adjoining it is a circular building, the *Laconicum*, an 'extra-hot' room with its own furnace. There were, of course, plenty of fragments of pottery and glass, metal objects, and a few jewels, but no human remains. In the bath-room some little animals, a small dog and its puppies or a cat with its kittens, had been lying when the building fell in at its overthrow, and there the poor little bones were found, too brittle for more to be said about them.

In spite of extensive excavation, the history of the fort still remains uncertain; the theory that Hardknott was an Agricolan fort is no longer accepted and it now seems that it was completed in the reign of Hadrian. One of the most exciting finds from the fort was a fragmentary inscription discovered in 1964 which appears to reinforce this view. It reads:

> For the Emperor Caesar Trajan Hadrian Augustus, son of the divine Trajan, conqueror of Parthia, grandson of the devine Nerva, Pontifex Maximus, thrice consul, the Fourth Cohort of Delmatians [set this up].

The date is thought to fall between A.D. 119 and 138 and the unit mentioned, the Fourth Cohort of Delmatians, was recruited from the Adriatic province of Delmatia, now part of modern Yugoslavia. One wonders what the troops from the sunny Mediterranean thought of their posting to the fort amid the cloud-catching fells of Brigantia.

From the terminus of the little railway at Dalegarth station you can follow the Whillan Beck up its gill, with many a pretty fall and so up to the moor. Half a mile north-west of Gillbank are several prehistoric cairns, a mile farther north is Burnmoor Tarn, solitary under Scafell. Hence the path leads easily across a hause between the Screes and Scafell to Wasdale Head, or one can climb Scafell without encountering the crags of its northern and eastern faces, and look down into Mickledore and across at the Pikes; or even, if one is accustomed to real climbing, venture down the Lord's Rake and so by the Pikes to Styhead or Wasdale. But that short cut leaves much unseen: we must return to the elbow of the valley.

Hence upwards, Eskdale is a glorious wilderness. Dungeon Gill and Wasdale Head Hotels are the nearest houses, five miles as the crow flies, but with Bowfell in the way of the one and Scafell in the way of the other: due north it is more than six miles in a bee-line to Seathwaite in Borrowdale over Esk Hause. You can play at being lost, and imagine a great lone land; yet the heights and distances are only big enough to give the illusion for a few hours' ramble, and you are sure—barring accidents—to come down somewhere into civilization before nightfall. We have no other bit of wild country like this, and hitherto it has not been spoiled for the purposes of a playground by too much meddling. A very little pathmaking and setting up of signposts would take away the charm of finding your own road, of attacking Nature single-handed, which is the thing that gives our homeland an advantage over more stupendous Alps, where you must take a guide, not to say more extensive mountain tracts where you cannot go without a whole caravan.

At Esk Force the valley branches: that to the right leads up to Bowfell, or over the Ore Gap to Langstrath; that to the left leads up to the grand inner valley, which is walled by the crags of Scafell, the Pikes, and Great End, successively emerging, each more impressive than the last. Continuing up the

The old bridge at Boot

A mountain pass

valley, you reach Esk Hause, and meet the track between Styhead and Rossett Gill. Sprinkling Tarn and Angle Tarn, though they are set among crags like the tarns of Coniston, are curiously different from them in their situation. Instead of occupying the bottoms of coves, combes, or corries, they are perched on watershed ridges. This is not uncommonly the case with rock basins too small to be called tarns, but here the peculiar structure occurs on a considerable scale, and with circumstances of scenery which make it not easily forgotten. On a cloudless, hot day, perhaps, when one is tired and thirsty, and the sun glares into every cranny of the rocks, cutting up the scene into weariful spottiness, one may pass this way without uplifting of soul. But let the mountains have something to talk about; let them dress up in their clouds or their snows, and act their parts: show what they can do with white dazzle against blue and black, or give you peeps of distant lake vignetted like a Turner sketch, or hints of crag behind crag and crest above crest, and now and then a swirl of grey, trailing over green tarn-banks and valley bottoms, lifting its curtain on new scenes, of which there is an inexhaustible store—for the mist has every sort of transformation trick ready; it is Nature's own stage-manager—and then you will see the drama of mountain gloom and mountain glory. Possibly, if it is so minded, the sun may help, and throw blazing searchlights on green and gold and lilac, or dewy rainbows, or even the rare fogbow, with your shadow in the centre, the true Brocken Spectre; possibly, climbing higher still, as you follow the frequent cairns that lead to the topmost cairn of the Pikes, you may feel the blue overhead penetrating the vapour, and suddenly stand above a waving sea of opalescence, with islands of hardly recognizable peaks blocked on the silent void. I have seen these things when folk below were kicking their heels and grumbling at the weather; but even if there is nothing but rain and rain, with a map and a compass, and some habit of mountain walking—without which the fear of being lost overbalances the pleasure—even then there is a delight in wandering here, through the heart of the hills, far beyond the easy amusements of sunny roads and lake shores.

The two separate mountains of Scafell and the Scafell Pikes are like two castle towers, between which would be a clear course but for a little gatehouse filling the gap. The gatehouse has a ridged roof, one end of which rests against the side of each tower. The northern tower, Scafell Pikes, has been so battered at the top that you can clamber down its ruined upper storey and get upon the ridge of the gatehouse roof. Then you are in Mickledore, the great gap; but when you have 'ridden the rough roofbeam,' like an Icelandic ghost, and reach the other side, thinking to climb the southern tower, Scafell, you find that it is not nearly so ruined. Indeed, it stands up with pinnacles and buttresses so high, and flanking precipices so deep, and even in places overhanging, that here, if anywhere in these mountains, one can get the impression of size and awesomeness which the usual quiet contour and unexciting altitudes cannot give. Right in front of Mickledore ridge the blocky volcanic-ash formation cleaves into a set of giant steps, as it were tilted from behind, so that the top of each step slopes outwards, and what should be vertical often overhangs. That is the Broad Stand,[1] accessible a little to the left of the ridge; but it needs a long arm, or, better still, a friend to give you a lift. Farther to the left is the Chimney, easy to climb for some distance, but near the top the trouble begins; and if you are not accustomed to climbing, the return from this point is dangerous. To the right of the ridge is the Lord's Rake, a gully which is the least difficult of the three routes to the top. There have been misadventures enough on this perilous edge to warn inexperienced wanderers to leave it alone. As a matter of scenery, the best points of view are from the other and safer side of Mickledore. Scafell can be climbed without risk from south or east or west; it is only this face that needs Alpine gymnastics; and when you are at the cairn on the Pikes you are at the highest point in England, without the danger of this lower summit.

Down from the Pikes an interesting route is by Piers Gill, following the right bank of the deep zigzag chasm, and, before the main tributary from the right comes in, crossing the breast of the mountain to look into Greta Force, the grandest in the district. Opposite and across the valley down which the Styhead path runs, Great Gable rises finely, with a band of precipitous rocks breaking the great descent of green and grey. One of these rocks, detached from the main wall, stands isolated, and about a hundred feet high; it is commonly known now as the Napes Needle, accessible to skilled cragsmen; its ascent was the discovery of Mr Haskett-Smith. It is pictured on all the posters of Lake District attractions. For the mere fell-walker there is a reward in beholding it near at hand, abrupt upon the slope, with the Isle of Man in the distance above the deep valley. The Great Gable itself is an easy climb,

---

1 The descent of this rock face by Coleridge in 1802 is classed by many as the first recorded English rock climb [Editor's note].

Wastwater

especially from Styhead, where the path from Wasdale to Borrowdale is at its
highest near the tarn. It is the old favourite mountain walk, enjoyed by
thousands as an escape from the regular coach-road, and all the more enjoyed
because there is no harsh artificial line to jar upon the wild harmony of the
whole delightful pass. From Seathwaite by quaint little Stockley Bridge,[1] and
up the steep dell past Taylor's Gill Force, and over the lofty bit of moorland
to the tarn, it is all perfect romance; and then, suddenly turning a rugged
angle where the rude track winds among broken rocks, Wasdale is before you,
below you, and great contours on either hand—all the might and majesty of
the hills. And you are a little thing among them, and the thread of a path that
marks your way, by the sufferance of the giants, leads you step by step—not
too easily, lest you should forget where you are and what you came for—down
to the valley, after a walk you will remember when car-drives and coach
excursions are long forgotten.

Wasdale Head is famous for its tiny church[2] and its former landlord, Ritson,
the wrestler and *raconteur*, who kept the inn until 1879, and had known
Christopher North and other worthies of the earlier age. At Wasdale Head
there are also sweet bits of beckside scenery and walks among the lesser dells,
beside these high places where we have been climbing. Up towards Black Sail,
the pass behind Kirkfell into Ennerdale, and up Lingmell Beck or towards
Burnmoor, or in those deep valleys opening on the northern shore of the lake,
there is the Cumberland charm of dainty detail in the midst of an almost
savage grandeur. Indeed, if the long line of the Screes, and their crumbling
precipices twelve hundred to fourteen hundred feet aloft, are not more than

---

1 Restored after the devastating floods of August, 1966 [Editor's note].

2 Dedicated appropriately to St Olaf, the patron saint of Norway [Editor's note].

Wasdale Head

almost savage, commend me to their betters in ferocity. But to enjoy this
neighbourhood you must go there out of the season; that is to say, any time
except the Easter and summer vacations.

Passing through Strands, we reach the ancient and interesting village of
Gosforth, in the valley of the Bleng, a little stream that comes down from
Seatallan and Haycock to join the Irt, which flows from Wastwater to Ravenglass. Gosforth is widely famous for its churchyard cross, a slender monolith
of red sandstone, standing fourteen feet high from its base to the top of the
wheel-cross head. There is a cast of it in the Victoria and Albert Museum and
a copy in Aspatria churchyard made for, and partly by, the Rev. W. S.
Calverley, who was the first to give a satisfactory interpretation of the curious
figures carved on it. They represent Loki, the demon of Norse mythology,
chained in hell, as the Edda relates, under a serpent which dropped its venom
upon him, so that he writhed under the torment, 'whence,' says the ancient
legend, 'there come earthquakes.' It was hardly believable, when this interpretation was first given, that a cross undeniably Christian, and bearing a figure
of Christ crucified on one face, should have this heathen symbol on the other—
all the more definite because Loki's wife, Sigun, is there to hold the cup that
caught the poison and spared her mate the pain until, the cup being full, she
had to turn aside and empty it, and then the drop fell on him. By this it is
seen that no conventional devil is pictured, but a real illustration to the Edda
is meant.[1] Dr Parker of Gosforth added to the discovery by pointing out more
allusions to Norse myths, and by finding another stone, now built into the
church wall near the organ, evidently representing the Edda story of Thor;
how he went fishing for the great sea-serpent which encircles the world and
holds it together; how he baited his hook with a bull's head and caught the

1 For a recent interpretation of the meaning of the carvings see Knut Berg, 'The Gosforth
  Cross', *Transactions Courtauld Institute*, XXI, 27–43 [Editor's note].

monster; and how the giant Hymir, frightened lest Thor should succeed and so break the bonds of earth, cut the line.[1] This was part of another cross of which the head is perhaps one built into the wall above. A third cross was cut down in the eighteenth century to make the present sundial. The two hogbacks, or shrine-shaped tombs—found at restoration under the walls of the Norman church, the twelfth-century church of which the curious capitals of the chancel-arch formed part—are of the same period as the crosses, earlier than Norman, but later than the composition of the Witch's Prophecy in the Edda, which is thought to have been the work of a Norse skald of the tenth century, who knew Irish and English beliefs, and brought the uncouth traditions of his ancestors up to date, so to say, as a rival system to Christianity. Many Vikings of that age were half Christian and half heathen, baptized and church-going at home, and praying to Thor in battle and at sea. This must have been the kind of folk for whom these monuments here at Gosforth were made, with Christ on one side and the heathen gods on the other, illustrating the Völuspá or Witch's Prophecy; and the period must have been about the year 1000.

Gosforth Hall, near the church, is the old house where Bishop Nicholson in the seventeenth century used to go courting Barbara Copley when he was a young archdeacon. Up the field from Gosforth Hall is a holy well, around which may be seen the foundations of a medieval chapel. Half a mile north-north-east of the hall, in a narrow bit of ground between two long walls, is the 'Dane's Camp,' not Danish, but an ancient homestead; and a mile and a half east-south-east of the hall is another old site, never yet properly investigated, but known as the 'King's Camp' at Laconby.

Seascale used to be not a village, but the old hall of the Senhouses, near which was a circle of great stones which the farmer buried, wise in his generation. We think him not so wise in ours, for it would have been another 'attraction' to the once-flourishing seaside resort which grew up round the perfect bit of bathing-sands.[2] From Seascale, or from the next station, Sella-

Near Gosforth

1 There are similar stones in Denmark and Sweden [Editor's note].

2 The circle was resurrected and restored in 1949 [Editor's note].

field,[1] we can reach the inland village of Calder Bridge. There the river tumbles over flat tables of sandstone, very picturesque in its quiet, lowland way. Near the village is Pelham House, on the old site of the manor-house of the Stanleys, who settled there in 1388; and down the stream a little way is Sella Park, another of the interesting old houses with pele-like walls and old oak, recalling the country life of three hundred years ago. But the glory of the neighbourhood is Calder Abbey, one of the most beautiful of all our ancient ruins.[2]

It was founded by Ranulf Meschines, lord of Copeland (the whole of this district is so called), in 1134 for a colony of monks from Furness Abbey. They had scarcely taken possession when they were driven out by a Scottish invasion; and in 1138 Calder was newly colonized from Furness. It was suppressed in 1536. The original buildings of the first colonists were burnt by the Scots; the second church, no doubt of wood, was replaced about 1180 by a small stone building of which the west door remains. About 1220 a new stone church was built, of which we can see the nave pillars and other parts. After the Scottish raid of 1322 this church was restored, and the chapter-house was built, with book-chambers on each side of its west door, as at Furness. Two of the effigies set up in the ruined chancel are probably those of a Sir John le Fleming of Beckermet (with joined hands and a fret on his shield), who died in the reign of Henry III, and of a Leyburne (with the lions on his shield) of Cunswick, near Kendal, connected with the Flemings in the later part of the fourteenth century. Another knight, like the last, cannot be identified (the one with his hand on the sword-hilt). A fourth very mutilated effigy has been thought to represent Sir Richard, son of Sir John le Fleming.

Calder Abbey

1 See Gazetteer [Editor's note].

2 Calder Abbey is privately owned and, sadly, there is no public access. However, the ruins can be clearly seen from the road and pathway [Editor's note].

Near Beckermet, a mile north-north-east from the village, are still traceable some remains of the burg or motehill of the Flemings, anciently called Carnarvon Castle. Sir Daniel Fleming has left us an account of the site, which resembled that of the elder branch of the family at Aldingham in Furness, in being a moated mound with a dyked base-court near it. In the village is the church of St John, a very ancient foundation, containing many curious and beautiful fragments of pre-Norman grave-crosses. Half a mile south-west of the village is St Bridget's, a thirteenth-century church, very picturesque and interesting in itself, but more widely known for its curious ancient crosses, one of which has an inscription which has puzzled antiquaries not a little. It seems to be eleventh-century Gaelic, with something about one named 'Iuan,' who, on the analogy of Saudar-Juan's or Sheep-John's cross in the Isle of Man, may simply be 'John.' The rest, at which many learned guesses have been made, is still obscure.

At Haile, up the valley, is another prettily placed and picturesque church with ancient pre-Norman stones: and at Ehenside, Gibb Tarn is the place where in the late nineteenth century, a number of prehistoric implements were found, one of them, a polished stone axe still in its haft, now in the British Museum.

Egremont Castle, now a ruin, was founded about 1120 by William Meschines, though some think the earthwork earlier. Parts of the masonry date from the twelfth century. The 'Boy of Egremont,' young William de Romilly, who was drowned at the Strid of Wharfe, as every reader of Wordsworth knows, was son of William FitzDuncan, nephew of David I of Scots (the same who ravaged Copeland and Calder in 1138), and Alice de Romilly, the heiress of Egremont. The Boy was thus one of the nearest in succession to the throne of Scotland, and the favourite of a majority of the nation. That was the reason of the 'endless sorrow' and great mourning made for him. Of his sisters, one married a de Luci, and it is of that family, so brought into possession of Egremont, that the story of the Horn is told, a legend versified by Wordsworth. The castle grew and passed to the Multons and Percys, but was finally destroyed, all but the courthouse, in 1578. The church, built or rebuilt about 1220, but now again rebuilt, has some curious fragments of twelfth- and thirteenth-century sculpture. The town got its market charter in 1267, and there is a street market every Friday.

Our tour through this mid-western part of Cumberland may fittingly close at St Bees, a spot where story and scenery are blended less strikingly but almost as intimately as at Hardknott. The legend is that about A.D. 650, when Irish missionaries were teaching English heathens the first rudiments of the Faith, before the Council of Whitby dismissed them from Northumbria, a certain Irish Saint Bega came with her nuns and begged a place for her settlement. The lord of the land—a Gallio—said they might have as much

ground as the snow covered at midsummer: and on Midsummer Day, behold
the snow! At any rate there was a pre-Norman church here with an Irish
name, Kirkby Begog—Begog being the regular Irish way of saying 'dear little
Bega,' that is, 'Saint Bega.'

This legend is medieval but fictitious, being built up from recognizable
sources. The name is from Bede and the story from common romances about
the saints. The reality is even more curious. In the thirteenth century they
still kept in St Bees church an ancient (Norse) arm-ring or fibula-ring, probably
of silver, on which litigants had to swear to the truth of their testimony, just
as in the heathen Norse temples; in fact, it had no doubt come down from a
pagan shrine. This Holy Ring (in Norse *Baugr*, in English of the day *Bēag*)
was in contemporary Latin *Sancta Bega*. There is only one other church of
St Bega, which is at Bassenthwaite; and there can be no doubt that the name
is simply the Holy Ring personified, like, for example, St Alkelda in Yorkshire,
the holy well that became a mythical person, from the old Norse *ölkelda*, 'ale
well,' or bubbling spring of effervescent mineral water.

Fragments of interlaced crosses may yet be seen in the churchyard and in
the church. One stone in particular is remarkable, the lintel set into the wall,
bearing a figure of St Michael fighting the dragon among curious early knots
and frets. This may have come from the neighbouring chapel of the saint at
Rottington on the headland. In the twelfth century a priory was founded by
William Meschines as a cell of St Mary's at York; it was burnt by the Scots
in 1315, but nevertheless was the third richest in Cumberland at the dissolution
of the monasteries. The church was spared, like that of Cartmel, and restored
in 1611 as the parish church, since when it has been altered somewhat, but
still remains a very fine relic of the Middle Ages. The west door and the
capitals of the tower piers date from about 1150; the west end of the nave and
aisles, the lower part of the tower, the north transept, and the west wall of the
south transept and chancel were built in 1200 or thereabouts; and the south
aisle of the chancel in the fourteenth century. Among the tombs is that of
Prior Cottingham, dated 1300.[1]

St Bees Public School, now co-educational, was established by Archbishop
Grindal in 1587, and reconstituted in 1881. The Head of Baruth, as it was
anciently called (*Barr-ruadh*, Irish for *Red-head*), rises in sandstone cliffs over
three hundred feet from the sea, the westernmost point and noblest coast
scenery of Cumberland.

---

1 During excavations in 1981 the body of a well-preserved man was unearthed. Believed to be
   that of a twelfth-century nobleman, the corpse was wrapped in a sheet of lead placed within
   a wooden coffin and packed with grey clay. It is thought to be the most complete medieval
   corpse yet discovered in Europe [Editor's note].

Troutbeck is one of the least altered villages in the Lake District; the main road by-passes the settlement and therefore change was minimized. On the fells to the north-east of the village, seen here, the Roman road from Ambleside to Brougham climbed to the summit of High Street.

V

ENNERDALE AND ALLERDALE

Whitehaven coal—Iron, ancient and modern—Antiquities of West
Cumberland—The first Lake poet—The three orders of mountain
architecture—Cockermouth Castle and its famous folk—Ancient
Workington—The Plumbland theft—'Speatry'—Villages on the
green—Forts or farms?—Imps or architects?—Michael Scot at
Wolsty Castle—The poisoned abbot—The unlucky church—The
country of *Redgauntlet*—Solway Sands.

A LITTLE to north of the red headland of St Bees there is a break in the cliffs,
and a bay with such a foreshore as gave boats in ancient times the desired
haven. Standing over it there is a white headland, cliffs which, at any rate, are
white in contrast to the red sandstone of the other promontory. In the
twelfth century the name Whit-hofd, 'white-head,' was already known; in 1295
Whytot-haven is mentioned. Three hundred years later a tiny fishing-hamlet
was all that folk knew by the name of Whitehaven. The Lowther family
acquired the Manor of St Bees in the early seventeenth century and in 1634
Sir Christopher built a pier at Whitehaven and began to dig the coal which
outcropped on the hillsides round the bay.

Sir Christopher's son, Sir John, who died in 1705, and grandson, Sir James,
who died in 1755, pressed the work forward. It was, of course, much to their
own interest to do so; but they were liberal and spirited in their methods and
fortunate in their employees, so that the Whitehaven mines not only became
exceedingly profitable, but they gave the opportunity for several important
engineering inventions and scientific discoveries.[1]

The first coal was got from the Bannock and Main bands by levels and
shallow pits. In a while it was necessary to go deeper, and then to pump out
the water that accumulated in workings below any drainable level. This was
done with horse-engines, 'ginns,' whence the name of a suburb of the growing
town. In 1709 there were seven pits, yielding weekly about eight hundred tons
of twenty-one to twenty-two hundredweight each, and the coal was shipped
from the wharf close by at 3s. a ton. In 1718 Carlisle Spedding became
engineer. He introduced the 'fire-engine,' as they called the steam-pump, one
of the first steam-engines in England. He investigated the fire-damp which

---

1 In 1642 the population of Whitehaven was 250; by 1713 this had increased to 4,000 [Editor's
note].

the deep borings revealed, carried it in tubes to light his office, and proposed to light the town with it. The town refused, and it was a century before gas came into use. He invented a way, in spite of the fire-damp, of lighting the darkness with the *steel mill*, a disk of steel revolving against a flint and throwing out a stream of sparks; a poor lamp, but better than none, and the only safe light until Davy's invention of 1816. Spedding, one of the greatest pioneers of industrial science, was killed in an explosion in 1755.

Another once-famous name is that of Dr W. Brownrigg, F. R. S., who died in 1800 at the age of eighty; he made important discoveries in the chemistry of coal-gas while he was in practice at Whitehaven. It was here that one of the earliest railways was laid down—with wooden rails and horse-trucks, a step in the evolution of modern travelling. In 1816, years before the first passenger railway, a locomotive was tried. But the first locomotives were modelled on the stationary pumping-engines; they were cumbrous and heavy, and the rails, though cast iron had been substituted for the primeval wood, could not carry the weight; so that the experiment was not at once successful. But Whitehaven by this time had grown into a town of more than seventeen thousand inhabitants, and its mines, extending for about a mile under the bed of the sea, were one of the wonders of the world. The late eighteenth century was the town's best time, since when other places have outrivalled it; but to many who pass this way and remember what they owe to the early engineers and men of science, Whitehaven may be even more classic ground than Calder Abbey or Hardknott.[1]

The smaller ports along this coast were Whitehaven's rivals, more or less unsuccessful. At Parton Mr Fletcher of Moresby tried to establish a harbour in 1705, but Sir John Lowther's opposition, in the interest of Whitehaven, was too strong; and a great storm in 1796 washed the pier away, and made an end of the place. Harrington port was built in 1760 by Mr Henry Curwen, who worked coal-mines near: in 1825 a great attempt to enlarge the workings ended, for the time, in a catastrophe; the sea broke in and the pit was drowned. Workington began to export coal before 1650, but it was only after 1730 that the Curwens and Lowthers developed the industry, which became enormously profitable, and made the old Roman, pre-Norman, and medieval port into a busy town. Maryport, another Roman and early medieval site, is still more modern in its present form. In 1750 there were only two houses, one just built, and one the original 'Golden Lion.' In 1774 Pennant on his tour of Scotland found above one hundred houses with thirteen hundred inhabitants, all collected by the opening of the coal trade on the estate of Humphrey Senhouse, who had named the place Maryport after his wife. Mr Christian of Ewanrigg, and his son, John Christian Curwen, M.P., and the Lord Lonsdale of the day

1 Sir Nikolaus Pevsner has argued that Whitehaven is the earliest post-medieval planned town in England [Editor's note].

The Abbey of St Mary of Furness was the Power and the glory of medieval Lakeland. Established in the remote valley of Beckansgill in 1127, this Savigniac and later Cistercian house became one of the major landowners in the fells, controlling thousands of acres in Borrowdale, Eskdale and all the territory between Coniston Water and Windermere. Today it is one of the finest yet least known of the monastic sites in Britain.

also worked mines on their lands near by, and shipped the coal from Maryport, which grew into a considerable town, with docks and a lighthouse and every promise of prosperity.[1] But these little harbours have 'cut one another's throats.' As if Whitehaven, Harrington, Workington, and Maryport were not enough, and undeterred by the fate of Parton, the Carlisle businessmen and manufacturers tried to set up their ports on the Solway. Port Carlisle was created in 1819–23, connected with the town by a canal. Despite grandiose schemes such as the extension of the canal to Newcastle, Port Carlisle did not prosper. In 1854–5 the canal was drained and replaced by a railway but this, too, was no great success. Then in 1859 docks were opened at Silloth, farther out seawards; but Silloth has not become great either. Indeed, none of the Cumberland ports have improved much upon the position they held nearly a

1 Maryport harbour closed in 1961 but the town's maritime past is recalled in an interesting museum. Today there are no underground coalmines in West Cumbria but extensive open-cast mining continues east of Workington [Editor's note].

*Like a huge galleon riding at anchor, Cartmel Priory completely dominates the
small south Cumbrian village. This Augustinian priory was founded in the late
12th century by William Mareschal, Earl of Pembroke. After the Dissolution,
most of the great church remained in ruins until 1618 when it was restored by
George Preston of Holker Hall. Today it is one of the finest medieval churches
in Cumbria.*

century ago. They are rather like a becalmed yacht race; each little puff sends
one and then another ahead, but there is not much progress.

Between the coal measures, which extend from Whitehaven to Torpenhow,
and the Skiddaw slate of the northern Lake mountains there is an outcrop of
limestone rich in haematite. As in Furness, this was worked of old. In the
twelfth century Holm Cultram Abbey worked mines at Bigrigg, near Egremont; and then, again, from 1635 onwards, those mines were pushed with
energy. Ancient oak spades have been found in the Bigrigg old workings, and
at Yeathouse oak spades with iron rims. The bloomeries, or small smelting-
hearths, are found in many places, as at Thornholme on the Calder, Smithy
Beck in Ennerdale, Whiteoak Beck near Loweswater, on the Irt and on the
Esk. These may be of any date up to the seventeenth century, when larger
furnaces came into use, such as we saw at Backbarrow, and in Coniston valley,
and at Duddon Bridge. In the middle of the nineteenth century modern
furnaces were built at Whitehaven, Workington and Cleator, but like coal

mining, this once great industry has contracted dramatically. One small iron mine continues near Egremont but elsewhere the rose red willow herb has replaced the blood red spoil tips of the haematite mines.

It might be thought that in such a region there was little to attract any sentimental voyager looking for scenery or story of more acceptedly romantic type; but this is not at all the case. The former coal and iron district is one of very great natural beauty in its way—between firth and fell, looking over Solway on the one hand to the Scottish mountains, and on the other over some space of rising moor to the high blue sky-line of the Lake hills. The actual shore is finely broken, here in high cliffs, there in a rugged rocky beach, with a steep backing of sandhills or grassy slope. The character of the country south of the Holm, and the flats which border on the Solway, is that of valley land, rolling and tumbled, with the interest rather at the bottoms than at the tops of places. Here and there you come upon extremely paintable groups of buildings, set in dells among wood and water; there are old houses, old churches, and sites of very interesting antiquity. At Moresby the churchyard partly covers a Roman fort. Going towards Distington, you pass the moated remains of Hayes or Aykhurst Castle (near the Castle Mill). At Distington church are several curious fragments of pre-Norman grave-crosses. Near Studfoldgate is the site of a megalithic circle of which eight stones remain on a circumference of one hundred feet. Dean, with an interesting church, was the birthplace of a forgotten poet (not without vogue and influence in his day), Dr John Dalton (to be distinguished from the famous early chemist),[1] whose poem on Keswick (1758) attracted the first tourists to the Lakes:

> Horrors like these at first alarm,
> But soon with savage grandeur charm,
> And raise to noblest thoughts the mind:
> Thus by thy fall, Lowdore, reclin'd,

—he rhymed away in the manner then understanded of the people, and brought poet Gray and parson Gilpin and other connoisseurs to view the landscape o'er. It was no small achievement to have set so lasting a fashion—to have been the first of the Lake poets. South of Dean, at Ullock, the old pack-horse bridge is interesting and picturesque.

Ennerdale means the valley of the Ehen (Egener-dale), as Allerdale (Alner-dale) is the valley of the Ellen. Above Ennerdale Water the stream is called the Liza (Leesa). There is a river in Iceland of the same name (Lýsá), meaning 'the bright water.' The genitive ending in -er, Egener, Alner, etc., is Norse, and many of the place-names hereabouts appear to suggest that it was under

---

1 Coincidentally, Dr John Dalton, discoverer of the atomic theory, was born in the neighbouring village of Eaglesfield in 1766, barely 25 miles from Calder Hall where the world's first atomic power station was opened in 1956 [Editor's note].

Ennerdale

Scandinavian settlers that the district of Copeland (*Kaupa-land*, 'a bought land,' i.e. not inherited) was brought into cultivation or habitable condition, being wild backwoods earlier, with only a sparse population of Cumbri and the descendants of a few Anglian colonists. Here, as elsewhere, the once thick forest has disappeared before wood-cutters, for building, charcoal-burning, and supply of fuel; and once cleared and turned into pasture any chance-sown growth is kept down by the sheep. The rock on both sides of the lake is a syenitic granite, but at the head of the valley it is the volcanic ash of the Borrowdale series, which has alternating beds of very hard and comparatively soft material, much broken and seamed with dykes. Hence we get the long precipitous line of the Pillar mountain, not unlike Wastwater Screes, and the isolated Pillar Rock on its side, like the Gable Needle. This rock was one of the first to be a sort of cragman's problem; even as early as 1800 Wordsworth made it the scene of a daring climb and a fatal fall (*The Brothers*). In the valley beneath it there are fine examples of moraine mounds, and at Bowness (*ból-nes*, 'the promontory of the dwellings') are remains of ancient homesteads. During the late 1920s and 1930s extensive areas of Ennerdale were acquired by the Forestry Commission and planted with softwood timber. Two thousand Herdwick sheep were displaced from their traditional 'heaf' and the action of the Commission was roundly condemned by the Friends of the Lake District and other amenity groups as wanton desecration of one of the finest valleys in the Lake District. (See H. H. Symonds, *Afforestation in the Lake District*.)

Near the head of the valley, which comes down from the back of the Great Gable, the Black Sail path goes over into Wasdale, with a fine sight of Scafell on the descent; and the Scarth Gap leads to Buttermere, with grand views of the Pillar mountain as you ascend and of the Buttermere mountains when the ridge is crossed. There are, of course, many possible routes from Ennerdale to Buttermere; by Floutern (flow-tarn, the tarn of the bog) over the moors to Scale Force or Mosedale; from Gillerthwaite up Red Pike, where you get a famous panorama of lakes, and down to Scale Force or to Sourmilk Gill; indeed, when you have once got up the rather steep banks of the valley, and find fair weather on the tops, you can make your route without much difficulty;

but the good old Scarth Gap is not easily bettered, especially if you walk along
the ridge of High Stile to Red Pike, to combine all the best that those fells
can show. The Lake mountains have a trick of giving you backs, grassy ridges
connecting summit with summit, easy and pleasant walking on springy turf
or old settled scree, where the air seems to lift you along, and the changing
view lends an impression of great speed and getting over an amazing range of
country. Such walks one can find along the backs of Coniston Fells, the Crinkle
Crag range, the Wastwater Screes, this Red Pike group, and perhaps best of
all on Helvellyn, where you get six miles of grass above the twenty-five-
hundred-foot contour line, with only a slight break at the Sticks Hause.

Red Pike is like a Three Shires Stone of the geological map, being conse-
quently the meeting-point of three sets of rather different scenery. To the
west and south is the syenite of Ennerdale, reaching to the foot of Wastwater;
south of that the Eskdale granite takes its place, reaching as far down as Bootle.
To the north and north-east everything is Skiddaw slate, all the hills on both
sides of Crummock, and between Buttermere and Keswick, and all Skiddaw
and Saddleback. To the east and south-east the mountains are built of the
volcanic ash of the Borrowdale series; not volcanoes, but the material ejected
from volcanoes into primeval seas, settled and stratified, pressed into intense
hardness, raised, contorted, and fractured in every direction, cut through and
through with dykes and seams, abraded by glacial actions, eroded by water,
and so made into these round-headed, rugged-sided, prettily varied Lake fells.
These volcanic rocks reach from here to the straight line of Coniston limestone
that cuts them off from the foot-hills, shearing across the map in two great
snips, Broughton to Brathay and Low-wood to Shap Wells. South-east of that
there are hills, but all of soft stone; north-west of this Borrowdale band there
are mountains, but of soft slate—but here soft and hard are stirred together,
and that makes the crags and gills we care for most. Red Pike is the meeting-
point of these different kinds of hill form, and Honister is the crag that shows
the Borrowdale type in perfection.

The Honister Pass

Pack-horse bridges, narrow, single-arched structures lacking walls and parapets,
are difficult to date accurately. Local tradition suggests that this one, near Calder
Abbey in West Cumbria, was built by the monks.

Honister crag is the steep north-eastern side of Fleetwith, which almost closes the head of Buttermere valley, its angular line so artistically contrasting with the soft curves of the dale, the Skiddaw-slate foreground, that every one has painted and sketched it as a perfect pictorial composition, ready made for artists. Looking at it more closely from the hause by which you come from Seatoller in Borrowdale over to Buttermere, you find the harder and more blocky mountain stuff sandwiched with what seems a different material. It is not so much a different material as the same paste more finely ground and more delicately tempered; prepared by natural cleavage for air and water to break up, leaving the belts and knots of rougher stone to stand out and rise up in crags. The cloven material we have seen already in the Coniston Fells, quarried for green slate, and here again are the great workings of Buttermere slate, practically the same as at Tilberthwaite. It is the best of all roofing, for it makes thin slabs, light in weight but as sound as steel and much more durable, with a beautiful colour of grey-green, far more pleasant than the livid

purple of the Welsh slates.[1] The size of Honister, about a thousand feet from
brow to base, is such that the quarries hardly detract from its impression as a
mountain, seen close from the hause; and, indeed, the workings are not without
interest: that men—such little creatures they look—should attack so stern a
giant's castle and win its treasures, and slide down the beanstalk path and
away.

In the two lakes we have almost had another Windermere, with merely a
bar and a few islands dividing the two basins; but the flat bit of green between
them is not without its charm, in contrast with the long range of heights over
against the village of Buttermere. The two chief waterfalls, Sourmilk Gill and
Scale Force, are among the most celebrated Lake District cascades; the one
conspicuous with its line of foam on the steep hillside, and the other a single
spout of water falling clear over one hundred feet in a tall dark cleft. In the
early days of the Lakers nobody could pass the 'Fish' without recalling the
story of Mary of Buttermere, the pretty daughter of the inn, who married a
swindling bigamist, giving himself out to be an Honourable and a Colonel.
When he was hanged for forgery (in 1803), the Lake poets and the chapbook
pedlars made copy out of the romance. Mary married again, and lived long
after at Caldbeck.[2] But the rather sordid incident lends nothing to the scenery.
Buttermere and Crummock are Nature's art for art's sake.

To taste the art with which Nature has arranged her treat, one ought
certainly to approach Buttermere from the lower valley: coming from Cockermouth, or from Keswick over Whinlatter, and quietly enjoying the Vale of
Lorton; halting at the Scale Hill Hotel for the point of view first found, or
first celebrated, by Father West, who was a connoisseur in points of view—
the Lanthwaite Hill 'Station'; giving a share of attention to Lanthwaite
Green with its nearly obliterated 'British settlement,' and to the prettiness of
Loweswater as a preface to Crummock, and making many a stay on the
splendid road under Grasmoor and Rannerdale Knott, with Mellbreak and
Red Pike and High Stile opening out, one after another, until you see Honister
and the wild head of the Gatesgarth dale. I always think of Buttermere as
made by Heaven for summer evenings and summer mornings: green floor and
purple heights, with the sound of waters under the sunset, or lit with the low
north-eastern sun into pure colour above, and the greyness of the dew upon
the grass.

At the mouth of the river Cocker, where it meets the Derwent, is the ancient
town of Cockermouth. Wordsworth was born here in 1770, and tells us in a

1 Most of the output from Lake District quarries is now 'cladding' slate, used to clad or clothe
   the exteriors of multi-storey buildings [Editor's note].

2 Mary became a *cause célèbre*; William and Dorothy Wordsworth, Coleridge, the Lambs, and
   Thomas De Quincey all wrote about her 'marriage.' And the story is still not played out—
   see Melvyn Bragg's novel *The Maid of Buttermere*, 1987 [Editor's note].

Near Buttermere

sonnet how he played as a child among the ruins of the castle, chasing butterflies on the green, climbing for flowers on the walls, and scared at the darkness of the dungeon. It was 'meet nurse for a poetic child.' For his sake as well as for its own this memorable ruin must have a page of gossip.

At Egremont we spoke of the Boy who would have been King of Scotland, but met his fate at the Strid of Wharfe; and how the great baronies in the North of England, which he would have inherited, passed to his sisters, and so away from the Scottish royal family. The youngest of the sisters, a second Alice de Romilly, had these lands of Allerdale for her portion, and married Gilbert Pipard. He seems to have built a castle at the site near Cockermouth where the Romans had once placed a fort, and from him the village is still named Papcastle (Pipard's Castle).[1] After his death she married Robert de Courtenai, who is said to have been a grandson of Louis le Gros, King of France—so curiously the Norman settlement brought folk together from north and south. After all, her lands went to her grand-nephew, William de Fortibus, Earl of Albemarle (1215), who was one of the turbulent barons of Henry III. In 1221 the Sheriff of Westmorland was bidden by the king to besiege and destroy the Castle of Cockermouth, which is then heard of for the first time. The earl found his way back to the king's favour and built his castle up again. Indeed, the lower part of the western tower shows traces of this siege; it must have been built early in the thirteenth century, and then thrown down, not utterly cleared away, and afterwards rebuilt. Earl William's castle was a triangular fortress on the brink of the hill, two sides protected by steep banks, and the third walled and ditched across, considerably within the area of the

1 Professor Eric Birley advanced an alternative theory—that the name was derived from the Old Norse *papi* meaning a hermit. Perhaps the Irish-Norse settlers in the tenth century found the remains of a hermit's lodge within the ruins of the Roman fort [Editor's note].

The quarrying of local green slate is one of the oldest and still one of the most economically important of Lakeland industries. However, the legacy of silent, dripping, moss-grown caverns like this one near Grassmere pock-mark the fellsides.

later castle; and there were round towers at each of the three corners. The masonry is not very well built; it was put up in a hurry, no doubt, to secure the place before the breeze of royal favour should change or a storm of war should blow from the North.

This earlier castle had several occupants whose names are well known in history. In 1269 the Lady Aveline brought it by marriage to the Earl of

The Wetheral railway viaduct, built in the 1830s, was one of the earliest in Britain. Gracefully spanning the River Eden, it carries the line from Carlisle to Newcastle and was the inspiration for Wordsworth's sonnet, Steamboats, Viaducts and Railways.

Lancaster, Edmund Crouchback, i.e. Cross-back, the Crusader, brother of Edward I. Piers Gaveston, the favourite of Edward II, was its constable, and then Thomas de Richmond; then Andrew de Harcla, the Earl of Carlisle, who, after his brave defence of Cumberland, despaired of English misrule and—so it was alleged—treated with the Scots; for which he was hanged, drawn, and quartered, as a traitor. His captor was Anthony de Luci, who received

Cockermouth as his reward (1323). Thomas de Luci, his grandson (*d.* 1365), seems to have rebuilt certain parts, but the great restoration and enlargement was under Henry Percy, Earl of Northumberland, who had married Maud, the heiress of the Lucis. While he was at work, and perhaps because the rebuilding gave them a chance, the Scots attacked the place (1387), and burned part of it; but that did not prevent Earl Percy from completing the eastern side, and adding a great gatehouse (the inner gate) with guardrooms, and— what is not usual in such castles—grim dungeons. For material he went to Papcastle and carried away the ready-cut Roman stones, so that a Roman altar appears on the north side of his gatehouse. The outer gate was built about 1400, thus completing the castle.[1]

In May 1568 Mary Queen of Scots passed a night here on her way from Workington, where she landed after the defeat at Langside, to Carlisle, where her long captivity began.[2] In 1648 the place was besieged by the Royalists for some weeks, but relieved by Colonel Ashton, after which it decayed. The later owners, the Wyndhams, kept up only the gatehouse, courthouse, and some rooms adjoining, and the rest of the buildings went to ruin.

The Derwent, which Cockermouth Castle overlooks, is one of those few rivers which are beautiful from source to mouth. It rises in Sprinkling Tarn, one thousand nine hundred and sixty feet above the sea, in the heart of our grandest mountains; flows through Borrowdale; forms Derwentwater and Bassenthwaite Lake, and then runs between steep banks, though charming scenery, past many historic places, to Workington, where not even ironworks can quite destroy its interest. It was at Derwentmouth that the monks of St Cuthbert, fleeing from the Danes, took ship with their precious burden, the reliquary that held his body (A.D. 870 or a little later). Before that there had been a Roman fort at Burrow-walls on the north bank; and already there must have been an Anglian church where now St Michael's stands. We noticed how there were Anglian monuments near the ancient ports, and here, too, there are some of that early period, and some of the rather later period when the invading Vikings in their turn became Christian, and set up crosses over their graves.

In the twelfth century the Culwens of Colvend, ancestors of the Curwens, built their first castle on the site of the Roman fort and out of its ruins, then moving to the finer position at the head of the long ridge, south of Derwent; so that Workington, like many other early towns, had its castle at the top of the hill and its church at the bottom, with traders' and retainers' houses

---

1 For a detailed description of the castle see Bernard Bradbury, *A History of Cockermouth*, 1981 [Editor's note].

2 It is possible that Mary spent a night not in the castle since the Earl of Northumberland was not in residence, but in the home of Henry Fletcher, a large house in the Market Place [Editor's note].

sheltered between the two. Workington Hall was built round a tower, for which a licence to crenellate was given to Gilbert de Culwen in 1379; in the next century a great hall was added, and then a kitchen. Effigies of the Curwens of 1450 are in the church. In the age of Elizabeth wings were thrown out to enclose the court. Here Mary Queen of Scots passed her first night of exile, and, as tradition says, left the agate cup called the Luck of Workington. Most of the house was rebuilt by John Christian Curwen (*d.* 1828) from the profits of his coal-mines; sadly, it is now a ruin.

Travelling up the Derwent, we come to the south side to Great Clifton, where there is a very interesting relic of the period before the Normans, the cross-shaft curiously carved with interlaced dragons, and made from a stone so chosen that one side is red and the other white. Brigham has its church of St Bridget with a Norman nave and many pre-Norman and medieval monuments: the old vicarage is an interesting example of domestic architecture, with pointed arches to some of the windows. Moorland Close, with arched entrance to the farmyard, was the birthplace of Fletcher Christian of the *Bounty* mutiny.

On the north bank of the Derwent, a little set back on the hillside and commanding broad views, is Bridekirk, another church of St Bridget. These Irish names came in with the Vikings who had been more or less converted in Ireland, the Hebrides, and the North of Scotland. Here there are more of these early monuments. The especial treasure is the celebrated font carved with dragons and strange beasts, and two quaint representations of the expulsion from Eden and the baptism of Christ, and on the fourth side a portrait of the artist with chisel and mallet and his autograph signature in runes of the twelfth century, 'Rikarth he me wrokte, and to this merthe gernr me brokte'— 'Richard he me wrought, and to this beauty eagerly me brought.'[1] It seems very likely that this Rikarth was the Master Richard of Durham, known as the greatest craftsman of the North in the later twelfth century. He was the man who carried always with him a precious relic, a bit of St Cuthbert's chasuble, which a French priest, when he was working at Norham Castle, once stole and threw into the fire; two hours afterwards Richard came back and found it still unburnt—so says Reginald of Durham in his book of the miracles of St Cuthbert.

Other early monuments are in the little twelfth-century church of Isel, in a most lovely situation by the Derwent. We often feel the want of fine river scenery in the Lake District; here, not far away, with the tops of Skiddaw and its neighbours looking over the lower hills, is a noble river with romantic and interesting sights to notice from point to point. Isel Hall is another of the

1 Pevsner ascribes a mid-twelfth-century date to the font and calls it 'one of the liveliest pieces of Norman sculpture in the county' [Editor's note].

Elizabethan mansions built round an earlier pele, and Hewthwaite Hall tells us by the inscription on its carved doorhead that

> John Swynburn Esquire and Elizabeth his wyfe
> Did make cost of this work in the dais of their lyfe. 1581.

From Isel it is only a step to Bassenthwaite, over Elva hill or up the river, and we should be in the Lake District again. But before going back to the mountains I should like to take you for a little round into the lower country, and show how much there is to see where no tourists go. It is not dull country, even for landscape. This is where Skiddaw nods to Criffel across the Solway:

> When Skiddaw dons a cap
> Criffel he wots well o' that.

And not only Criffel and Skiddaw, but ranges of blue mountains line either horizon. Solway Firth, after all, is one great valley, visibly delimited by the hills. From any of the higher summits you can take it in at one glance. It is only down below, and then not always, that you lose the grip of surroundings; and there are few valleys where such dramas of history have been played out.

There was the Roman age, when this bit of shore was the end of the world: we can see how it was fortified with the Wall and the network of forts against outer barbarians who came from the unknown—yonder—to unsettle the Pax Romana. There was the mysterious Cymric Age of Cunedda, Rhydderch, and Kentigern: we have many hints of that in legends and place-names, a few possible relics in hill forts, allusions in bardic songs, shadowy, but enough to repeople the landscape in imagination, if not enough to reconstruct solid history. There was the period of Anglian settlement, which has left us traces in its place-names, by which our villages are still known, and when the Angles grew in culture, their fine monumental sculptured stones; still more of the following age of the Vikings, to whom this was the centre of the world they called their West, between York and Dublin, close to their Galloway haunts. Then we have early Norman churches and castles, the abbeys and peles of the Middle Ages, and the halls of the Tudor and Stuart days. At every step fuller light falls on the old-world life that has hardly yet died out here and there. In all this Allerdale and Solway-side are rich, so rich that in such a sketch as I can give, I can do no more than indicate the facts and point out the road to reach them.

At Maryport we have seen how a modern town sprang up; but there is the Roman fort still to be visited,[1] and the burg or mote-hill at the south end of

---

1 The Netherhall collection of altars from the fort is one of the finest in the country. It is hoped that they will soon be on public display in a new museum near to the site of the fort [Editor's note].

Wastwater is the most Scandinavian of all the lakes. Here, above all, is the place
to remember those Norse colonists who tamed the landscape, left their names on
fell and dale, cleared thwaites at Burnthwaite, established seters at Seatallan,
and built booths at Bowderdale.

the Castle hill, showing that some importance attached to the harbour in early
medieval days as the meeting-place of useful Roman roads. Near it, Dearham
has its pre-Norman church; the grave-cross, Scandinavian in type of ornament,
shows the antiquity of the site, and Norman work in the church proves the
continuity of its history. Crosscanonby, on the other side of the Ellen, finely
overlooking the seashore, is another of those early places, with valuable

monuments in stone telling us of its otherwise forgotten story. At Gilcrux and
Plumbland, again, there are similar remains. 'Plumbelund [the wood of plum-
trees] in Alredale' is the scene of a fine story told by Reginald of Durham, the
twelfth-century monk who gives such lively pictures of the North Country in
his age. He describes the invasion of William the Lion (1173); how the people
fled to this church of St Cuthbert for sanctuary and built huts thatched with
hay and straw in the churchyard, putting their goods in 'arks or little kists'
into the church; how a thief picked the lock of one which held the money of
a rich knight, Cospatric, son of Ulf, and was found out when he tendered a
stolen coin. The coin happened to be a Scottish penny, and when he offered
it at the ale-house, 'Nay,' said the mistress, she would not take the money of
a king who was fighting our good King Henry. So the other folk asked to look,
and it went from hand to hand till it came to a lad who was servant to the
knight. 'By chance,' says the chronicler, 'by God's ordering, he had seen the
aforesaid penny in his lord's hands, and so now most easily knew it again.'
Whereupon he told his lord in all confidence, and begged him to look at his
box in the church—and, lo, the bag of pennies was missing! But when the
thief was caught and had confessed, 'God forbid,' said the worthy rector, 'that
we should hang him. Has not St Cuthbert shown a miracle in this discovery?'
And from that day to this, adds Reginald, Plumbland church has been the
safeguard of the countryside. This is the church about which the old rhyme
runs:

> The queerest sight that ever was seen
> Is Plumbland church on Arkleby Green.

If the joke lies in the difference of names, it can be matched by Windermere
church at Bowness Bay, Addingham church at Glassonby, and several other
fine old crusted anomalies, due to the shifting of population.

'Aspatrick' (perhaps 'Patrick's Ash,' not necessarily the saint's) was the old
name; 'Speatry' in the vernacular. It is a former mining village, but not without
picturesqueness. Although St Kentigern's church at Aspatria was rebuilt in
the middle of the nineteenth century, the doorway to the vestry has a genuine
Norman arch and there are several Anglo-Scandinavian stone carvings, including a remarkable hog-back tombstone, important documents, so to say, in the
early history of Cumbrian art. Blennerhasset, a rustic village, has its old
market-cross; Torpenhow, retired and picturesque, has a most interesting
Norman church; above Bothel is the Beacon Hill, with the old beacon station
on the top, and below it, to the south, the remains of a great Roman earthwork,
Caermote. There is another curious entrenchment at Snittlegarth, and another
near the tarn of Overwater; others at Aughertree and Thistlebottom, all on
the northern slope of the Skiddaw group, at the head of the Ellen valley. Some
of these may perhaps be the garths of early settlers, Anglian or Scandinavian,

who planted themselves in the woods among the hills, safe in their retirement, the pioneers of that pastoral life which bred the Dalesfolk. Such places hardly come into the system of Roman frontier fortifications, and they have no military value. On the other hand, it was the custom of Northern farmers in ancient days, when they had 'stubb'd Thurnaby waäste,' to run a dyke round it, enclosing a larger or smaller area, which was their *tún* or homefield. There were wolves, if not thieves, to be kept out; ditch and bank, with the usual stockade on the top, would do this, where such slight defences would be of no use against armed troops. This is certainly the real meaning of many earthworks to be seen in Cumberland, and of others on record at sites where they have disappeared.[1]

Uldale and Ireby are villages where a sketcher might find many subjects. Ireby, perhaps, ought to be called a town, for it had a market as early as 1237, of which the old cross is the outward and visible sign, and it was an important centre of the corn trade over two hundred years ago. At the old church, a mile to the west, there are medieval tombstones. Bolton old church, with its stone-vaulted ceiling, was said to have been built by imps in a single night, at the command of the wizard Michael Scot. Near Wearyhall is the site of another earthwork, a medieval castle, and at Whitehall another mote-hill.

Leaving the valley of the Ellen, and travelling northward past High Aikton and Bromfield with its prettily kept twelfth-century church and many early monuments, we come to the flat breadth of land between the Irish Sea and Moricambe, the broad bay formed by the estuaries of Waver and Wampool. This is the Holm, and its chief interest centres in the history of the abbey, which dominated it as Furness Abbey dominated the corresponding plot of ground to the south of our district. At Abbey Town is the old church which, though largely rebuilt, incorporates the major part of the nave and the west door of the famous Cistercian monastery of Holm Cultram.

It was founded in 1150 by Prince Henry, son of David I of Scotland, at the time when Cumberland was more Scottish than English, and it was a great and wealthy place. The church was bigger than that of Carlisle; seven priests could say mass without interrupting one another. The present church is only a fragment, about half the length of the original; but behind the sixteenth-century porch you can see the twelfth-century door, and in the side walls you can see the pillars which once merely marked off the nave from the aisles. In 1216 the place was pillaged by the Scots, on whom Heaven showed its vengeance by drowning them all in a sudden tide as they returned over the Solway, 'like Pharaoh's host in the Red Sea.' After that, the monks built Wolsty Castle (due west, on the coast) as a defence and a refuge. Here, it is said, Michael Scot came, wearied of his wizardries, to find rest for his old age.

---

1 It now seems likely that many of these banks and ditches date from the Iron Age [Editor's note].

Sir Walter, his namesake, shows his grave at Melrose, but the real place is not known. If he came to Holm Cultram about 1290, and died in 1291, it is more likely that he was buried at this abbey as some traditions relate. A little later this was in the thick of great events. Edward I made this shore of Solway the base of his attack on Scotland, and for eight years army and fleet were quartered on the Holm. The abbey got some reward in various privileges, among which was a market charter for Skinburness; but no sooner had they established their port and town there than a great storm and flood destroyed the harbour; upon which they chose a new site, and built the church of Newton Arlosh; its pele-tower was added as a stronghold for their tenants. Nevertheless, the Holm was often raided and invaded—after Bannockburn, and again in 1322, when Robert Bruce pillaged the abbey; and in 1385 the Earl of Douglas forced the monks to ransom themselves for a year by payment of £200. This was reckoned treason to England, and it was with difficulty and self-abasement that they got pardon for the offence of paying blackmail.

One of the greatest of the abbots was Robert Chamber (1507–31), who built the present porch and beautified the place and its dependencies; you will see his rebus, the R.C. and 'chain-bear,' and his inscriptions, and some fragments of his elaborate tomb within the porch. The next abbot, Matthew Deveys, died suddenly, and others who had eaten with him were struck with mysterious illness; it pointed to poison, and suspicion fell on one of the monks, Gawen Borrodaile. The reports of the trial give every reason to believe that he was guilty; but he had strong friends. He not only escaped, but returned to Holm Cultram some years after as abbot. Gawen Borrodaile was, in fact, the last abbot, but with his luck and cunning managed to remain in possession as vicar for many long years after the Reformation. The church was kept for the use of the parish, as at Cartmel, dilapidated and frequently restored on smaller and smaller plans. On New Year's Day, 1600, the steeple fell; in 1604, while restoration was going forward, a workman, looking with a candle for his chisel, set fire to a jackdaw's nest, and the whole building was in flames. The vicar, Edward Mandeville, was charged with some connivance or contrivance towards this mishap, but repaired the chancel at his own expense; and so it went on until about 1730, when the present queer mixture of medieval work and early Gothic revival was fabricated.[1]

Kirkbride, at the mouth of the Wampool, is a very early site, and a very pretty one to any who cares for river and trees, a pleasant variety of broken ground and tidal creek with the hills always looking in from the distance on either hand. The twelfth-century church is restored, but the village is picturesque. I suppose that this was where the *Jumping Jenny* in Scott's *Redgauntlet* landed her smuggling cargo, and Alan Fairford started on his

---

1 For further details see F. Grainger and W. G. Collingwood, *The Registers and Records of Holm Cultram*, 1929.

*The Newlands Valley near Keswick was once the site of important mining
activity. In the 16th century, German miners of the Company of the Mines
Royal worked the fellsides for silver and lead ores; today their spoil tips are
long overgrown with bracken, the haunt of sheep and the occasional fell wanderer.*

night ride. It was not at Crackenthorpe's inn by the Solway that they ran the
brandy: that would be too audacious. Sandyside, near Burgh, is said to have
been the usual smugglers' landing; but in the novel it is clearly made out that
the pack-horses came across country (from Skinburness?) to meet Nanty
Ewart, who had sailed up the Wampool. Scott's curious ignorance of the
Cumberland dialect gives the only jarring note in his picture of Solway shores
in the old smuggling times; he loved this landscape, and drew it again and
again as the background to his favourite creations. It is still beautiful country,
all the more worth visiting because it is not, like the Lake District, submerged
with trippers; and so undisturbed that for most of the time we can still, with
Wandering Willie, hark to the roar of the Solway.[1]

1 Aerial photography has recently added considerably to our knowledge of settlement patterns
   and fortifications of this Solway coastal plain. Although evidence of a Roman fort at Beckfoot,
   three miles south of Silloth, existed in 1879, an aerial photograph taken in 1949 by Dr K. St
   Joseph revealed the walls, ditches, and internal buildings of the fort in amazing detail. Within
   the last decade Professor Barri Jones has discovered scores of settlement sites from the air in
   areas previously thought to have been uninhabited. Collingwood would have been fascinated
   by such developments [Editor's note].

VI

'MERRY CARLISLE'
AND THE BORDER

The Roman Wall—By the side of the Solway—The Throstle
Nest—St Cuthbert's prophecy—Carlisle Ha'—The Archers of
Inglewood—The vexillary's record—The mote-hills of the Irthing
valley—Lanercost Priory—Naworth Castle—Belted Will—Scott
at Gilsland—Mumps Ha' and *Guy Mannering*—The moors—King
Alcfrith's grave—Young Lochinvar—The Battle of Arthuret; St
Kentigern and Merlin the Seer.

BOWNESS-ON-SOLWAY is the westernmost point on the Roman Wall, though a
system of fortlets continued along the coast almost to St Bees. The Wall is so
famous, and its importance as the beginning of history in Cumberland is so
great, that one must not return to the Lakes from Bowness without looking
for some of the traces of its course. We can hardly take up the end of the clue
without following it farther. Indeed, I think for many reasons we might do
worse than attempt the pilgrimage of the Wall, up to the frontier of Cumberland. It will lead us into many places of interest, and into very charming
scenery. Though the Wall in Cumberland is not so scenic as in parts more to
the east, still there are castles and churches by the way, and delightful valleys
as fine in their kind as any Lake landscape. Farther eastward there are the
Geltsdale and Bewcastle hills, running up above fifteen hundred feet, with
glorious wild moors and distant views, surpassed by none of the tourist
panoramas at the Lakes. This section, then, shall deal with North Cumberland,
the land of Carlisle, Inglewood, Edenside, Gilsland, and the Debateable Land;
afterwards we will return to more familiar haunts round Keswick.

The Roman Wall runs, as every one knows, from here to Wallsend on the
banks of 'coaly Tyne,' just beyond Newcastle. Old maps mark it as the 'Picts'
Wall'; some writers call it the 'Great Barrier of Hadrian,' for it is certain that
the Emperor Hadrian, who visited Britain A.D. 122, or rather his officers, had
by that time built most of the system of works which we usually group together
under the name of the Wall. It grew out of the intention to mark rather than
to defend the frontier against the northern barbarians; the Roman idea being
that, if any attack were made, Roman soldiers were quite able to repulse it,
and needed no defensive works in front of them. First of all a chain of forts

was built across the narrowest part of the island, which not being sufficient to prevent smuggling and petty raiding, a definite mark was drawn on the ground with the big trench, miscalled by old antiquaries the Vallum—useless for defence and evidently never intended for such a purpose. That it is later than some of the forts is seen by the way it turns out of its course to evade them. But it was not allowed to remain in use for more than a very few years; it was felt that something more substantial was wanted, and they soon began to put up a rampart, at first of turf, to be replaced by stone. The line of this turf Wall was not exactly followed by the stone Wall; and in one place, Appletree (a little west of Birdoswald), part of it can be seen as an isolated mound or dyke, running south of and near the stone Wall which borders the present road on the northern edge. At first the Wall was meant to be ten feet thick. It was begun at Newcastle and carried as far as Heddon before the engineers decided that such thickness was unnecessary, and a narrower gauge of seven feet six inches was adopted from there to Carlisle and Bowness-on-Solway. About every four miles a large square fort was built adjoining the Wall, and at every mile between these were smaller forts (called 'mile-castles') with turrets between them at intervals of a third of a mile. Southward were forts to support the line of defence; in front—in the country of northern barbarians—were other outposts; together making a very complete system of fortification, and, if well garrisoned, unassailable before the days of gunpowder.

West of Carlisle the Wall can hardly be seen, though its position is known by tradition and by digging; but the Vallum and ditch of the Wall appear in various places. East of Carlisle the traces grow more distinct; where the stones are not visible you can often feel them underfoot, for the foundations have been turned into a road here and there. Just north of Lanercost a large piece of the original masonry, refaced, stands up to nearly ten feet; you see it again near Birdoswald, and can trace it thence to the vicarage at Gilsland, where the original facing is left, and the ditch and Vallum show finely. At almost every step along its track stones of the Wall can be seen built into churches, cottages, halls, and castles.[1]

At Bowness the Wall ended, just to the west of the last place where Solway is fordable; the fort was close to the church on the north side. The sea has carried away all the Wall on the northern part of the fort at Bowness, but the west ditch was deepened in medieval times, perhaps when Edward I refortified the place at his visit, shortly before he died. He was at Holm Cultram on 6th July 1307, the day before his death, but the defensive works had been going on since 1304 or earlier. Drumburgh Castle was built by Lord Dacre in the time of Henry VII, of stones from the Wall here; Leland, writing in 1539,

---

1 For recent research on the Wall see D. J. Breeze and B. Dobson, *Hadrian's Wall*, 1976 and D. C. A. Shotter, *Roman North-West England*, 1984.

calls it 'a pretty pyle (pele)[1] for the defence of the country.' Through a
farmstead to the north-west of this you find the garth of a medieval house on
the site of a Roman fort. The dyke you see is not Roman work, though it was
always supposed to be so until excavation showed the facts.

From this little hill eastward there is a wide stretch of marshland, which
may not have been so swampy in Roman days. It is possible that the Wall
crossed the marsh and has been lost: at any rate there are no traces of it, and
the Vallum is not seen westward of Burgh-by-Sands (pronounced Bruff).
Here, the fort occupied part of the site where the church now stands. It is a
most interesting twelfth-century church, built of Roman stone (much restored
now), with a pele-tower added as a refuge for the parishioners in the frequent
Scottish raids. You see the grille which, with an inner door, shut them into
their ark of safety. Its lintel is an early carved stone, very grotesque in design.
The view from the roof is extensive and interesting. Northwards, on the edge
of the marsh, is a pillar, marking the spot where Edward I died in 1307.

Inland hence, at Kirkbampton, there is another twelfth-century church,
with rudely carved and much defaced tympanum over the door, several old
tombs, and Roman stones built into the walls; so far did they carry the spoils
from the quarry. Farther south, a mile beyond Wigton, is the site of a very
important Roman fort at Old Carlisle, near Cunningarth. Wigton itself is an
ancient market-town, and a considerable centre of trade. It is noted as the
birthplace of R. Smirke, R. A. the first genre-painter of the old English school
(1752–1845), father of the architect of that name. Ewan Clark was also born
here—one of the eighteenth-century Cumbrian poets; indeed Wigton was
known as the Throstle Nest, from its very many local singers; a remarkable
fact when you remember that it was the headquarters of Puritanism in the
Civil Wars.[2] Cockermouth, the other Roundhead town, produced Wordsworth,
though his family came from Penrith.

Returning to the Wall, at Beaumont (pronounced Beemont) the church is
on a mote-hill which was on a Roman fort. Kirkandrews's ruined church is
also on a mile-castle. Here the Wall and Vallum come close together. East of
this, the Wall makes for Grinsdale and the Vallum diverges a little. At
Knockupworth they meet again and run close to the high bank of the Eden,
and so we lose them in the outskirts of modern Carlisle, but the Wall crossed
the river just north of the castle. We can pick up the trail again across the
river at Stanwix, where there was a great fort underlying St Michael's church.
From Stanwix, which was anciently written Stan-wegges, 'the stone way,' an

---

1 Note the use of 'pele' by Leland, which excuses it in modern writing, though disallowed by
   some.

2 The literary and artistic tradition at Wigton continues—the novelist and broadcaster Melvyn
   Bragg was born there in 1939. For a detailed account of Wigton see his book *Speak for
   England*, 1976.

Nestling under the flanks of Cross Fell, Milburn in the Eden Valley is a fine example of a village built around a large, rectangular green, perhaps for defence. However, most of the houses date from the 18th century and it is possible that the enclosed green afforded additional winter grazing.

old road goes on the foundations of the wall to Tarraby: this was the Carel-gate (i.e. Carlisle road), the main track before the military road from Newcastle to Carlisle was made by General Wade after the 'Forty-five. Here you can see one of 'these roads before they were made, and hold up your hands and bless General Wade,' as the old rhyme says. The Wall and Vallum can be traced through fields and through Brunstock park to Walby, where for a time the old road runs upon the Wall again; then to Wall Head and Old Wall, and so to Newtown. But we must not wander too far from Carlisle; we can return to the Roman Wall afterwards.

Luguvallium was a wealthy Roman civil settlement covering about 74 acres. Excavations in the 1970s showed occupation of many periods but the earliest seems to have taken place during the governorship of Agricola (c. A.D. 78–84). In 1978 in Annetwell Street, the remains of a gateway to a Flavian fort were excavated; this fort was later replaced by the fort at Stanwix which housed a cavalry unit of 1000 men. As Caerluel, it was a British capital for two hundred

An old spinning gallery at Hartsop

and fifty years after the Romans left. In the legendary accounts, which are all
we have of the period, it is associated with Cunedda, the first great king of
the Western Cumbri (Cymru) and Rhydderch the Magnificent, who extended
his power thence over all Strathclyde, late in the sixth century. 'King Arthur
lived at merry[1] Carlisle,' the ballad says, but that is fiction; no doubt, however,
the kings of this district, whose battles with the encroaching Angles are
traditionally remembered in the romances, made Carlisle their headquarters.
But by about 680 the Angles had prevailed, and their king, Ecgfrith, gave the
town to St Cuthbert. The story of the saint's visit, A.D. 685, and his walk
round the Roman walls with the townsfolk—local antiquaries of the day—
and his sudden trance while they were showing him the fountain, is told by
the Venerable Bede, and has been often quoted. It was at the hour when he
leaned on his staff, looking fixedly at the ground and then sadly at the heavens
with the mysterious words, 'Peradventure, even now, the hazard of battle is
over,' that Ecgfrith, his friend and patron, was overthrown and slain at the
battle of Nechtansmere. We should like to be certain of the spot where stood
this Roman fountain 'of wonderful work,' and still more wonderful legend.
The deep well in the castle-keep is usually said to be Roman, but there is not
enough evidence that the Romans occupied the castle-hill: they planted their
town on the cathedral-hill.

1 i.e. pleasant, fair.

Anglian Carlisle has left few remains, but these few are proofs of some wealth and art. The chief of them are the cross-heads from graves of the ninth century. The Danes ruined the town soon after 876, and it never regained its position until William Rufus, in 1092, drove out Dolfin, the lord of Norse or Danish name, and built a castle, and colonized the town afresh.

The castle was built on the hill overlooking the Eden, already moated by the Roman Vallum, which cut the neck of the headland across. Within that there seem to have been two other moats and a tower. Later in the Norman period, and during the Edwardian age, the castle grew. Richard III, while Duke of Gloucester, was constable, and is said to have added the Tile Tower, which you see to the left in the wall which runs from the castle to join the west walls of the city. Henry VIII adapted the interior for cannon. Mary Queen of Scots was imprisoned here; kept in a not very rigorous captivity in a tower to your right as you face the chief entrance, and permitted to ride out hunting the hare and watching football matches in the fields below. It was after her time that Kinmont Willie was rescued by Buccleuch, who burst in, one night in 1596, and broke the prison 'with coulters and with forehammers.' In the keep, Major Macdonald, the real Fergus MacIvor, was confined, with other Jacobites, after the 'Forty-five. After the gruesome executions for high treason, the heads were exposed over the Scotch gate of the city. It is said that one was a lad's, with long yellow hair; every evening and morning a lady unknown came and looked at it; one day both the head and the lady were missing. When, later, a Highland regiment had to pass Carlisle, it was halted outside the town, so that the men might not see the still lingering trophies.

To catch the sentiment of the place, one should see the castle from Stanwix rising proudly over the broad green fields that border the Eden. Imagine the Eden bridges away, and the somewhat formal trees which break the line of the ancient Battail-holme, then the view may almost pass for what they saw in old times—'Carlisle Ha', wi' its castle and bastions and a',' the river being in medieval times unbridged and forded. Then crossing the 'bridges,' as the Eden bridge is called locally, find your way by Castle Street to the walks round the walls—lofty walls above and steep bank below—and then enter the gateway, and, looking not to the left hand and its hideous barracks, pass the

Carlisle

Brough was once one of the most strategically important centres in Cumbria. In order to defend the road over Stainmoor, the Romans built a large fort here, and the Normans founded their castle on the same site. Destroyed and refortified several times, today's ruin is a gaunt reminder of Cumbria's troubled past.

inner gate and climb the stairway beside the keep to reach the battlements. It is not all as it was when Wallace (1297) and Bruce (1315) were driven from the walls, or when de Luci marched in by broad daylight and seized Sir Andrew de Harcla in his own hall (1323), nor even as Carlisle looked when Lesley besieged the Royalist city for nine long months in 1644–5, and starved it utterly out; or when in 1745 the town surrendered to Prince Charlie, only to fall a few months later before the Duke of Cumberland's cannon.[1] There is change, but not everywhere, and much clearing and restoration have been done lately. Still the main features of the scene remain; how much the nobler for their memories, for the glamour of Border romance and the echoes of many an ancient passionate tale when 'the sun shines fair on Carlisle wall.'

The west wall of the city is actually over the railway; you find little of the old effect there. Near the station are two monstrous round towers, the

---

1 The Duke of Cumberland contemptuously dismissed the castle as 'an old hen coop.' It is now in the care of English Heritage and is open to the public [Editor's note].

*Hidden away on the banks of the River Esk, St Catherine's chapel at Boot must
have one of the most attractive settings of any Lake District church. The
churchyard contains the gravestones of many Wasdale Head folk who had to be
carried by pack-horse over lonely Burnmoor for burial here in Eskdale.*

courthouses built early in the nineteenth century, representing Henry VIII's
citadel. Thence the old wall ran down Lowther Street, and turned to rejoin
the castle. To the left of the courthouses was the English gate, where, I
suppose, Adam Bell and Clym of the Clough broke in to rescue William of
Cloudesley from the mayor and his poleaxe beneath the gallows-tree in the
market-place. These archers of Inglewood seem to have flourished in the
thirteenth century; the ballads relating their exploits in the 'English wood'
and 'merry Carlisle' are as fine as anything we have in the way of popular
poetry, and sketch a picture of old Cumbrian life, not only brilliant and
effective, but very possibly historical. The 'proud sherrif of Notyngham' of
the ballad was probably Ralph de Nottingham, sheriff of Westmorland for
some years about 1250. The sheriff of Nottingham, properly so called, could
have nothing to do with Inglewood. It must have been this sheriff's surname
that remained in popular memory and was adopted in the ballad.

The cathedral is the old priory church, once very magnificent, but partly destroyed when General Lesley's army of Presbyterians occupied Carlisle during the Civil Wars. The Norman nave, or rather the part of it that is left, with the two short transepts, look like antechapels on an enormous scale to the choir, which seems to be, and really is, the main and important part of the building. Near the south entrance is a pane of glass in a frame against the wall, covering a stone on which is scratched in twelfth-century runic characters—'Tolfihn yraita thaesi rynr a thisi stain,' which needs little interpretation to make you understand that 'Dolfin,' not the lord of Carlisle in 1092, but some namesake half a century later, 'wrote these runes on this stone.' The most interesting points in the aisles are the ancient paintings behind the choir stalls, representing scenes from the life of St Cuthbert, St Augustine and St Anthony, the capitals of the piers, and the splendid east window; there are also some monuments of medieval and modern times, more fully noticed in the gazetteer at the end of this volume. In the old priory precincts are the fratry, once the canons' dining-hall, and the square tower of the deanery, once the prior's lodging; the modern houses in the 'Abbey,' so called, are the residences of the cathedral canons.

Since 1974 Carlisle has been the administrative centre for the new county of Cumbria, yet it still retains its market-town character. The eighteenth-century Town Hall and the seventeenth-century market cross where in 1745 Bonnie Prince Charlie proclaimed his father king, are now marooned in a complicated traffic flow system but the cathedral precinct remains a haven of tranquillity, and nearby Tullie House is a fine example of a late seventeenth-century mansion. Of course, the twentieth century has intruded though 'concrete and carbuncle' architecture is not as obtrusive as in some northern towns; indeed, the new Lanes shopping development with its splendid new Library successfully blends the new with the older buildings which surround it and augurs well for the future prosperity of the town.

The bishop's residence is seven miles south of Carlisle, at Rose Castle, which grew out of the pele built by Bishop Halton in the thirteenth century. In 1322 it was destroyed by Robert Bruce, and restored by Bishop Strickland in the fifteenth century. In the Civil Wars it was captured by the Parliamentarians and used as a prison; after recapture by the Royalists it was again taken and burnt. Bishops Rainbow and Smith rebuilt it, and at the two Jacobite rebellions it narrowly escaped attack; in the 'Forty-five—so the tradition runs—the Highlanders arrived while the christening of Bishop Fleming's little granddaughter was going on; Captain Macdonald gave the baby a white cockade and gallantly withdrew his men.

All this country between Carlisle and Penrith is Inglewood, the Forest of the Angles, where they seem to have effected their first settlements after the taking of Carlisle by Ecgfrith. Being traversed by a Roman road, used for centuries as the main route north and south, it was exposed to every invasion, and as the Anglian power declined it seems to have lost population. When the Normans came in it was made into a royal forest, that is, hunting-ground. It was doubtless uninhabited except for a few settlements here and there, and, as the story of Adam Bell shows, it was the resort of deer-stealers and outlaws down to the time of the Tudors. The growing villages were frequently raided by Border riders, and there are various forts and earthworks which were used by the countryfolk as refuges. Some of these, no doubt, date back to very early times; some are perhaps Anglian garths; but of some—for instance, at Southernby and in Castle Sowerby—there are traditions which suggest their use down to the Elizabethan age. With such a history Inglewood is quite a land of romance, full of legends, full of curious antiquities. No part of Cumberland is richer in appeals to the imagination; no part can tell you such tales, from the dimmest of Celtic traditions down to the folk-lore of peasant life of the last century.

Then the Eden river is worthy of its name,[1] if a broad and winding stream, lofty wooded banks, castles and churches and pretty villages, can make an earthly Paradise. It is hard to modulate the strain of praise and to measure the appeal of this kind against that kind of landscape; to many people these river-banks are more beautiful than Scafell; our greatest artists have shown more enjoyment in painting dales than peaks, and here you have this manner in perfection.

Following the stream there is Edenhall—who does not know about the Luck of Edenhall? There are Langwathby and Little Salkeld, two quite different styles of charming rusticity. There is the wonderful stone and circle of Long Meg and her Daughters, Addingham church with its crosses, and Kirkoswald, the delightfully rambling old market-town, with its ancient church, college, and ruined castle. Then you come to pretty Croglin, and

The Eden at Langwathby

1 Warwick Hall gardens lie along the bank. The lady of the place was teaching a class of Sunday school girls, and asked: 'Where did Adam and Eve live?' 'Doon watter side,' said one; 'in Pairker's garden.' But, of course, Eden is a Celtic river-name found elsewhere. The Hall was rebuilt this century after a fire destroyed the earlier building. It is now occupied by Benedictine nuns [Editor's note].

Long Meg and her Daughters

Nunnery, the gorge of Eden deepening into still more beautiful strength; Armathwaite, and near Armathwaite Castle the site famous in ballad and romance where King Arthur fought the giant of Castle Ewain beside the Tarn Wathelayne. And so down to the ravine that divides Corby Castle on its wooded cliffs from the ruined fragments of Wetheral Priory. Down among the trees by a little path from the priory you reach the Safeguards, or St Constantine's Cells, cut into the face of the sandstone wall of rock, near some Roman inscriptions, and built up with medieval masonry; hermitage of the British king whom St Kentigern called to missionary labour and martyrdom, or of his votary, for the priory was dedicated to him; and later perhaps a refuge in times of trouble. Over the pleasant village green and past the cross you find the church, with curious architecture and ancient effigies, and Nollekens the sculptor's masterpiece in the Howard Chapel. A little farther down stream you reach its confluence with the Irthing and the unique old church of Warwick, remarkable for its Norman apse and narrow lights, and walls like the walls of a castle.[1] I know I have been galloping through many a place where you would linger, but we have still farther to go and still finer things to see before we return to Carlisle.

Our course now lies up the Irthing; open here with a broad valley, but gradually narrowing and then entering the hills, until it loses itself on the lofty moors behind Bewcastle, where the heights rise to seventeen hundred feet above the sea. To the right of the main road, a little above Warwick Bridge, is Hayton and its moated castle-hill. Soon we cross the Gelt. It was at the Hell Beck that Lord Hunsdon, Queen Elizabeth's cousin, defeated Leonard Dacre (1569), and put an end to the Rising of the North. A mile up-stream

An Anglian fragment in Addingham church

1 'The most memorable Norman village church in Cumberland'—Pevsner.

from Low Gelt Bridge is the Written Rock, like that at Wetheral, with a Roman inscription, which, as Tennyson wrote:

> The vexillary
> Hath left crag-carven o'er the streaming Gelt,

to record the working of the quarries, A.D. 207, under the Emperor Severus. Half a mile up river, on the opposite bank, is Pigeon Crag where names of men of the sixth legion are carved.

Brampton lies in a valley between the Gelt and the Irthing. In the middle of the town is the market-place, and in the middle of the market-place is the Moot Hall, now an Information Centre, built 1817, and enlarged 1897; the iron stocks have been preserved, and are still to be seen, replaced in the square. In the modern church are fine Burne-Jones windows; a mile west, on the site of a Roman fort, stands the chancel of the old church with its Norman north window. At the east end of the town is a fine mote-hill or early castle which used to carry a beacon. The house in High Cross Street, called Prince Charlie's House, was the young Chevalier's headquarters for a week in 1745; here he received the Major and Corporation of Carlisle when they brought him the keys of the city.

Across the river is Irthington, where there is the twelfth-century church of St Kentigern and between it and the river another mote-hill. Near the bridge by which we crossed the Irthing from Brampton is a third, and, to anticipate a little, a fourth and a fifth are at Denton Hall and at the interesting early Norman church of Over Denton. These mote-hills were the abodes of the first Norman settlers, before stone castles came into general use. A wooden house was built on the top, to which one climbed by steps from the palisade fencing the base of the mound, crossing the ditch by a drawbridge. Most of the early Norman lords did not at once build stone castles; the pele-towers are two or three hundred years later than the Conquest; these mote-hills were the castles of the eleventh and twelfth centuries both here and in Normandy. One may perhaps leave the reader to imagine their inconvenience as residences of the nobility.

At Newtown we find the Wall and Vallum once more. In the garden of Castlesteads was a station which has yielded many altars and other remains. From Walton a lane runs along the Wall past the sites of three mile-castles, and just before you reach the road leading down to Lanercost is the place where the Wall stands nearly ten feet high; the facing stones now seen are a more recent addition to preserve the remains.

Here we can turn off to Lanercost and Naworth. The ruins of the priory are second only to Furness Abbey in interest as ruins, and they stand in much more delightful scenery, in a broader valley, with loftier hills around and a fine river running past them under richly wooded banks. This priory of Austin

Canons was founded by Robert de Vallibus (de Vaux) about 1169. Edward I stayed here in 1280, 1300 and 1306, when the place was at its prime. In 1311 Robert Bruce, and in 1346 David, King of Scots, invaded and left the place ruined and crippled for ever after. At the dissolution in 1536 it was given to the Dacres of Lanercost, who made their manor-house out of part of the buildings. The west gateway of the precinct is still standing, through which you enter a broad green field with the church opposite and on the right the parsonage, built around a pele which may be the work of Edward I. On the left is the base of a cross; the shaft with inscription dated 1214 is inside the church.

The priory buildings are late twelfth and thirteenth century, and consist of the great church, with the cloister, to the south of which is a range of buildings, with a crypt now used as a museum for Roman antiquities found in the neighbourhood—though Lanercost itself was not a Roman station. West of the cloister is the Dacre Hall and Tower. The chapter-house, formerly on the east of the cloister, is destroyed. The west end of the church is restored for use; behind it is the ruined chancel in which are various monuments. One of these is an effigy of about 1400, on which an inscription for 'John Crow, 1708,' has been rudely cut. Another is the fragment of an effigy of Roland de Vaux of Triermain, a name familiar in poetry; the verses once on his tomb are reproduced on a tablet in the church, though the date there given is too early. In the choir is the altar-tomb of Thomas, Lord Dacre (*d.* 1526) and his wife. Thomas Dacre commanded the horse at the battle of Flodden. Scott brings him into the *Lay of the Last Minstrel*, but, with a romancer's disregard for the verities of chronology, makes him contemporary with 'Belted Will,' who was not born until after his death. It was this tomb which was robbed of the coffin and corpse in 1775, and a rather naïvely worded advertisement was published

Near Lanercost Bridge

in the papers of the day: 'Whereas, some evil-disposed person did sometime this spring enter into the ruinous parts of Lanercost Church or Priory, and did feloniously take away from out of a vault in the said church a lead coffin' and so forth, offering ten guineas reward. At that time the place was neglected, and it is said that some of the corpses in the vaults were lying exposed, among them a venerable man with a long white beard. Now, however, you see at every turn the evidences of good feeling and good taste, preserving the charm of the ruins; even though part of the ancient site is turned to modern use, it is to a congenial use, not out of harmony with the surroundings and associations. You have not to look far for the reason; the more recent monuments—interesting in themselves as the work of Boehm and Burne-Jones—tell you that Lanercost was in the keeping of the artist-lord of Naworth Castle. Today the ruins are cared for by English Heritage.

The history of Naworth—the New-ward—does not begin very early, though it became the greatest and most famous of the Border castles on the western side. In 1313 Ranulf de Dacre—so named from the place near Penrith, which Bede called Dacore, not from the town of Acre in Palestine—married Margaret de Multon, the heiress of the barony of Gilsland; in fact he ran away with her from the custody of the Earl of Warwick. In 1335 he got the usual licence to crenellate, which implied that he was building a fortress on the angle of hill between two streams where Naworth stands; and Ranulf made it into a castle on the plan of other castles we have visited, cutting the neck of land across with a moat, enclosing a court with a curtain wall, and building therein a tower with some chambers and offices adjoining. Humphrey Dacre was Warden of the Marches in the time of Richard III. His son Thomas carried off another heiress—Elizabeth of Greystoke—and it was she who enabled him to enlarge and adorn the castle, building the great hall in which are the four great beasts—the Bull and Griffin of Dacre, the Dolphin of Howard of Greystoke, and the Sheep of Multon, besides many interesting old pictures. He built also the tower carried on arches, known as Lord William Howard's Tower. His successors lived chiefly at Kirkoswald Castle; but when the last male heir died—a little boy who was killed by a fall from a vaulting-horse—Naworth came by marriage to Lord William Howard, son of the Duke of Norfolk. Leonard Dacre, the uncle of the heiress, disputed her title and seized Naworth; we have seen how he fought at the Hell Beck and how the Rising of the North came to an end.

Lord William Howard was sent to the Tower of London, and it was only after paying a fine of £10,000 to Queen Elizabeth that he got possession of his barony (in 1601). Thenceforward he lived chiefly here until 1640. From these dates it is easy to see that Bauld Willie, as he was called, was not the great scourge of the moss-troopers whom Scott represents under the name of Belted Will, though he was a magnate of the Border in the reigns of the first James

The bridge at Lanercost

and Charles. His real character was scholarly rather than warlike; he was interested in antiquities, such as the Bewcastle cross and his library. There is a story that once when he was deep in his books, word was brought of the capture of a notorious Scot: 'Hang him!' grumbled the student, and they hanged him. But this, we are assured, is a myth and a libel. Lord William did much for the repairs of the castle and also built the bridge that leads to Lanercost. From him Naworth descends to its present owner, the Earl of Carlisle, whose ancestor, Sir Charles Howard, received the earldom from Charles II in 1661.

In the park is a lofty double ring-embankment, known as Tower Tye or Tortie, and it is possible that such ramparts were serviceable in Border troubles before the age of peles, but much later than the Stone Age, to which it has been referred.

Passing Denton Hall, an ancient manor-house, and the small ancient church of Over Denton, built of Roman stones in the earliest Norman period, we come to Gilsland. The name is properly the name of the whole district, i.e. the land of Gilles, a Celtic name which, like Malise, means 'the servant of Jesus.' Gillēs, son of Bueth or Boyd, was the owner in the early part of the twelfth century; of Gallgael or Galloway Viking descent, as it seems from the mingled Norse and Celtic names of his connections.

Gilsland is associated with Sir Walter Scott, who stayed at the Spa in 1797 and there met his 'fate' in the person of Charlotte Carpenter, whom he married in Carlisle Cathedral on Christmas Eve that year. The Popping Stone is the local name for the spot where he 'popped the question'; strangers have chipped half the stone away for relics (charms indeed), and the place has been vulgarized by trippers, but it is a very lovely and romantic neighbourhood, with its wooded cliffs and gorges, valley below and moors above. Here Scott rambled and read up local antiquities in Sandy Gordon's *Itinerarium* and gathered the impressions from which he afterwards drew the scenery of the opening chapters of *Guy Mannering*. Mumps Ha' was the tavern where Captain Vanbeest Brown met Dandie Dinmont. Tib Mumps was the mistress of the house—Margaret Teasdale, whose tombstone is in Over Denton church, recording her death on 'May 5, 1777, aged 98 years,' with these verses:

> What I was once, some may relate;
> What I am now is each one's fate;
> What I may be, none can explain
> Till He that called me calls again.

A strange epitaph for a life of lawlessness, of which gruesome tokens were found in her house. Beside the great fireplace is a cupboard; behind it was a secret door leading to a stairway in the chimney; there they found, some years ago, the skeleton of a child, and in another part the bones of a hand.

At Gilsland you find the Roman Wall and Vallum once more. Eastward they run into Northumberland, where we must not follow them. Westward they cross a bend of the Irthing, where we can rejoin them by taking the road to Birdoswald. Here the Wall coincides with our road, and behind the farm is a very famous fort, known to the Romans as Amboglanna or Camboglanna, where the turf wall can be traced by its ditch running into the fort from Wallbowers on the west.[1] The Vallum, between the turf wall and the lofty banks of the river, makes a curve, as excavations have shown, to avoid the fort. Part of the Vallum has disappeared by the crumbling of the cliffs along which it was carried. The view over the Irthing below, and Denton beyond, and the distant hills with Skiddaw far away, is very beautiful; the walk northward along the track of the Roman road, which Scott and other writers after him miscalled the Maiden Way, is well worth taking—even if you wander from the direct line, as you probably will. It is a wild country of desolate moors, up and down among heather, and bent, and bog, crossing deep dells with roaring streams at the bottom of them, and wide stretches of brown hill, dotted with sheep and with the famous black cattle they breed on these lonely farms. Curlew and peewits whirl overhead; the distant plain rises into view as you climb Gillalees Beacon. From this height, over a thousand feet above sea, you get 'a glorious vision of deep blue distance, and the Solway all silver, and Carlisle like a toy-town with every tower detailed against its wreathing smoke, and on either side Skiddaw and Criffel shouldering back their companies of mountain-tops, that seem to represent the old opposing powers of two king-doms, eyeing one another before the battle.'

1 Cumbria County Council is currently (1987) engaged in a major excavation of the site and a visitors' centre is planned [Editor's note].

Then you drop down upon Bewcastle. It can be approached by road from Brampton, passing Lanercost and the Wall, and the Dacres' old castle of Askerton, a fine ride of twelve miles; but the moorland walk is a grander introduction to this most interesting of Border sites.

Down at the bottom of a deep valley, surrounded with high moor and mountain, the stream winds sharply round a rocky headland. Below, there is a ford with a bridge and a cluster of cottages; above, the church and castle ruins rise behind the rectory, which is perched on the brow of the bluff. Here stood a Roman fort, an advanced post beyond the Wall, and here stands one of the most famous of Anglian crosses.[1] In A.D. 670, or thereabouts, died King Alcfrith, son of the great Oswy of Northumbria. He was the friend of St Wilfrith, by whom first the arts of Gaul and Italy were brought over to England, to adorn the newly planted church. Alcfrith was the person whose influence mainly contributed, in the famous conference at Whitby (664), to turn English Christianity away from the rude, though zealous, Irish missionaries, and to attach it to the civilizing organization of Rome. He was the instrument of the conversion of the Midlands, and to his memory this cross was set up, not in the first year of his brother Ecgfrith's reign, as the fragmentary runic inscription seems to read, but some time, perhaps as much as a century, later.

In the eleventh century, Bueth, the father of the Gillēs who gave his name to Gilsland, had his fortlet here, whence the name of Bewcastle.[2] Later still, the existing castle was built—the scene of innumerable raids and repulses. In the fourteenth century, during the reaction after Edward I and his great successes against Scotland, Bewcastle was so ruined that there was no priest to the church for many years. After Flodden, it regained its importance as a Border hold. Jack à Musgrave, captain of Bewcastle, doubted by the English and dreaded by the Scots, held it in Tudor times; and even when the days of Border wars were over, the Bewcastle folk were known up to the nineteenth century for a rough and dangerous crew. It used to be said, though the gravestones prove it a libel, that only the womenkind were buried here: the men were all hanged, sooner or later, at Carlisle!

Northward, up the Bailey, a few miles of hill road bring us to the Kershope burn and Scotland. At Kershope foot we turn to the south-west and pass down beautiful Liddesdale by Stonehouse Tower and Canonbie to the waters-meet of Liddel and Esk. High on the cliff are the great embankments of the Moat or Liddel Strength, an early Norman fortress, first named in the twelfth century; not Roman, as used to be said. Here Sir William Selby and his

---

1 'Perhaps the first extant masterpiece of Early English Stone carving'—Professor Robin G. Collingwood.

2 However, it is also possible that the name is derived from the Old Norse *budh*, meaning booth or dwelling [Editor's note].

garrison were starved out by David Bruce, and the brave defender was beheaded after the Scots had strangled his two sons before his eyes. Pleasanter associations attach to Netherby, where the young Lochinvar of Scott's ballad won his bride, but he was Scott's own invention. The hall of the Grahams is built round a pele-tower on a Roman site; on the opposite bank of Esk is another pele near the church. In the Debateable Land, on Sollom Moss, Sir Thomas Dacre in 1542 overthrew a great host and took twelve hundred Scotsmen prisoners, the flower of their nobility. It was for this King James V died of a broken heart, so the popular story ran, leaving his crown to the new-born Mary Queen of Scots.

But there is a much older and more dreamy romance haunting the place. The story is that St Kentigern, praying in retreat among the forests of Strathclyde, met a strange being, 'naked and hairy,' the ancient Latin 'Life' says, 'a wild madman: who, bidden speak and tell his name, replied, "I am Merlin, once a prophet; dreeing my weird in the wilderness. For it was I that egged them on to fight—all those who were slain yonder in the great battle betwixt Lidel and Carvanolow."' This battle, we learn from various other sources, was fought A.D. 573, and gave the Celtic Christians the decisive victory which placed Aidan on the throne of Dalriada (the Western Highlands), and made Rhydderch of Carlisle king of all Strathclyde, with Kentigern as his bishop. It is famous in Welsh annals and poems as the battle of Arthuret (Ardderyd or Armterid). The leader of the pagan enemy was Gwenddoleu, whose caer or castle, Carvanolow, is identified with Carwhinelow or Carwinley close at hand. But how comes Merlin the Seer among all these historical verities or romantic probabilities? The fact is that we must not allow much historical value to the far later statements of Welsh chronicles and pedigrees about this period. There may be a grain of truth in the story; but at Arthuret and in the neighbourhood not a scrap of evidence has ever been found to justify the legend of a great battle, or of any battle at all, except Solway Moss.

One might dream many poems at Arthuret under the quaint churchyard cross; but you must not forget that Archie Armstrong is buried there—King Charles's jester, who said to Laud, 'Wha's feule now?' when they had bad news from Stirling about the Liturgy. And for poet as for prelate, imagination is a good servant but a bad master.

VII

KESWICK AND THIRLMERE

Legends of Derwentwater—The stonesmith's workshop—The great circle—Shoulthwaite Castle—St Kentigern and St Herbert—The Norse settlement—The origin of the statesmen—Old-time Dales-folk—The Lake District farmhouse—Borrowdale 'gowks'—Ancient customs—The German miners—Pencils—Keswick worthies—Coleridge and Southey—The spectres of Southerfell—Borrowdale beauties—Haunted Armboth—*The Shadow of a Crime*—Old roads and new—The Steading Stone and the Rock of Names.

IF one area could be said to characterize the Lake District, it surely must be the region around Keswick and Derwentwater, Thomas Gray's 'Vale of Elysium.' Geologically there are rich contrasts; to the north lie the huge whale-backs of Skiddaw and Blencathra, some of the oldest rock in the Lake District, while to the south the volcanic ashes, tuffs and lavas of Borrowdale create a wild and rugged landscape which so frightened and thrilled the early tourists. Indeed, at Hollows Farm near Grange it is almost possible to physically straddle two major geological epochs by standing with one foot on the Borrowdale Volcanic rocks and the other on Skiddaw Slates. But the area is no less rich in history; from Portinscale and elsewhere comes evidence of Neolithic communities roughing out stone axes from the fine-grained ashes found on the Langdale Pikes and Scafell ranges, and perhaps, somewhat later, the same people were sufficiently organized and motivated to construct the great stone circle at Castlerigg. Long Meg by the Eden is grander, and Swinside near Millom is in wilder scenery; but the circle is the most beautifully placed—Skiddaw, Blencathara, Helvellyn, and all the mountains looking at it, at the ring of great grey stones, a mysterious conclave. What could they tell us if we asked them rightly? They might say with some scorn that they are ages older than the Druids, and that they know nothing about shrieking holocausts and fiery Moloch-worship. Were they the sepulchre of some great chief, as so many of the smaller circles were? No; so far as we have been able to inquire of them—putting the question with pick and spade—these greater circles are not sepulchral, but meeting-places of the primeval folk for their rites and tribal observances.[1]

1 Some recent researchers have suggested that the Castlerigg Circle and others in Cumbria could be Stone Age astronomical calendars but the theory has not found universal favour in the archaeological world [Editor's note].

Away from the circle, up that narrow dell to the right of the Benn which hides Thirlmere, is a lofty rock standing precipitously above the ravine. The peak of the rock is joined to the mountainside by a narrow green neck of land, and on this neck are three great trenches. This is Shoulthwaite Castle, said to have been used by the Dales-folk as a refuge in times of raid, but of unknown antiquity. The Castle Crag of Borrowdale was no doubt used as a stronghold at many different periods. Near the foot of Bassenthwaite Lake, near Peel Wyke, there is another such ancient fort on a steep rocky hill, now overgrown with trees, but with a little imagination you can see what a commanding site it is, what a view of lake and mountain the guardians of the place must have had before their eyes. It was just over the hill from here, at Embleton, that the famous sword now in the British Museum was found, an iron blade in a bronze sheath, with red and green jewels on the hilt—the Excalibur of some ancient Briton not without wealth and art.

Of Roman settlement in the Keswick neighbourhood there is little to be certain about, though there is the strong suspicion that the town overlies a Roman camp. After they left, the Cymric Age gives us the story of St Kentigern: how (about A.D. 550) he came into these mountains from Carlisle to preach to the half-savage and heathen hill-folk. Jocelin of Furness, who compiled a life of the saint from Irish records going back, no doubt, to very early times, tells us that he set up a cross in a thickly wooded place, called Crosfeld, where, when Jocelin wrote (about 1180), a church had lately been built and dedicated to St Kentigern. Now *feld* in English is the Norse *thwaite*, and at Crosthwaite St Kentigern's church was built in Jocelin's day. This is fact, if the legend of the saint's visit be doubted.

Rather more than a century after Kentigern, wild and remote Derwentwater was chosen for his hermitage by St Herbert, the friend of St Cuthbert. Bede tells us that every year the friends used to meet; what adventurous travelling among unknown fells and foes! The two saints prayed that they might die on the same day, which was granted to them in the year 687. As the twelfth-century church revived the remembrance of St Kentigern, so the fourteenth

Bassenthwaite Lake

century revived St Herbert's; a cell was built upon his island—his own hut had long since disappeared, of course—and annual pilgrimages were instituted. It is a curious fact that there was found, near the stone axes just mentioned, and about the same time, a little mould for making such crucifixes as were sold to pilgrims. It was close to the old road called Finkle Street, leading to Nichol-end landing near Portinscale, where folk would take boat to visit St Herbert's island. Perhaps there was a booth and workshop there to catch the pilgrims on their way. How little the medieval lead-founder guessed that another and very different craftsman had been at work, ages before, on the spot; and that the relics of both would be shown—as they are in the Keswick Museum—to quite a new sort of pilgrim in the twentieth century.

After St Herbert there is a long silence. We have no reason to suppose that the Angles of Northumbria made any considerable or permanent settlements within the fells of the Lakes, though they did in the surrounding country. In the neighbourhood of Keswick nearly all the place-names have a Scandinavian form. There are a few Celtic. Derwent, like the other great rivers, naturally keeps its early name, but Greta is Norse, and all the *becks* and *gills, forces* and *tarns*. There are a few *glens* and a *strath*, but *dale, scarth, gap, door*, and so forth, are Norse. Blencathara is a Welsh mountain-name; Glaramara, Helvellyn, and Skiddaw are doubtful but possibly Norse. But all the *fells, bells, pikes, bowes, nabs, snabs, sides, seats*, and *moors* are Norse or Middle English. Of village names most are Norse *thwaites*, or have some reference to farming, as we noticed before. *Lath* or *laithe*, a barn; *sty*, a ladder or steep path; *rake* and *gate*, a path; *carr*, a swampy coppice; *ness, hause, holme* (often dropping to *ham*), are all very common. *Seat* usually means a 'sæter' or outlying chalet, as in Seathwaite and Seatoller; the last part of Seatoller in former times was -*haller*, possibly for Halldor, a Norse name.[1] In Gutherscale, near Swinside, we seem to have the *skáli* or shed of Guthred or some such name, like Gutterby near Bootle; Hestholm, the early name for Derwent island, meant the place where the landlord kept his horses (*hest*) out of mischief, and so on. Of course the original tongue of the Viking settlers gradually became more and more like English, but it lasted long enough for many twelfth-century places to have Norman names of quite Norse form: for example, Rickerby, Botchardby, Aglionby, and even Parsonby. I suppose one might even now build a new house and call it, say, Mossgarth, which would be quite Norse; so that it must not be inferred that every such name implies an original Viking settlement. But the name Borrowdale is a good proof that not only Norse, but grammatical Norse, was spoken by the people who finally settled here. In the Furness Abbey records—for that abbey held it, whence their 'Grange'—it is written *Borcheredal*, that is *Borgardalr* in Icelandic, the 'dale of the Borg' (Castle Crag,

---

1 An alternative might be 'the saeter among the alder (Old Norse *alor*) trees' [Editor's note].

The shores of Derwentwater

I suppose), *borgar* being the proper genitive. The *r* of the nominative *dalr* has dropped out in all English-Scandinavian names, as it has in Norway; if indeed it was ever sounded by the folk who settled here. In addition, there are several early medieval inscriptions in Cumbria written in Scandinavian runes, indicating that a debased form of Norse was being written, and in all probability spoken, at that time. One more name we must mention, and that is most puzzling of all. Many guesses have been made at 'Keswick.' It was Kesewic in c. 1240, which can only mean 'cheese dairy.'

So we have those farming colonists gradually going farther up the dales from Norse settlements in the lower ground, clearing the woods and keeping their horses, cattle, and sheep on the fells: this would be in the tenth and eleventh centuries. They were not left in peace, for King Edmund in 945 and King Ethelred in 1000 invaded Cumbria, obviously because the great kings of the south, to whom Vikings of all sorts were natural enemies, distrusted any such encroachments on their borderland. But whatever damage and devastation was done by these and other wars, the descendants of the Northmen became the ancestors of the Dalesmen.

At first the farmers of the dales were free men, squatters in the woods of no-man's-land. During the twelfth century even the mountains began to feel the grip of the Norman settlement, barons and abbots from their lowland castles gradually getting more and more hold of the hinterland. Not without resistance the dalesmen became tenants of feudal lords, but even so they were not in the condition of the villeins of other counties; they kept many customary privileges, amounting to something very like independence. When an explanation of this unusual state of things was required, it was said that they held

their lands on condition of repelling Scottish invasion—a constant and heavy
task, which entitled them to greater advantages than other tenants: they held
by Border tenure. When the Scottish Solomon became James I of England,
he argued that Border service was out of date, and that much money might
be raised by driving that fact home to its logical conclusion. The Crown was
lord of many manors in which the farms were held by Border tenure; Border
service need be no longer given, therefore the Crown might seize the lands.
Other lords of manors followed the king's example, and there were riots and
lawsuits, and it seemed as if the Star Chamber would, as usual, carry out the
king's will. But old use and immemorial rights prevailed over the king and the
lords and the great legal fiction of Border tenure. The English courts decided
that the estates of the tenants were 'estates of inheritance at the will of the
lord, descendible from ancestor to heir according to the several customs of the
several manors whereof they are holden'—quite apart from service against
raiders and invaders; and thus the statesmen (estatesmen) of the Lake counties
came into being.

It was this independence that made the Dales-folk such interesting characters. They were practically their own masters all through the times of the
Stuarts and the Georges. Their life was like that of the Swiss or the Icelanders,
where every farm is a separate estate; every farmer was almost his own landlord.
There were few gentlefolk, very few great folk, and no sort of notion about
emulating the grandeurs of town or castle. Every one's position was assured
in a way we can hardly realize now; it did not even depend upon the state of
the market, for each family raised and manufactured its own food and clothing,
and wanted no more. They were forced to be careful, but they had no one to
cringe to. The priest, as they still called their clergyman, was usually the only
superior person in the dale, but he was often one of the poorest, ekeing out a
'living' of £5 a year with annual gifts of clothes and clogs, and getting his
daily dinner at other folks' houses—whittlegate, they called it, the run of his
knife. He was one of themselves, a farmer's younger or less sturdy son, who
had been kept at school, and had not risen in the Church. Some rose high,
for with all their rusticity the Dales-folk had brains, and produced many
eminent clergy, lawyers, and merchants. Odd things happened when they
came back to visit their relations. The late Miss Noble, in her *History of
Bampton*, tells how the great Bishop Gibson, Anglo-Saxon scholar, editor of
Camden, and so forth, came to see his sister, and sat by the fire while she
cooked the dinner. He thought her cooking was not quite clean, and said so. .

'What,' she said, 'we mun all eat a peck of dirt before we dee.'

'Yes,' said he, 'but not all at once, Mary, not all at once.'

Some of the clever dalesmen stayed at home. In Bampton it was said they
drove the plough in Latin. At Ulpha some college lads asked for their bill in
Latin and got it in Greek. There were several noted mathematicians among

A lakeland farm

the cottage-folk of a hundred years ago.

The Lake District house, the ordinary statesman's house, is a comparatively modern type. Before the Civil Wars poor folk lived in a ruder kind of cottage, still sometimes seen in outhouses. They set up two pair of 'siles,' rough crooked beams forming a Gothic arch; then thatched a roof nearly down to the ground on each side, and built up the rest with wattle-and-daub (the clay daubings) or with stones, where stone was handier than clay. This was enlarged by adding another bay, with another pair of siles. But in the seventeenth century the statemen began to build better houses in imitation of the Jacobean manor-halls, and evolved a type of their own—the low, rough-cast building with porch and penthouse (outside stair and gallery), dead-nailed door and massive thresh-wood, house-place with mullioned windows, and behind the rannal-balk a great open fire-spot where peats burned on the cobble-paved hearth, under the pot hanging from the ratten-crook; upstairs was the long loft, where the family slept unashamed, as in the Icelandic *badstofa*.[1] The exterior was charming, especially with the big trees that overhung the mossy slates, and the massive chimneys, sometimes round and sometimes square. A bit of garden, in which you saw the rock sticking out, and a few clipped yews, and a humble imitation of the Elizabethan courtyard formed by the outbuildings, made the homestead a most picturesque feature, absolutely in harmony with the landscape.

Sheep were the chief care; the Herdwick sheep that keep their heads to the wind, and know their own 'heaf' on the fells where they are pastured in summer, every flock to its own 'stint.' Before winter most were killed off and the mutton-hams hung in the chimney; there is no better mutton than the Herdwick sheep.[2] Oats were grown and made into porridge, a few cows gave

1 See W. Rollinson, *Life and Tradition in the Lake District*, 1987.

2 It was served at the Coronation banquet of Queen Elizabeth II [Editor's note].

the milk, and the farmer's wife brewed ale. There was a certain amount of illicit whisky-distilling, too, in the later times, of which many a tale is told; and there was some drinking on market days; but the folk were mainly sober, hard-working, self-reliant, cautious, close-fisted, hospitable, humorous mortals.

Borrowdale was the Gotham of Cumberland. Every one knows the old stories: how they built a wall to keep the gowk[1] (cuckoo) in, so that it might always be summer; but it just hopped over the comb of the wall—another stone would have held it!—how the rain fell on the lime and the carter tumbled it into the beck to put the fire out!—how they were puzzled by a mule, and called it a peacock (I have myself heard a child at a fell farm ask if a donkey was a camel!)—and how the old farmer stuck fast in his stirrups, a new invention, and sat on horseback all night, till at a bright idea he was lifted off, saddle and all; and at last, by the scholar's advice, they hoisted him out of his clogs.

Some of the old customs were curious: the sweet-butter (with sugar and rum), always eaten at a birth; the 'Old Wife Do' at the month's end, when the women jumped the can with a besom stuck in it, and the lads raided the house and stole the sweet-butter; the wedding-race home from church; the bride throwing her stocking at the lasses; the 'laiting' or 'bidding' to the funeral, and the lifting of the coffin; the procession by some traditional corpse-road, flood or snow notwithstanding, and often a journey of miles over the fells; the arvel bread doled out to the mourners: these were survivals from very early times. The calendar was marked by Christmas merry-nights; New Year stanging (making churlish wayfarers ride the pole); Candlemas business-settlements; Collop Monday and Pancake Tuesday; Carling Sunday, when they ate fried peas at Mid-Lent; the pace-eggers' mummery at Easter; April noddies and May goslings; Mayday and midsummer bonfires; Whitsuntide hirings and holidays; waking the holy-wells; rush-bearing on the Saints' days, and the kurn (i.e. churn) suppers at harvest home—these, with ploughings, clippings and clay-daubings (gatherings to shear a neighbour's sheep or build his house), popular fairs, hunts, and wrestlings, kept them from stagnation. Some of these customs have not died out. 'Pace' eggs are still dyed at Easter in the Furness area and until the 1940s arvel or funeral bread was distributed to mourners at funerals and the custom of 'telling the bees' of a bereavement in a family continued at least until the 1950s. Tradition, like dialect, dies hard in Cumbria.

In the Keswick neighbourhood a curious foreign element was introduced with the German miners of Queen Elizabeth's days.[2] The mines had been

---

1 *Gauki* is the Icelandic word for the cuckoo [Editor's note].

2 See W. G. Collingwood, *Elizabethan Keswick*, 1912, reprinted 1987.

worked long before; they are mentioned under Henry III and Edward IV, but about the year 1565 a German company began working some of them with improved science and skill. It is very striking, in view of the modern development of scientific manufactures in Germany, to find that the Germans, more than three hundred and fifty years ago, were far ahead of the English in mining and metal-working; not only then, but two hundred years earlier, it was so. In 1350 the Alston silver and lead mines were managed by a German from Cologne, named Tillmann. In 1565 Thomas Thurland and Daniel Höchstetter asked leave to bring German miners to Keswick. The colony was very ill received by the exclusive Dales-folk; assaults and even murders are mentioned, and the Germans had to be lodged on the northernmost of the larger islands to keep them safe. They built copper-smelting works at Newlands, and on the Greta at Brigham near Keswick; mined also at Coniston and elsewhere, sent a colony to Neath in South Wales, and some of them certainly made their fortunes, for the Höchstetters, Tullies, Raisleys (originally Ritseler), Steinbergers, and others descended from them, took rank among the county families. Indeed, Tullie House, the finest mansion of its time in Carlisle, was built, it is thought, with money made in the Keswick mines. But the Civil Wars put an end to their operations.

It was not agreeable for the old landed gentry to see these new-come foreigners prospering where they had failed. The Radcliffes of Lord's Island are especially mentioned among their enemies. The Radcliffes had got the manor in the time of Henry VI through marriage with the heiress of the Derwentwaters, who had been lords of the neighbourhood since the time of Edward I. They too became mine-owners under James I, and enriched themselves out of the Alston mines. James II gave them a peerage, the earldom of Derwentwater; and they remained staunch to the Jacobite cause. The last earl joined in the rising of 1715, and was beheaded in spite of powerful friends and the prayers of his young wife. The story goes that she escaped from Lord's Island up the Lady's Rake (path), a steep gully in Walla Crag, and so made her way to London on the fruitless errand; but this is doubtful. Pennant (1774) alludes to the place as the Lady's Leap. Some nights after the earl's execution there was a great display of aurora borealis, and the countryfolk thenceforward called it 'Lord Derwentwater's Lights.' After the Civil Wars their mansion on Lord's Island was left to ruin. A bell that used to hang there was used as the clock bell for the Keswick courthouse or town hall, and it has puzzled many antiquaries by its inscription, 'H D 1001 R O'; one thing is certain, that it does not date from A.D. 1001: probably an error in casting for 1601.

The town got its market charter from Edward I, and was something of a business place—what with the mining population and the old woollen industries, as at Kendal, and later in its history the pencil manufacture. At the end of the eighteenth and early in the nineteenth century pencils were made by hand, each separately and laboriously, from the famous Borrowdale 'wad,' 'black cawke,' or black-lead, got at the mine near Seathwaite; before that the 'wad' was used in casting shot and shells. The mine was worked before the seventeenth century, and it was so valuable that an Act was passed under George II to make any theft from it a felony; they had even to protect the mine with firearms from determined and organized robbery. The pencil-making still goes on though the mines are closed and the raw materials are imported. One of the most recent attractions at Keswick has been the opening of a museum devoted to pencil manufacturing.

Among the earlier worthies of Keswick were Sir John Bankes, Chief Justice of the Common Pleas under Charles I, and the Speddings, of whom one has been mentioned in connection with the Whitehaven mines together with Dr Brownrigg of Ormathwaite (1711–1800), the eminent early chemist. When the first tourists were discovering the beauties of the Lakes, on the tracks of Gray the poet, Pennant the antiquary, and Mrs Radcliffe the novelist, the chief figure at Keswick was Peter Crosthwaite (1735–1808), a native who had been in the naval service in the East Indies. He opened a museum in the Square (1780) with local antiquities and natural history, which was a great attraction until its dispersion in 1870, since when the museum in Fitz Park has been formed. He also organized the once famous regattas (1781–90), made maps of the Lakes and meteorological observations, and assisted John Dalton in the chemical researches which led to the atomic theory. Jonathan Otley, whose *Guide* was published in 1827, was a geologist of more than local renown.

But the chief celebrities of Keswick were 'off-comers,' outsiders who settled there. In 1800 S. T. Coleridge, already a poet of some reputation, came to settle at Greta Hall. His wonderful *Christabel* was inspired by Lake District legends; but after Southey joined him at Keswick he wandered away (1804), and though visiting the place occasionally never identified himself or his work with it. Robert Southey, who lived at Greta Hall from 1803 until his death in 1843, became the genius of the neighbourhood. Some of his work, like the well-known *Lodore* (and the 'Knitters of Dent,' which, though not his writing, was published by him in *The Doctor*), illustrated his adopted home; but neither of the Keswick poets made the Lakes their theme as Wordsworth did.

A curious little picture of Greta Hall is given by Sara Coleridge: 'Two houses interconnected under one roof; the larger part of which my parents, and my uncle and aunt Southey occupied, while the smaller was the abode of Mr Jackson' (the master-wagoner of Wordsworth's poem).[1] 'How gravely and earnestly used S.T.C. and W. Wordsworth and my uncle Southey to discuss the affairs of the nation, as if it all came home to their business and bosoms; as if it were their private concern!' And then they used to read their poems,

1 Jackson had built the house in the 1790s [Editor's note].

and poor little Sara, a child of six, was terrified at her uncle's ballads, especially at the *Old Woman of Berkeley*. 'Oh! the agonies I have endured between nine and twelve at night [late hours for a little girl!] before mamma joined me in bed, in presence of that hideous assemblage of horrors, and the horse with eyes of flame.' It seems that uncle Southey only thought it funny, but Coleridge let the child have a lighted candle in her room. 'From that time forth,' she says, 'my sufferings ceased. I believe they would have destroyed my health had they continued.' One sees why Southey, in spite of enormous cleverness and success, has been found wanting.

His eminence—he was appointed poet laureate in 1813—brought many pilgrims to Keswick. Ruskin as a little boy in 1830 went reverently to Crosthwaite church in the hope of seeing the great poet, and wrote in his rhyming journal:

> His dark lightning eye made him seem half inspired,
> Or like his own Thalaba, vengefully fired.
> We looked, and we gazed, and we stared in his face,
> Marched out at a slow stopping, lingering pace;
> And as toward Keswick delighted we walked,
> Of his face and his form and his features we talked.

At the same church we can see his grave. It is outside, near the north-west corner of the tower: and inside is the monument with Wordsworth's verses in his memory.[1] It was partly in praise of the scenery, and partly in praise of his friend Coleridge, that he had written in 1801 in an access of patriotism:

> What was the great Parnassus' self to Thee,
> Mount Skiddaw? In his natural sovereignty
> Our British Hill is nobler far; he shrouds
> His double front among Atlantic clouds
> And pours forth streams more sweet than Castaly.

Skiddaw has a claim upon us as one of the first mountains that tempted climbers for the sake of the scenery. There had been travellers and explorers, hermits and hunters before; but I do not think it often happened that people went up to the heights for the mere pleasure of going there. Bishop Nicholson in his diary for 20th May 1684, records that he went up Skiddaw with some friends, and about this time it seems to have been a well-known point of view. Housman, who tells the story of his climb in 1798 which he 'inconsiderately undertook to perform without a guide,' says that towards the northern extremity of the summit of 'this stupendous mountain' where 'chasms of enormous depths in the bowels of the mountains, forming steeps of slaty

1 For other monuments and details see gazetteer, under Keswick.

shiver, yawn upwards with frightful grin, and threaten to swallow inferior hills,' there were ruins of a hut. 'It is said,' he continues, 'that this building was made in 1689 by Mr John Adams, the geographer, of a sufficient size to contain his telescopes and optic glasses, whereby he was enabled to give a better description of the two counties; but being arrested by his engraver, and death soon following, his labours were lost.' But by Housman's time there was already a track to the top; Mrs Radcliffe, who wrote *The Mysteries of Udolpho*, had published her account of the great adventure. She began by saying: 'We stood on a pinnacle, commanding the whole dome of the sky,' and concluded: 'The air on this summit was boisterous, intensely cold, and difficult to be inspired, though the day was, below, warm and serene. It was dreadful to look down from nearly the brink of the point on which we stood upon the lake of Bassenthwaite, and over a sharp and separated ridge of rocks that from below appeared of a tremendous height, but now seemed not to reach half-way up Skiddaw; it was almost as if

> 'the precipitation might down stretch
> Below the beam of sight.'

We who walk up Skiddaw as unconcernedly as we take a stroll in the park may smile; but we don't get half the pleasure those old folk got.[1]

Saddleback, or to call it by the older, romantic name, Blencathara, is more interesting as a mountain, for it really has a bit of sharp ridge over Scales Tarn which can give a not too hardened climber the sense of mountain height. Ruskin wrote in 1867 about his walk up Saddleback, how he went up the steep front by the central ridge to the summit. 'It is the finest thing I've yet seen,' he said—meaning in Cumberland—'there being several bits of real crag-work, and a fine view at the top over the great plain of Penrith on one side, and the Cumberland hills, as a chain, on the other. Fine fresh wind blowing, and plenty of crows. Do you remember poor papa's favourite story about the Quaker whom the crows ate on Saddleback?'—Helvellyn, he meant, in vague remembrance of Christopher North's coarse travesty of the story which Scott and Wordsworth had told in sentimental verse. 'There were some of the biggest and hoarsest-voiced ones about the cliff that I've ever had sympathetic croaks from:—and one on the top, or near it, so big that Downes and Crawley [his servants] having Austrian tendencies in politics, took it for a "black eagle." Downes went up capitally'—Downes, when I knew him a little later, was distinctly stout—'though I couldn't get him down again, because he *would* stop to gather ferns. However, we did it all and came down to Threlkeld—of the *Bridal of Triermain*:

---

1 The late Graham Sutton suggested that 'Steep rock went to our forefathers' heads.' Perhaps he was right [Editor's note].

Seatoller, Borrowdale

> 'The king his way pursued
> By lonely Threlkeld's waste and wood.'

Southerfell is the last height in the range, its name meaning not that it stands to the south, which is not the case, but evidently like the Icelandic Saudhafell—sheep-hill. It is famous for the curious mirage seen there on midsummer eve, 1735. A farm-servant thought he saw troops marching over the mountain, and of course was ridiculed for the tale. Two years later the farmer's whole family saw the same thing, and they too were thought to have gone mad. So, at midsummer, 1745, they invited a large party, and all saw an army with carriages, which could not possibly be, on the top of the fell. Next day they went to look for the footprints, but in vain. It came out that the Jacobite army had been parading or marching that evening, somewhere to the north, at a great distance; and it was supposed that this was the reflection of their figures 'by some transparent vapour, similar to the *fata morgana*.' The same thing was seen on Helvellyn on the eve of the battle of Marston Moor; and the *Lonsdale Magazine*, which collected the accounts, gave a number of similar instances, but no real explanation.

It is not easy to write of Borrowdale without becoming too lyrical. There are no eagles now on Eagle Crag as there were a hundred and fifty years ago. Lodore—we may keep Southey's spelling, though I suppose the real name is Low-door—cannot now be dissociated from that memory-puzzling accumulation of epithets. The beck-side at Grange under the old fir trees, beside the famous glaciated rock, has been walled up; the quarries have spread, and the Bowder Stone with its ladder and air of Cockney sight-seeing is an offence to many. But when you have passed these you are in ancient Borrowdale. If you

Old houses at Grange-in-Borrowdale

are on foot, and can ramble up behind the Castle Crag, or among the woods
of Longthwaite and Seatoller, or by the lovely path and over the moor to
Watendlath with its little tarn and quaint old bridge and perfect Cumberland
beck, broken into tiny cascades among the rocks; or if you explore the
Stonethwaite valley, the queerest of hamlets, and the most idyllic of rocky
garths and ferny, briery paths, leading suddenly round a crag-corner to wild,
desolate Langstrath, 'Glaramara's inmost caves,' and the Stake Pass; or the
Seathwaite valley and lonesome Stockley Bridge, and the grand ascent to
Styhead: if you can linger here you will have your fill of beauty. It is not this
part of the district which gains so much in winter, for its charm is in the
richness and daintiness of foliage and frondage in the midst of strong rocky
surroundings, each helping the other by the contrast; but I do not know any
place where that effect is so perfect and where there is so much of it, in such
variety and grace, as in Borrowdale.

Then the walk over to Thirlmere. You can get to Thirlmere by the road
from Keswick or Grasmere; thousands pass that way every summer, but they
miss the one thing which Thirlmere has yet to show—the magnificent sight
down and up, to right-hand and left, when you come, after crossing the moor
by Watendlath or Blea Tarn, to the brink of the fell and see Helvellyn in all
its mass above you, and the lake in all its length below. Helvellyn has no peak,
and hardly any crags on this side, but it has a huge mass, and an effect of size
enhanced by the broken edges of the steep fell-side on which you stand.
Thirlmere has no expanse, but it once was the richest in story and scenery of
all the Lakes. Its conversion to a reservoir in 1894 was regarded by many as

an outrage and desecration of the worst sort; the destruction of the small
rustic footbridge which formerly crossed the lake at its narrowest point, the
inundation of the hamlet of Wythburn and the addition of a pumping station
masquerading as a pantomime medieval castle offended those who remembered
the charm of its shores. Today the memory has faded and the beauty of
Thirlmere can be recalled only through ancient photographs, engravings and
paintings. Nature trails and a degree of public access have gone some way to
mollify public opinion but the contentious question of reservoirs within the
Lake District remains unanswered.

Armboth farm used to be thought a haunted spot; there were tales of a
nocturnal marriage and a murdered bride; strange lights appeared at the
windows and uncanny figures were seen; there was a black dog that swam the
lake o' nights. Dalehead opposite was also a weird place; sometimes a fire
blazed out along the roadside, above the trees, throwing showers of sparks,
and disappeared leaving 'nowder a black pleàce nur a bit o' gurse swing't nur
nea udder mark o' t' fire.' There was a murder there once, and wherever a
murder has happened the countryfolk plant a cutting from the ancient Yggdra-
sil of myth-lore, and it flourishes. Sir Hall Caine worked the legends and
scenes of this dale into his novel, *The Shadow of a Crime*, and they make fine
material for an effective story. There is something of a romance in real life
attaching to Armboth. The Jacksons of that place were a very old landowning
family, and their representative, Miss Jackson, married a Russian Count
Ossalinsky. When the Manchester reservoir scheme required the land the
corporation offered a large sum, but the lady asked thrice as much, and the
courts decided in her favour. The Countess Ossalinsky died in 1902, aged
eighty-one.

Old writers make much of the Castle Rock of St John's Vale; you face it
when you look east from Smaithwaite Bridge, where the now diminished river
runs from one valley to the other. Sometimes it is called the Triermain Rock,
only because Scott mentioned it in the course of his *Bridal of Triermain*: he
was versifying Hutchinson's *Excursion* (1776), which says that 'the inhabitants
near it assert that it is an antediluvian structure,' but so bewitched that when
you approach it the whole thing changes into a mere heap of rock. On the
rock there are the ruins of an old building, perhaps a fort—but there is no
record of its history. If Scott had known the neighbourhood he would have
found a much finer subject in Shoulthwaite Castle, which is a real ancient
fort, and strange enough for any amount of romance. The valley of 'St John,'
too, should be 'of St John's,' from the little church—once belonging to the
Hospitallers of Jerusalem—on the hause between this valley and Naddale,
through which the main road runs.

At the church is buried John Richardson, a dialect poet of much fame in
Cumberland. He was born at Piper House in Naddale, 1817; began life as a

mason, then became schoolmaster at Bridge House, just under the church; and died there in 1886. To strangers the unnecessarily uncouth spelling of his songs is difficult to understand, but nobody better painted the later Dales-folk—not the statesmen of the fine old days, but their already degenerate progeny in the nineteenth century. His old farmer, like Tennyson's, is all for 't' brass' and a good match for Sarah. He dreams that the bank has broken, and what then?—

> Theer three clips o' woo up i' t' woo-loft;
>   Them Kendal chaps bad me elebben;
> I thowt I sud hev twelve an' sixpence,
>   And noo, dang't, it's com't doon to sebben ...
>
> I's rayder sleepy; bit mappen
>   I'll dream that ill dream ageàn;—
> Bit what! hang them Wakefields—they'll brek nin
>   If I nobbut let them aleànn!

It is perhaps necessary to tell that 'Wakefields' was the old-standing bank of the district.

Through this narrow rocky dale ran an ancient road—fancied to be Roman, but really medieval—from Penrith-way past Wanthwaite to Legberthwaite, and then over the Wath and wooden bridge, once the chief beauty of Thirlmere, and so by the western shore of the lake, up and down the crags, and round the bays to Stenkin (Stane-weg-ing) and Wythburn.

Where this old road crossed Launchy (i.e. Lancelot's) or Deergarth Gill was the Steading Stone. Here manorial courts were held, and a local parliament which had written bylaws called 'The Pains and Penalties of Wythburn,' among which were fines for turning out too many sheep on the fell, letting horses and cattle stray, or fouling the becks. This stone is now submerged, but up the beautiful gill you can see the Cop Stone, Thirlmere's Bowder. Above Launchy Tarn from which the stream flows is the big Web Stone where, in the plague of 1665 when markets were stopped, traders met the Dales-folk and bought the webs and yarn they had manufactured.[1]

Opposite Deergarth is Clark's Lowp, where a henpecked dalesman drowned himself. The story goes that his widow only remarked 'he had often threatened it, but she never thought the fool had the courage.' Near it was the Rock of Names, with Wordsworth's and Coleridge's initials; it has recently been removed to the safety of the Wordsworth Museum, Grasmere. The isolated hill north of Dalehead is Great How, where Wordsworth's 'George Fisher, Charles Fleming, and Reginald Shore' built 'a man on the peak of the crag.'

Legberthwaite is the general name for the scattered houses at its foot, in

---

1 There is now a Nature Trail through the forest at Launchy Gill [Editor's note].

In Borrowdale

the side-valley of Helvellyn Gill; here is the old 'King's Head,' where John Stanley set up for sign:

> I, Stanley lives here, and sells good ale,
> Come in, and drink before it grows stale.
> John succeeded his father Peter,
> But i' th' old man's time 'twas never better.

One dark night a bagman rode to the door, and asked how far he was from the 'Nag's Head'—the rival inn at Wythburn. 'Only t' length o' t' neck,' said Stanley; but he had to explain his joke next morning.

The scene of the 'merry night,' in Wordsworth's *Waggoner*, was the 'Cherry-tree' at Wythburn, now demolished. Budworth, in 1792, enjoyed a second breakfast here after coming down from Helvellyn; mutton-ham, eggs, tea, etc., and the charge was sevenpence. The 'Red Lion' at Grasmere did even better for him. Robert Newton, the landlord, provided a dinner of roast pike and anchovy sauce, boiled fowl, veal cutlets, and ham, beans and bacon, parsley and butter, cabbage, peas and potatoes, wheat bread and oat bread, butter and cheese, preserved gooseberries and cream; and the charge was tenpence each. It is not the price that is wonderful, for in those days food was cheap, and travellers drank for the good of the house. But the plenty and variety show that the pre-Wordsworthian dalesman was no stranger to the comforts of life.

'Wythburn's modest house of prayer' was built in 1640 and enlarged in 1872. There is a tale often told, but not made the most of, about an ancient Wythburn clergyman who had only two sermons, and kept them in a crack of the wainscot behind his pulpit. Some wag pushed them down one day out of his reach, and the people smiled while he fumbled. At last he turned, and began: 'My brethren, the sermons are down the grike [crack], but I'll read ye a chapter in Job worth the pair of them.' That was what they didn't expect.

Another scrap of Wythburn wit is given me by a native of the dale, known to many under his pen-name of Rowland Thirlmere. He met a late vicar's son, who had been in a stockjobber's office. An old farmer came up, with 'Eh, Mr B——, so you're back again. And what may ye be dewin?'

'What do you think?'

'Oh, happen you're abease [cattle] jobber?'

'No, I'm a jobber in *stock*'—which, in one sense, is the same thing.

Hence away to Dunmail Raise, and you are back in Westmorland. The cairn used to be thought the burial-place of the 'last king of rocky Cumberland,' whom Roger of Wendover calls Dummail. Others have derived the name conjecturally from Dun (Gaelic), Moel (Welsh), and Raise (Norse), all meaning a hill or heap. It is needless to point out the absurdity of such an etymology. But Domhnall, son of Owain, was really King of Cumbria, and was defeated in 945 and 946 by Edmund of England. As this was always a highway into Cumberland, it is quite possible that the fight took place hereabouts; but Dummail himself was not slain. He lived for thirty years longer—perhaps in Strathclyde, where there was some mention of him—and died at last a pilgrim in Rome.

VIII

FROM HELVELLYN
TO STAINMOOR

Catstycam—Gough and his dog—Striding Edge—Mountain
names—Patterdale, its saint and its king—Lyulph and his tower—
British forts—Roman road and red deer—Dacre Castle—The four
Bears—Mayburgh and King Arthur's Round Table—The bishop
as general—Giants' caves and holy-wells—The Countess of Pem-
broke—Swindale stories—Bolton and Bewley Castle—Appleby
Castle and town—The Kaber Rigg Plot—The Bound Devil of
Kirkby Stephen—Lammerside and Pendragon.

IT is only the back of Helvellyn you see at Thirlmere. Most of our mountains
have a back, sloping and grassy, and a front, steep and rocky; 'crag and tail'
on a large scale, resulting mainly from the effects of glaciation. The backs are
not always without interest. Helvellyn, by mere mass, we found impressive
from Armboth Fell, and when we climb it from Legberthwaite or Wythburn
there are grand gorges and abruptnesses, not to speak of an ever-growing
panorama of lake and mountain, which opens and spreads and complicates
itself, until it gives you in one sweep of the horizon all the great summits,
most of the great lakes, and peeps beyond to far-away Scotland and the Irish
Sea and the distant hills of the Pennine chain. For such a view Helvellyn is
the most central. You overlook the whole of the little Lake District so
completely that it is no great wonder people thought this point the highest in
the days before surveying was a science, or coupled it and its neighbour with
Skiddaw in the old doggerel:

> Skiddaw, Lauvellin, and Castican,
> Are the highest hills climbed by Englishman.

Castican, Catstycam, or Catchidecam means the comb or ridge of the cat's
ladder, a homely way of calling it uncommon steep. It is the tip of Swirrel or
Swirl Edge, which matches Striding Edge—twin buttresses of Helvellyn,
enclosing the Red Tarn beneath them. The legend of the place every one
knows—how Charles Gough died there, and how his dog never left him for
three months. Scott and Wordsworth visited the spot with Sir Humphry Davy

in the autumn of 1805—the accident was in the spring before—and both poets told the story in verses which have paid the usual penalty for effectiveness in becoming commonplace.

'The general sympathy with this tragic event,' wrote De Quincey, 'was not derived from the unhappy tourist's melancholy end, for that was too shocking to be even hinted at by either of the two writers (in fact, there was too much reason to fear that it had been by the lingering death of famine)—not the personal sufferings of the principal figure in the little drama—but the sublime and mysterious fidelity of the secondary figure, his dog.'

Canon Rawnsley was at great pains to hunt out all the facts of the case; to prove that the dog, a little yellow terrier named Foxey, did not eat her master, as had been unkindly hinted; to find the spot where the body lay, and to place a memorial stone above it. There has been many an accident as sad, and many an incident as touching; but—with De Quincey's leave—our sympathy would never have been so roused if Scott had not drawn us the picture of the dog's vigil:

> How long didst thou think that his silence was slumber?
> When the wind waved his garment how oft didst thou start?

Or if Wordsworth's lines had not been closed with such a haunting cadence:

> He knows, who gave that love sublime,
> And gave that strength of feeling, great
> Above all human estimate.

Striding Edge got a bad name from this mishap, but it is far from dangerous. There is just one bit between the long roof-ridge and the wall of Helvellyn which needs a little care on the part of inexperienced climbers, but even in fog or snow there is no necessity to consider it impassable.[1] The grandest crags in the immediate neighbourhood are to the south of this, round the head of Grisedale and Deepdale. Here Fairfield and Helvellyn, which look so grassy and innocent from the Ambleside or Coniston direction, break into a series of grand ridges and gorges, where you can find opportunity enough for breaking your neck. From the top of Fairfield there is a splendid view of Helvellyn as a long ridge, foreshortened in violent perspective, a most interesting study in mountain-building; and the Eagle Crag and St Sunday's Crag rise magnificently from the pass between Patterdale and Grasmere as you go up between them. The name of St Sunday reappears in St Sunday's Beck in the Kent valley; it may possibly be St Sanctan, as Santacherche is the Domesday form of Kirksanton, which again resembles a name in the Isle of Man derived

---

1 Provided one is well shod! [Editor's note].

At the foot of Kirkstone Pass

from Sanctan. But Dollywaggon Pike is a more puzzling name; it can hardly mean, as the late Mr Robert Ferguson suggested, the pike of the Norse chief's servant 'Wagen.' Budworth, almost two centuries ago, said it was so called 'in remembrance of some rustic fun.' I should like to believe it was named from the Norse *dólgr*, 'fiend' or 'giant,' for it has all the look of supernatural architecture when you see it from the Grisedale side, quite the 'Troll's work.'

This group of valleys, branching from Patterdale, is full of good things—ancient Hartsop Hall and craggy Dovedale, Kirkstone with its boulder 'that gives the savage pass its name' and northward views towards Ullswater, Hayeswater Gill and its wild cove below the top of High Street, Angle Tarn on the open moor, and Boardale Hause, leading over into Martindale. But Patterdale, itself the head of Ullswater, gives the grandest impressions of Lake scenery. Nowhere else do the contour lines fall with such broken and cliffy impetus into the level floor of water; there is nothing, now that Thirlmere is no more, to equal the effect of Place Fell and Stybarrow crowding upon the lake as you come round from Airey Point to Householme, and the winding waterway leads you right into the heart of the mountains.

Patterdale was in the thirteenth century 'Patricdale,' but I suspect Patric was the owner, not the saint. The church is only an Elizabethan foundation, but pretty with its yews and interesting from its holy well. The legend, however, is unfounded that St Patrick on his wanderings through Britain preached and baptized there. The Dales-folk here were not so republican as in most parts: they had a neighbour more important than the average statesman. Nicolson and Burn (1777) said of him: 'This Mr Mounsey and his forefathers for time immemorial have been called kings of Patterdale, living as it were in another world, and having no one near them greater than themselves.' But in

1824 their dynasty came to an end, and the Marshalls reigned in their stead.

Lyulph's Tower is not as old as it looks, though said to be on the site of a real old tower, taking its name from 'the first baron of Greystoke, L'Ulf, the wolf, from whom also Ullswater is named.' So say the staple county histories and their copyists: but Lyulph, the name of the twelfth-century lord, is simply another form of Ludolph (Liotulf); the name is also given as Siolf, i.e. the Norse Sigulf; and Ulf's-water must have been so called from a person named Ulf. The present strange, castellated building was constructed in 1780 for the Duke of Norfolk.

The moorland north of Gowbarrow and Watermillock does not equal the lake-shore in beauty, but Caerthanoc or Maiden Castle on Soulby Fell is an interesting antiquity. Dunmallet, at the foot of the lake over Pooley Bridge, is still finer as an ancient fort with well-marked ramparts at the top of an isolated hill, somewhat like the castle at Peel Wyke near the foot of Bassenthwaite Lake, though both are now wooded. Too little is known about these ancient strongholds; they were used in post-Roman times, but that is all we can say of them as yet, until further exploration.

South of the lake Hallin Fell stands boldly between the deep valley of Sandwick, the outlet of Martindale, and Howtown at the mouth of Fusedale with the mass of Place Fell on the one hand, and Swarth Fell on the other. No lake can show such a varied margin, and none is so interesting in its formation; for the series of basins in which it lies, instead of giving us two main deeps as at Windermere, gives three or four quite distinct and independent hollows with very remarkable features. The highest basin, between Patterdale and Householme, is nearly filled at one end by the deltas of Goldrill and Glenridding Beck. The reach between Cherryholme (opposite Glenridding Beck) and the Waterhead is only about fifty feet deep. Off Glenridding is Wallholme, north of which the lake-bottom falls steeply to one hundred and fifty feet. At Householme is a bar separating this south-west basin from the long and deep middle reach, which goes down to two hundred and five feet between Airey Point and Birk Fell. This gradually shoals up eastward until at the narrows between Hallin Fell and Skelly Nab there is a bar little more than seventy-five feet below the surface. Just to east of the narrows and north-north-west of Howtown, a depth of one hundred and twenty-five feet is reached, which gently rises to less than fifty feet opposite the Brackenrigg Hotel. Below that is yet another shallow depression before the water runs out under Pooley Bridge. I think it may be said that all our valleys are made in this form. They are not long gouge-grooves, but chains of basins, once far more accentuated than now, but gradually crumbled down at the edges, and filled up at the bottoms by the action of ice and water, which have rubbed off the knobs and filled up the holes. Hence the variety, the sudden turns, and the cleverly arranged scaffolding of the scenery.

From Pooley Bridge it is an easy walk of a couple of miles to Moor Divock, where the path crosses the Roman road which we tracked in our second chapter past High Street and Kidsty Pike. Scattered about the moor are many interesting prehistoric cairns which have been found to contain interments, some of burnt bones in urns and one of a skeleton in a cist, or stone coffin made of slabs. Martindale Common contains a protected herd of red deer. Although the area is not open to the public, the deer can often be seen, especially in winter, on the shores of the lake.

Dacre is not only a very pretty spot, but its castle is worth seeing, though only the keep remains, with some earthworks. It is a square tower with large turrets at the angles, built about the middle of the fourteenth century, and altered in the seventeenth by the insertion of square-headed windows and addition of doorway and steps. The hall, once also the kitchen, has the old open fireplace and oven, also a fourteenth-century piscina which has been taken to indicate a religious use, but is merely the medieval wash-hand basin. Above is the solar, which once had a wooden minstrel-gallery. This room is called the king's chamber, and a bogus tradition connects it with the three kings, Athelstan, Constantine, and Owain (father of Dummail), who met in 926 at Dacor (William of Malmesbury says) or Eamot (says the Anglo-Saxon Chronicle). The castle is four hundred years later, but it may be hereabouts that their meeting took place. Bede tells a story about a wonderful cure at a monastery by the river of Dacore about the year 698, and the ancient cross-shafts in the church prove that there were pre-Norman graves here of some importance. Moreover, excavations between 1982 and 1984 confirmed the existence of pre-Norman buildings to the north of the church. Are these the remains of the monastery? In the churchyard are the four Bears which probably sat on the top of the keep, like the four stone figures which once existed on the roof of Dalton Castle. Despite many ingenious and fanciful attempts to unravel the mystery, the secret of the four Dacre bears remains hidden and will probably remain so.

North of this, near Greystoke and Newton Reigny, are ancient forts or camps, but the most celebrated of such antiquities are Mayburgh and the Round Table, close to Eamont Bridge. Mayburgh is a huge circular embankment of stones three hundred and eighty-three feet from crest to crest in diameter, with a hollow space in the middle and an opening towards the east. A standing stone nine feet two inches high in the enclosure may be the last of a circle. There are traces of a modern wall on the crest which must not be taken for part of the original work. The purpose of the great undertaking is not known; one old fancy made it out to be a Roman amphitheatre, and the standing stone was for the criminals to dodge behind when the wild beasts were pursuing them!

King Arthur's Round Table is easily found a little way to the south of

Eamont Bridge. The Round Table is like a big cockpit, and it was formerly used for games, which went on in the middle, on the raised platform, while the spectators sat on the banks around. Some writers have thought that this was its original purpose, but any attempt to explain this earthwork must be speculative. Both Mayburgh and King Arthur's Round Table are henge monuments of the late Neolithic–early Bronze Age period.

Across the bridge and up the hill we are soon in Penrith. The old local pronunciation of the name is Peerith, but as it was spelt Penrith in 1110 we may take it that local pronunciation is no help to the meaning of the name. Etymologists propose *Pen-rhudd*, the red headland or head-place of the district; it is a red-sandstone neighbourhood and was certainly a place of importance from very early, though not Roman, times. The nearest Roman sites were at Brougham, a mile across the river, and at Plumpton, five miles to the north. But the ancient crosses and hogbacks in the parish churchyard, long since rearranged to form what is called the Giant's Grave, and the isolated cross called the Giant's Thumb, must be a thousand years old, more or less, and their size and number prove that great folk once were buried there. The church, except the tower, was rebuilt in 1720–2, and contains many interesting monuments, including the chandeliers, given by the Duke of Portland in thanksgiving for the retreat of Charles Edward Stuart and the Jacobites from the area.

The town of Penrith was especially open to Scottish raids, both as lying on the highway from the north and as one of the places claimed by the Scottish kings under the grant which gave them (1242) certain manors in compensation for abandoning the whole of the northern counties to England. When in 1285

Eamont Bridge

the Scottish dynasty had come to an end and Edward I resumed these manors it was, of course, a grievance, and every good Scot felt it his duty to make the robbery worthless. So in 1311 the raids began again; Bannockburn was fought in 1314; in 1347 Douglas wasted Penrith; in 1382 it was burnt. From about 1397 the Nevilles held it for half a century, and built the castle of which we now see the ruins. Later, it was the residence of Richard III, then Duke of Gloucester.

So protected, Penrith flourished. It had received a market charter in 1223; as early as 1340 a school is mentioned, and Bishop Strickland, about 1400, brought a water-supply to the town from the Petterill. There was a little-known priory of Austin Friars at the Friarage, where the buildings, though old, are later than the suppression of the monastery in 1542–3. After that time the castle was disused; Penrith as a manor formed part of the dowry of successive queens, and Border unrest did not reach so far. The town became in the seventeenth century what it still is, the market of the neighbourhood. The old moot-hall, cross, stocks, and shambles were removed a hundred and fifty years ago; but there are still several buildings of antiquity; especially the early sixteenth-century Two Lions Inn (Gerard Lowther's house), and Robert Bartram's on the west side of the churchyard with a bay window dated 1563.

The Beacon Hill, rising on the north-east to nine hundred and thirty-seven feet above the sea, commands a wide view. It was in 1745 that the beacon was lighted in earnest for the last time. At the previous Jacobite rising the *posse comitatus* was drawn up on the fell under Lord Lonsdale and Bishop Nicholson—in his coach and six—to withstand the invaders. Neither the bishop nor the viscount was a soldier, and the local levies were a mere mob with guns, scythes, and pitchforks. When the Highlanders appeared the countryfolk ran; 'Lord Lonsdale presently galloped off to Appleby, and the bishop's coachman, whipping up his horses, carried off his master, *willy-nilly*, to Rose Castle. It is said,' Chancellor Ferguson adds, 'the prelate lost his wig while shouting from the carriage window to his coachman to stop.'

Three miles east of the town, on the north bank of the Eamont, are the caves known as 'Isis Parlis,' or Sir Hugh's Parlour, where the legends of the neighbourhood say that Sir Hugh Cesario the giant lived—he that was buried at the Giant's Grave, they add. In old times Penrith folk used to go there on the third Sunday in May to drink the water with Spanish juice; on the first Sunday of the month the meetings were at Skirsgill, on the second at Clifton, and on the fourth at Dickey Bank well. These well-wakings were common in all parts of our district, but the early nineteenth century found that they led to mischief, and stopped them. At the Gosforth holy-well wine was poured into the water, and the people caught it as it came out of the spout below— too much diluted, one would think, to hurt anybody's morals.

Nearly opposite the caves is Ninekirks (St Ninian's), an ancient church rebuilt by the Countess of Pembroke in 1660. She was the great lady of the age. Anne Clifford, heiress of the third Earl of Cumberland, was born at Skipton Castle in 1590, brought up in Queen Elizabeth's court, and married at eighteen to Richard Sackville, Lord Buckhurst, who soon became the Earl of Dorset. Seven years later she came to Brougham Castle to visit her mother, and at the spot where they parted she afterwards erected a monument by the roadside—a quarter of a mile from the castle—still known as the Countess's Pillar. Her marriage was unhappy, and after Lord Dorset's death she married Sir Philip Sidney's nephew, the Earl of Pembroke; but he turned out to be even worse as a husband. At last, in 1649, she came into possession of the great estates in the north which had been willed away from her by her father, and she then began to repair the ruin of the Civil Wars. She more or less rebuilt the castles of Skipton, Pendragon, Brough, Appleby, Brougham, and Bardon Tower, with seven churches. She was one of those who 'feared God and took her own part'; extant diaries and memoirs witness to her piety and pertinacity. Sometimes her struggles were rather comic, as when she claimed the 'boon hen' in addition to manorial rents. A Halifax clothier resisted this bit of antiquated feudalism, but the law courts found for the lady. So the countess asked the clothier to dinner, and the first dish was—the hen.

'Come, Mr Murgatroyd,' she said, 'let us be friends. Since your hen is served at my table, I will give you half.'

She lived at all her castles by turns—saying she would not go to Charles II's court 'unless she might go in blinkers'; but for nearly thirty years she was the real Lady Bountiful of Westmorland, and towards the end the very model of spirited old age. Her last words were: 'I thank God I am very well.'[1] Her castle is now a ruin, looking almost as venerable as the Roman fort beside it; but the bright and intimate detail of her autobiography makes her a very living figure even yet, as one travels through the neighbourhood where her name is still written so large.

Brougham Hall was once the seat of a very ancient family, one of whom, the celebrated lawyer and politician, was raised to the peerage in 1830 as Lord Brougham and Vaux. The Hall was demolished in 1934. The church near it was a Norman building restored by the Countess of Pembroke, and containing St Wilfrid's well, which once filled the font.

The neighbourhood of Penrith is full of old halls and churches which are a treat to the antiquary and the architect, or to any one who likes to see what is picturesque and curious in ancient buildings, placed among hills and dales, and within sight of the great mountains. Many of these old halls are now farms, but still retaining interesting features in their peles, or their carved windows and doorways, or old panelling and plaster-work inside. The fol-

1 See Martin Holmes, *Proud Northern Lady*.

Once the home of the Earls of Lonsdale, Robert Smirke's Lowther Castle is today merely a shell, a spectacular mock-gothic pantomime back-drop recalling past glories.

Bampton

lowing will repay visits: Barton, Sockbridge, Yanwath, Blencow, Catterlen, Greystoke Midfarm, Greenthwaite, Johnby, Hutton, Hornby, Clifton, Hackthorpe, Askham.

On our way to Haweswater we pass the great ruined mansion of Lowther Castle, former seat of the Earl of Lonsdale,[1] and its church of St Michael, beautifully placed in the park on the steep bank of the rocky Lowther. To an antiquary the three Anglo-Scandinavian hog-backs in the church porch are especially interesting. Thence through the village of Askham—a most picturesque place—and the quaint hamlet of Helton you ascend the valley past the medieval 'camp' in Setterah Park opposite Whale, to Bampton, famous chiefly for its ancient Grammar School (now no more), where they made bishops out of ploughboys in the old Dales-folk days. Higher up the stream is Thornthwaite Hall, an Elizabethan building where, tradition says, Lord William Howard (Belted Will) died. The Standing Stones, higher up the fell, look like a couple of disused gateposts; but this moor is full of ancient relics— old farmhouses, old roads, old enclosures; and from various points there are grand views across Haweswater to Naddle Forest and up to the Mardale mountains.

The first edition of this book in 1902 contained the following paragraph:

'At Mardale you can see the old Lake District with few modern improvements. Indeed, it is less populous than formerly; several houses, once inhabited, have fallen into ruins, for nowadays the little farm, which just supported a family of the old type, does not pay, and field is added to field. The valley is a *cul-de-sac* to carriage company; there is no road above the Dun Bull, but splendid mountain paths—up Riggindale and over Kidsty Pike to Patterdale; up the Rough Crags, leaving Bleawater in its dark combe on your left, to High Street; past Smallwater over Nan Bield into Kentmere; up the glen to the east

1 The castle was designed by Robert Smirke for the fifth Earl of Lonsdale. Completed in 1811, the cost of maintaining the building eventually became prohibitive and the house was abandoned and the interior demolished in 1957. Only the shell now survives as a spectacular and romantic façade [Editor's note].

of Harter Fell over Gatescarth into Long Sleddale; or eastward over the moor into Swindale. Like Patterdale, Mardale gets the cliffy sides of hills which are less exciting on their southern slopes; from Troutbeck or Ambleside you would hardly guess what there is at the head of Haweswater.'

Today there is little at the head of Haweswater for in the 1930s the lake was turned into a reservoir to satisfy the growing thirst of Manchester. Like the earlier destruction of the community at Wythburn on the shores of Thirlmere, the village of Mardale was destroyed. In 1936 the seventeenth-century church of Holy Trinity was demolished and the remains of those who had rested beneath the shade of the ancient yew trees were re-interred at Shap. The old school which was founded in 1713 escaped the rising water level—it was carefully dismantled and rebuilt at Walmgate Head where it is now a private residence, but the famous Dun Bull Inn, the home of the Mardale Shepherds' meet, was not so lucky; the last meet was held there in 1935 when, it is said, the 'wake' continued from the Friday evening until the following Tuesday. During the drought conditions of July 1984, it was possible to visit the site of the village, to inspect the bee-boles near to the remains of the Dun Bull, to cross Chapel Bridge and stand within the former churchyard and examine the stumps of the felled yew trees. For many this was an interesting and memorable experience; for a few who had lived in the village it was a sad and poignant occasion.[1]

For a lonesome walk through scenery less mountainous, but very characteristic of rugged Westmorland, there is the path over the heathery moor into the secluded valley of Swindale. Today the dale is one of the least populated in the Lake District yet in the eighteenth century it was populous enough to need a Grammar School. John Hodgson (1780–1845), the historian of Northumberland, was born here and was educated at Bampton, a few miles away. Like most Lakeland valleys, Swindale has its heroes and folk stories, many of which, no doubt, improved with the telling. Once, it is said, a dispute arose at church as to whether it was really Sunday: 'T' parson's reet; gang on,' said old John Fell. On another occasion the bottle of wine for the communion was accidentally broken; so they used some rum. One clergyman, when the parsonage had become too ruinous, lived from house to house, and carried his box of sermons with him. He took one out of the top, when Sunday came, without much picking and choosing, until the old lady with whom he lodged told him to 'stir up that box; they're beginning to come varra thick,' as if they were porridge, which of course in the North is a plural noun.

In the next valley are the ruins of Shap Abbey. The Premonstratensians or White Canons originally founded their house at Preston-in-Kendale in 1191 but around 1199 it was moved to the wooded valley of the Lowther where it remained until the dissolution of 1540, the last of the Cumbrian monasteries

1 See Geoffrey Berry, *Mardale Revisited.*

*Together with churches at Burgh-by-Sands and Newton Arlosh, St Cuthbert's
at Great Salkeld in the Eden valley is a fortified church. The 14th century
tunnel-vaulted tower is, in effect, a pele designed to protect parishioners against
Scottish raids.*

to be extinguished. Today the western tower is the most impressive part
remaining but the ground plan can be easily traced; the ruin is in the care of
English Heritage and is open to the public. Across the fields to the south-east
of the abbey is the hamlet of Keld with its sixteenth-century chapel now
owned by the National Trust. Of the famous Shap Stones not very much
remains, but this high moorland reaching from the Lowther valley to the

Although it is almost entirely a man-made beauty spot, Tarn Hows attracts almost three-quarters of a million visitors each year. Despite this popularity and the countless thousands of images reproduced on gaudy tourist souvenirs, it remains essentially the Lake District landscape in miniature.

Eden, and south to the Lune, is crossed by the Roman road, and is full of cairns, tumuli, circles, and ancient 'camps'—at Gunnerkeld, Oddendale, Crosby Ravensworth, Penhurrock, Asby, Orton, Raisbeck, Sunbiggin, Ravenstonedale. These we must leave for the present, and take our road north and east, passing Little Strickland (some inscriptions in the church), Thrimby Old Hall and Grange, Newby Hall, and Morland Old Hall, to Bolton, by the Eden, which flows in a noble stream through a finely-wooded and cultivated valley. The village is—like so many others—interesting ground. The church is curious for its Norman door and most unusual carved relief of two jousting knights on horse-back at the back of the building. A mile up the stream are the ruins of Bewley Castle, once a residence of the bishops of Carlisle. Crossing the Eden by the bridge at Bolton, to the right of Redlands Bank we see the site of a Roman fort, and taking the footpath to the left through the fields, we soon reach the little town of Kirkby Thore.

This was an important point in Roman times, because from here on the 'Second Iter,' from Brougham to Stainmoor, ran the Maiden Way over the fells to Alston and Carvoran on the Wall. At Burwens, between the church and the main road, which here follows the line of the Roman road, was a large fort, Bravoniacum, which has yielded many altars, fibulae, and other relics, some of which are in the Tullie House Museum at Carlisle. Outside the fort was a 30-acre civil settlement which, at some stage, became a walled town. The name Kirkby Thore used to be connected with the Norse god Thor, but it is more probable that it is a reminiscence of an early owner called Thorír, or some such name.

Hence one could make an interesting round through pretty scenery—for the hills, though not craggy, are full of sweet little nooks, and rise gradually to lofty moors. There are Newbiggin with its old hall of Christopher Crack-enthorpe, 1533, and Milburn church, set high above the dell that moats it on two sides, with Norman door and rude red sandstone architecture; and then at some distance the village, quaintly surrounding its broad green and central cross; and Howgill Castle, with massive towers and walls ten feet thick. Then by Knock and Dufton we could reach Long Marton, on the wooded banks of the Troutbeck, and across the valley its ancient church, with grotesquely sculptured tympana over the doors, and 'long-and-short work' in the doorway. Then we could regain the 'Second Iter'—the Roman road—and its bee-line would lead us to Appleby.

There is a drawing by Ruskin which gives a bird's-eye view of Thun in Switzerland, standing in its broad flat valley with distant blue mountains beyond. When you look into the tangled detail of roofs and winding river, interrupted by the gables and chimneys of the town, you begin to find why it was that such a point of view was chosen, and what historical interest the picture was intended to convey. You see how—before any town was there—the river took a bend round the bluff, and some early chieftain seized on the height as a place to fortify. You see how there grew up a castle with central towers and curtain-wall, building up the slopes of the hill into impregnable steepness. On the landward side a gate opens, strongly fortified, while the road seems to wind round the cliffs and under them for the inspection and—if necessary—repulse of the visitor, and so into the stronghold. On the lower end of the hill, but nearer the river, is the church within the walls; and between the castle and the protecting stream a crowd of little houses, packed together for safety, has grown into a town. Then in peaceful times, to gain breathing-space, bridges were thrown over the river, and beyond it a suburb grew up, more loosely planned, more modern in its manner of life. And finally the modern roads, with their dreary lines of poplar, stripe the plain. It is a complete object-lesson in history.

Now, Appleby is just such a place as Thun. There was a loop of the river, with a steep-sided hill in it; the neck of the headland was cut across with great trenches and ramparts (perhaps in pre-Norman times, though this is by no means proved), and a castle placed on the highest point. Sheltered by the castle a little town grew up, with its church at the other end of the one street of the town. Across the river was a suburb, in this case perhaps an earlier village, called about A.D. 1300, 'Old Appleby where the bondmen dwell,' which already had its pre-Norman church, as the hogback built into the existing St Michael's testifies. As to the name of the place, there has been much ingenious guessing, to evade the unromantic idea that the whole town got its title from an original farm where the orchard was a speciality; but we have seen that most names in these parts were farm names to begin with.

In the twelfth century there was the keep of the castle, later called Caesar's Tower (though not Roman), and no doubt some surrounding cottages. Then came the Scottish invasion under William the Lion in 1174. Gospatric, son of Orm, 'an old grey-headed Englishman,' and grandson of the Scottish Earl of Dunbar, made little resistance, and was fined two hundred marks by the English king a year or two later for his surrender. But the town now began to grow. It got its first charter in 1179, built its church of St Lawrence, and became a centre of trade. Under Edward I it had a mayor, and returned members to Parliament. It had eight thousand or ten thousand inhabitants in the Middle Ages, and was in every respect the county town. But the Scots burnt it in 1314 and in 1388, and in 1598 it was depopulated by plague, and never regained its size, though it kept its prestige and retained its title as the county town of Westmorland until 1974. When the ancient county was abolished by Whitehall bureaucracy, the town assumed the name Appleby-in-Westmorland. Its medieval school, one of the oldest in Cumbria, was refounded 1573 by Queen Elizabeth. Its old corporation lasted until 1885, when it was reformed; it sent members to Parliament from Edward I until 1832. The market-house and the high and low crosses at each end of the street are not earlier than the beginning of the nineteenth century, but they recall, like so much else, the features of the antique town not yet obliterated by modern growth and change. There are no great smoky suburbs here; you go out of the streets into the country, as in some old continental city; and the river with its cliffy and wooded banks, overtopped by the great mass of the castle, has a

Elterwater is one of the smallest lakes in Cumbria. It takes its name from the
Old Norse Elptarvatn *meaning 'the lake of the swans' and, appropriately, it is*
sometimes visited in winter by whooper swans from Scandinavia.

charm quite comparable, I think, with scenes which we go much farther to find.

Ormside, or Ormshed, has an interesting old church and some old houses; Warcop can show several old halls and sites of antiquity, and near it is held the celebrated Brough Hill fair. Brough-under-Stainmoor is a place of great antiquarian fame. A little way south of the town, on the bank of the Swindale beck, which comes down from fells more than two thousand feet above sea, is the fort known to the Romans as Verterae, the first great station west of the Pennine range on the main road from Eburacum to Luguvallium. When the Normans came this was still the main road from York to Carlisle, and they built their castle on the Roman site, as at Brougham. The Norman poet, Jordan Fantosme, who wrote the story of the Scottish king William the Lion's invasion in 1174, has a vivid description of the siege of Burc, as he calls it; how the Flemings and Border men assaulted and took the portcullis, and then the defenders, shut up in the keep, were burnt out and surrendered. But a new knight had just joined them, and he kept up the defence alone, hurling javelins and killing his man each time. When the javelins were spent he threw sharp stakes at the Scots from behind two shields which he had hung on the battlements to protect him, 'E tuz jorz vait criant: Jà serre tuz vencuz!' (and kept on shouting, 'You will soon be conquered, all of you!'). At last the fire caught his shields, and he had no cover left—'nor was he to blame if he surrendered then. So Burc was overthrown and the best part of the tower.'

A little south of this is Kaber, known in history for the Kaber Rigg Plot. In 1663, after the restoration of Charles II, an insurrection of the Republican party was intended; there were plans for a general rising all over England and Ireland. In these parts the head of the movement was Robert Atkinson of Mallerstang, who had been a captain of horse under Cromwell, and had led the commoners of the barony of Appleby in a great suit with the Countess of Pembroke about things more important than a hen. His enemy was Sir Philip Musgrave, and the particular object of the plot in Westmorland was to capture Sir Philip in the first place, then to take Carlisle and Appleby, and finally to force the king 'to perform his promises made at Breda, grant liberty of conscience to all but Romanists, take away excise, chimney-money, and all taxes whatever, and restore a Gospel magistracy and ministry.' The rising failed; they were betrayed; Atkinson was captured, and finally hanged; and this scare put back the clock most sadly for all dissenters and suspects throughout Westmorland.

Kirkby Stephen can boast one of the finest ancient churches in the county, with monuments as curious as any. Near the font on entering you see the famous 'Bound Devil,' the figure of Satan, or, as some think, the Norse Loki, as at Gosforth, chained and horned; a fragment from some grave-cross of the Viking period. In the Musgrave chapel, south of the choir, are other early sculptures and capitals of the Norman church, with an effigy which used to be called that of the celebrated Sir Andrew de Harcla, or Hartley, who took his name from Hartley Castle near this town (see p. 81). A later opinion[1] makes it represent Sir Richard de Musgrave (about 1420–30) about whom the story is that he killed the last wild boar in the district; and curiously enough, when the tomb was opened in 1847 a wild boar's tusk was found with the bodies. On the other side of the church is the Wharton chapel, with the effigies of Lord Wharton (d. 1568) and his two wives, with Latin verses which were parodied in the eighteenth century thus:

> Here I, Thomas Wharton, do lie
> With Lucifer[2] under my head;
> And Nelly, my wife, hard by
> And Nancy as cold as lead.
> Oh! how can I speak without dread?
> Who could my sad fortune abide,
> With one devil under my head,
> And another laid close at each side?

The Whartons were the great family of Wharton Hall, a very fine place, partly in ruins, to the south of the town. This Lord Thomas was Warden of the West Marches under Henry VIII, and the rebuilder of the hall. He also made the deer-park in Ravenstonedale, which he had bought, turning out the tenants and building the great wall (yet remaining) to enclose the place, which, after all, was never stocked with deer. It seems, however, that the place had been a decoy or preserve of the Sempringham monks, whose priory has left its traces at Newbiggin near at hand; and that the tales of Lord Wharton's tyranny were exaggerated. He was struck blind on Ash Fell, they said, as a punishment for his crimes, and dared live no longer here, but was forced to shelter himself in Yorkshire. One of his last acts, however, was to found Kirkby Stephen Grammar School. The last of the family was the Duke of Wharton, whose portrait by Van Dyck as a handsome young man is so well known; he was an eccentric, who flirted with free-thought and Jacobitism; but after he had been raised to the dukedom by George I he squandered his livelihood and reputation, and came to a sad end in Spain. These estates and the hall were confiscated; the magnificent banqueting-hall where James I was royally entertained is a ruin, but enough remains to show what the architecture of the place was in its prime.

Lammerside (i.e. Lambert seat) Castle is said to have belonged to the Warcops in the fourteenth century; but little is known about it. Pendragon

---

1 Pevsner supports this later theory [Editor's note].

2 Really the crest of his helmet—a bull's head.

Once regarded with awe and apprehension, Kirkstone Pass holds no terrors for today's visitors, and coaches and cars sail effortlessly over the summit where, not too long ago, passengers had to alight from their horse-drawn vehicles and walk up the steepest sections. The name is derived from a large boulder which has the appearance of a sturdy Dales church, built foursquare against the winds.

Castle commands Mallerstang, the uppermost valley of the Eden, and local legend connects the place with the mythical father of King Arthur:

> Let Uther Pendragon do what he can,
> Eden shall run as Eden ran.

Though lacking the dramatic, craggy background of Buttermere, the neighbouring lake, Crummock Water is overshadowed by Grasmoor in the east and Mellbreak in the west. Crummock shares with Buttermere that haunting lucidity of light from the western sky.

As a structure this fortress can claim no such antiquity. When or why it came to be called Pendragon does not seem to be recorded; but under Edward III the stories of King Arthur were especially popular. It is quite possible that this was a fancy name given to it by the Cliffords who owned it in 1314. The name at any rate does not come down from Arthurian days of the sixth century. It is a Norman building, burnt by the Scots in 1341, and restored; burnt again by the Scots in 1541, and rebuilt by the Countess of Pembroke in 1660. As a piece of scenery it is worthy of its name, standing on its isolated hill, in the midst of the remote, though now partly cultivated, valley, with wild fells around—a place where you might well let your imagination loose to dream idylls of King Arthur or romances of Norman barons and Scottish raiders, or to picture the noble old lady driving up the rough lane in a coach and six to read her Bible in the haunted solitude and write her memories of the spacious times of great Elizabeth.

We are on the extreme borders of Westmorland, between two of the loftiest summits of the Pennine range. Ingleborough and Whernside themselves are only a few feet higher than Wildboar Fell and High Seat, which stand on either side of Pendragon and rise to more than two thousand three hundred feet above the sea. From Mallerstang the road and railway rise to nearly two thousand feet at the pass which takes them into Yorkshire; from Nateby, snug in its deep dell, a gloriously wild path leads over the bleak fell to Muker. North of the hause are the Nine Standards, a group of stones conspicuous from below and commanding a broad view of the Eden valley and the massive summits of the backbone of England. Thence you can follow the watershed to Stainmoor and that important Roman road which once crossed the Pennines, linking Luguvallium with Eboracum. We have seen it before, leaving Carlisle, through Inglewood by Voreda and Brocavum, passing through Kirkby Thore, and Brough; and here is the last little outpost on this side of the range, at the Roman fort of Maidencastle. The earthworks rise high over the gill, and look down far into the valley. Around and above the bare hills rise heavily. There are no trees; nothing but bent grass, sombre and bleak. Without a crag or a cliff, there is a wonderful feeling of the hugeness of mountain and moorland scenery.

The road climbs forward: you looked for a sharp ridge and a prompt sight of the farther side, but here is only widening solitude. This way came the armies of old; Roman troops to their exile, Angles to the conquest of the Briton, Danes and Northmen going and returning between distant Dublin and wealthy York. Once it seems—about the year 950—a great host came up by the road you are treading, King Eric of the Bloody Axe and his confederate kings, to win back the realm of Northumbria: here on the moor they were met by all the levies of the East, and the tide of invasion rose no farther.

At last by the side of the open road there is a grey pillar of stone on its grey mouldering base. It is a thousand years or thereabouts since it was set up for some hero's grave, fallen in fight, perhaps, in some forgotten battle. For nearly a thousand years it has been the boundary mark between east and west. This is the Rey Cross of Stainmoor. Here our pilgrimage ends.

GAZETTEER

ABBREVIATIONS USED: E., East; N., North; S., South; W., West; m., miles. A.O.N.B., Area of Outstanding Natural Beauty; N.T., National Trust.

ABBEY TOWN The village, formerly market town, at which are the remains of the Holm Cultram Abbey (p. 87). Arts festival in June. North of the abbey church is a moated mound, probably a burg: Nearby is Raby Cote farm, the sixteenth-century seat of the Chambers family.

ADDINGHAM A parish on the Eden, S. of Kirkoswald; no village now of that name. Church between Glassonby and Long Meg, with 'spiral' cross in the churchyard. Anglian fragments (seventh or eighth century) in the porch.

AIKTON A village 3½ m. E.N.E. of Wigton. Church of St Andrew, a Norman foundation. At Down Hall, a moated mound, probably the burg of the earliest de Morvilles. The parish includes Biglands, Gamblesby (Gamel's-by), Wiggonby, Wampool (Wathen-pool), and Drumleaning.

AINSTABLE A village 2 m. E. of Armathwaite, formerly Aynstapellith, where a nunnery was founded under William Rufus, afterwards removed to Staffield. Parish church modern, with tombs of a Denton, fifteenth century, and of Aglionbys of Nunnery.

AIRA FORCE A waterfall (*foss*, Old Norse, waterfall) 80 ft. high on Aira Beck (*airidh*, Gaelic, 'shieling' or 'chalet'). Lyulph's Tower, near it, is eighteenth century on the site of a possible pele; scene of Wordsworth's *Somnambulist*. The fall is easily reached from the main Patterdale–Penrith road.

ALDINGHAM A scattered parish in Furness. The church, Norman to Perpendicular, with sun-dial 1753, and tomb of Godith de Scales (thirteenth century?), is 4 m. S. of Ulverston. The mote-hill is probably the early Norman burg of the Flemings (p. 38), finely placed on the sea-cliff.

ALLEN CRAGS The central summit, 2,572 ft., from which Eskdale, Wasdale, Borrowdale, and Langdale radiate.

ALLERDALE Valley of the Eden (Alner-dale). The barony of Allerdale-below-

Derwent at first included the country between the Derwent and the Wampool; later it comprised the country bounded by the Waver and Shawk Beck to the N. E. with the valley of the Derwent (except Workington). Allerdale-above-Derwent was the rest of West Cumberland, including Copeland or the district of Egremont, and the land between Esk and Duddon.

ALLHALLOWS A parish between Aspatria and Wigton named from the church of All Saints. Whitehall was the seat of the Salkelds in the sixteenth and seventeenth centuries; near it is a mote-hill or burg with base-court. Harbybrow, a sixteenth-century hall with a pele tower, was the seat of the Highmores and later of the Blencowes, who also owned the adjoining manor of Upmanby, anciently Uckman-by, from an early lord.

ALLITHWAITE A village between Cark and Kents-bank stations. Wraysholme Tower, $\frac{1}{2}$ m. S., is a ruined pele, forfeited by the Harringtons after the battle of Bosworth, and granted to the Stanleys, whose crest is on a bit of stained glass still preserved.

ALLONBY A manor on the coast between Maryport and the Holme, called Alan-by from the second lord of Allerdale. Captain Jos. Huddart, F. R. S., lighthouse builder and marine surveyor, born here 1741; died 1816. The coastal area is an A.O.N.B.

ALSTON A mining district in the upper valley of the S. Tyne, 17 m. by road N. E. from Penrith over a pass 1,800 ft. Two m. E. of summit the Maiden Way crosses the road. Alston (anciently Aldeneston) is the diocese of Durham, though in the county of Cumbria, because in the twelfth century it was more convenient to pay the king's dues on the mines to Carlisle than to Newcastle. The lead and silver mines were worked about 1350 by Tillmann, a German from Cologne; for a century before 1715 the Ratcliffes, earls of Derwentwater, owned them; after the Jacobite rising, in which the last earl was implicated, they were given to Greenwich Hospital. Later the London Lead Co., in the hands of Quakers, worked the Garrigdill and Nenthead mines with philanthropy and profit until 1882, when they were sold to the Nenthead and Tynedale Lead and Zinc Co. Alston is an old market town; church of St Augustine built 1769. Garrigill (Gerard's-gill) is a chapelry 4 m. up the Tyne valley with a camp said to be Roman in a field called Chesters, S. of the river. Nenthead is a village and chapelry 5 m. from Alston up the Nent.

AMBLESIDE A town at the head of Windermere, one m. N. of the Waterhead terminus of the Windermere lake steamers. A market town in 1650, with market cross restored. On the Kirkstone road is the old church of St Anne, rebuilt 1812; in the valley is the church of St Mary with conspicuous spire, built 1854. Rush Bearing ceremony on the first Saturday in July. Stock Gill Force, 120 ft. high, is a series of cascades $\frac{1}{2}$ m. E. from the White Lion Hotel. The way to

Wansfell is well marked. The Knoll, home of Harriet Martineau, is on the left of the Rydal road; on the opposite side of the valley, by footpath and across Miller Bridge then to the right, is Fox How, the house of Dr Arnold of Rugby. The famous 'house on the bridge' over Stock Beck was probably a seventeenth-century summer house for the now demolished Ambleside Hall. Loughrigg Fell (pronounced Luffrigg, 1,101 ft.) can be climbed by a path from Miller Bridge, or from Clappersgate ½ m. S.W. of Rothay Bridge; good panorama from the summit and easy descent N.W. to the Redbank road overlooking Grasmere, or by the Grasmere and Skelwith road to Loughrigg Tarn and Langdale. Pretty walks to Rydal; by Sweden Bridges N. of the town, up Scandale to Little Hart Crag and by Caiston to Patterdale; and up the Stock Gill valley to Kirkstone Pass. Roman camp Galava between Waterhead Hotel and mouth of the Brathay, in Borrans Park. Stagshaw Gardens, N.T., open to the public.

ANGLE TARN The source of Langstrath Beck, under Bowfell, 1,760 ft. above sea, on the path from Langdale by Rossett Gill to Styhead.

ANGLE TARN On the ridge between Patterdale and Bannerdale, 1,572 ft. above sea.

ANGLER'S CRAG A steep rock of syenite, rising 450 ft. above Ennerdale Lake on the S.W. side.

ANNASIDE A hamlet S.W. of Bootle (formerly Anderset), near which was a megalithic circle, now destroyed.

APPLEBY-IN-WESTMORLAND Former county town. The castle is of Norman origin (*see* p.139), restored by Lady Anne Clifford in 1651; the Great Hall contains the famous triptych of Lady Anne and her family. The Rare Breeds Survival Trust occupies part of the grounds of the castle and there are examples of rare British farm animals. Church of St Lawrence, Norman and thirteenth century, restored by Lady Anne in 1665, contains her tomb and that of her mother, the Countess of Cumberland (*d.* 1616). The church of St Michael, Bongate (now redundant), has on the S. side a Norman (?) horse-shoe arch with an Anglo-Scandinavian hogback as lintel. Sixteenth-century Moot Hall in the middle of the main street; market-house or cloister at the foot of Borough-gate, built 1811; Low Cross near it and High Cross at the upper end. St Anne's Hospital, a group of alms houses, was founded by Lady Anne Clifford in 1651. Grammar School was one of the oldest academic institutions in Cumbria; it originated in two chantry bequests of 1286 and 1331 and was re-founded by Queen Elizabeth in 1573. Appleby Horse Fair is held on the second Tuesday and Wednesday in June.

APPLETHWAITE A village N. of Keswick under Skiddaw where Sir G. H. Beaumont (1753–1827), the celebrated amateur artist and donor of pictures to the

National Gallery, proposed to settle Wordsworth in 1804; whence the sonnet:

> Beaumont! it was thy wish that I should rear
> A seemly Cottage in this sunny Dell,
> On favoured ground, thy gift.

ARMATHWAITE At the foot of Bassenthwaite Lake; the hall, formerly the seat of the Vanes, is now an hotel.

ARMATHWAITE-ON-EDEN In the twelfth century written Ermitethwaite, i.e. hermit's field, a chapelry on the Eden. The castle (modernized) was the seat of the Skeltons, 1461–1712. The church was built 1688. Near it is fine river scenery, and the site of Castle Ewain and Tarn Wathelayne (p. 100).

ARNSIDE A seaside resort at the mouth of the Kent. Ruined pele; pretty rock, wood, and water. Station between Carnforth and Barrow-in-Furness.

ARTHURET The Ardderyd of early British history (p. 107), 1 m. S. of Longtown. Church built 1609, with cross, near which, it is said, lies buried Archie Armstrong, jester to Charles I.

ARTHUR'S ROUND TABLE At Eamont Bridge; an oval trench enclosing a platform 78 by 72 ft. The trench is surrounded with an embankment 7 ft. high at the highest part. To S.E. is a gangway to the platform; another used to be opposite, but is now shaved off by the road. It was formerly used for games; origin unknown. Pennant's plan (1769) shows a second ring embankment to the S. called the Little Round Table. *See also* Mayburgh.

ASBY A scattered parish S. of Appleby, anciently written Askeby. Great Asby contains Asby Cotesforth or Cotsford, from the family which held it from the twelfth century till late in the fifteenth, and Asby Winderwath (Wynanderwath) from a family owning it in the fourteenth century. Near the parish church is St Helen's well, said to be medicinal. The rectory is built round a small medieval pele. Old hall with arms of the Musgraves over the door, and date 1694. Asby Grange belonged to Byland Abbey (Yorks), and Shap Abbey had three houses in the parish. Garthorn Hall was seat of the Bellinghams from James I to Charles II. Prehistoric settlements $\frac{1}{2}$ m. S. and $1\frac{1}{2}$ m. S.W. of the church.

Little Asby, said to be the older site, is 2 m. S.S.E. of the church; it had anciently a chapel of St Leonard. Near it is a unique earthwork, a flat platform or court, 80 by 26 yards in area, surrounded on the three sides by artificial banks rising to 15 ft. Toward the S. end of the platform is a mound, E. of which a spring supplies a drain leading to another wall at the N. end.

ASHNESS A farm S.E. of Derwentwater; fine view from Ashness Bridge leading up to it from Barrow House (Youth Hostel).

ASKERTON A castle of the Dacres (fifteenth and sixteenth century), ¾m. N.E. of Kirkambeck. Remarkably, the timbers in the hall have retained their fifteenth-century numbers applied in the woodyard to facilitate accurate assembly.

ASKHAM A village on the Lowther, 3 m. S. of Eamont Bridge. Hall, close to the river (here very beautiful), was seat of the Sandfords from Edward III until 1680, including an Early English chapel of which arches are inserted in the gateway. The fifteenth-century pele adjoins a late seventeenth-century wing, opposite to which are Elizabethan buildings around the gateway. The hall contains an oak staircase of Charles II's time and heraldic shields. On the W. bank of the Lowther, at Setterah Park, is a camp where Roman relics have been found.

ASPATRIA An ancient parish, formerly Aspatrick. Church of St Kentigern (1846–8) on pre-Norman site with tenth- or eleventh-century churchyard cross (S. of the church), and early sculptures built into the vestry within and without.

Pre-Norman hogback; curious medieval font and fragments of the Norman church. Medieval grave-slabs in the churchyard wall, E. side. Copy of the Gosforth cross by the late vicar, W. S. Calverley, F.S.A., author of *Early Sculptured Crosses in the Diocese of Carlisle*, and C. Dickinson.

Aspatria Castle has now disappeared; Hayton Castle, seat of the Musgraves from the early fifteenth century, now a farm, is said to have stood a siege by the Parliamentarians in the Civil Wars. At Beacon Hill, N. of the town, a celebrated tumulus was opened in 1789 and found to contain a skeleton 7 ft. long with arms of the Viking age. In this parish are Allerby (Aylward's-by) and Oughterside (Uchtersat or Uchtred's Seat, see the gravestone of Bartholomeus de Uchtersat in Aspatria churchyard), where a colliery was worked before 1681.

AUGHERTREE A village 1 m. N.N.E. of Uldale. On the fell are three settlement enclosures or ring-embankments surrounded by ditches, each about 85 yards diameter, somewhat like the British settlements at Hugill, etc.; near them is a tumulus in which were found twelve British burial urns. *See* T. Clare, *Archaeological Sites of the Lake District*.

BACKBARROW A village on the Leven with the remains of an ancient charcoal ironworks. The former ultramarine works has been successfully converted into an hotel, timeshare and leisure complex.

BAISBROWN The mountain (2,120 ft.) between Styhead Pass and Gillercombe, also written Basebrown.

BAISBROWN A farm in Great Langdale under Lingmoor. Formerly Basebrun, i.e. 'borran or stony ground of the cow-shed.' Once a dairy of Conishead Priory (*which see*).

BAMPTON A parish in the valley of the Lowther. Bampton Patrick was so called after Patricius de Culwen, ancestor of the Curwens, not from the church and well, of which the dedication to St Patrick is probably more recent. Bampton Cundale or Carhullen is in the valley of the Cowdale, or Cundale Beck. The parish was once famous for its Grammar School, founded 1623, which educated Dr Mill, editor of the New Testament, Bishop Gibson, translator of Camden, and other celebrities; the most famous master was the Rev. J. Bowstead (1776–1832). A free library was established in 1710. Archbishop Curwen (d. 1568) was a native. At Thornthwaite Hall (Elizabethan) 'Belted Will' is said to have died. On Knipe Scar, 1 m. N.E. of the church, are two pairs of concentric stone circles, in which burnt matter was found. Due N. of Measand 1 m. are two Standing Stones, old road and enclosure; and 1 m. N. of the Standing Stones is Towtop Kirk, an ancient homestead. The annual Shepherds' Meet, once held at Mardale (*which see*) is now held near Bampton in November.

BAND The spur of Bowfell dividing Mickleden from Oxendale. *Band* in the dialect means 'boundary,' and is often used of ridges dividing valleys.

BANNERDALE (formerly Cumberland). A dell under crags between Scales and Bowscale Tarns.

BANNERDALE (formerly Westmorland). A valley in Martindale between Angle Tarn and Rampsgill.

BANNISDALE The upper valley of the Mint; hence the name of a series in the Upper Silurian slates resembling the Wenlock and Lower Ludlow shales.

BARBON A chapelry E. of Lune, through which passes the Maiden Way, in Domesday written Berebrune. On the E. Barbon beck comes down a deep valley from Lord's Seat (over 2,000 ft.).

BARDSEA A village on the coast, 2½ m. S.S.W. of Ulverston; in Domesday Berretseige. In the twelfth century there was a Hospital of St John of Jerusalem here, which was given to Conishead Priory. Bardsea Country Park includes 175 acres of woodland and shingle foreshore. *See* Sunbrick.

BARF A mountain (1,536 ft.) W. of the head of Bassenthwaite Lake, with a white rock called the Bishop. Behind Barf is Lord's Seat (1,811 ft.), pretty ascent up the gill from the Swan Inn.

BARNSCAR The Borran-scar or ridge of ruins on Birkby Fell, 1 m. W.S.W. of Devoke Water. Prehistoric settlement and cairns, in which Bronze Age burial urns have been found. It is not, as was once commonly said, a 'Danish city.'

BARROW A house on the E. side of Derwentwater, above Barrow Bay (boat-

landing), with a waterfall (over 100 ft. high in two cascades). Now a Youth
Hostel.

BARROW-IN-FURNESS Unashamedly a nineteenth-century upstart; an early nineteenth-century agricultural hamlet which grew into 'the Chicago of England'
with its prosperity based firmly on iron, steel and shipbuilding. Today the iron
and steel works, once, in the 1870s, the largest Bessemer plant in the world, has
been demolished but the shipyard continues to produce atomic submarines and
other naval vessels. The grandiose town plan of Sir James Ramsden, the former
Furness Railway engineer who became the town's first mayor, may still be seen;
the wide streets and the major entrance to the town—the longest tree-lined
boulevard in Britain—are his lasting memorial and evidence of his foresight
and ambition. *See also* Walney Island, Piel Castle and Furness Abbey.

BARTON A parish with church 3 m. S.W. of Eamont Bridge, originally consisting
of a little Norman chancel, to which a later tower was added, perhaps as a pele,
and then a nave, approached from the chancel by a small archway under the
tower. Subsequently a S. aisle was built nearly the whole length of the church,
and a N. aisle to the nave. In the sixteenth century a N. aisle was built to the
chancel; and in the seventeenth the porch was added. About 1860 the church
was restored and the interior disguised in plaster. Brass of W. Lancaster, 1575.
Near it is the vicarage house of Dr Lancelot Dawes, 1637; and Barton Church
Farm, an Elizabethan hall with fine plaster ceiling on the first floor, site probably
of an early fortified house once in a swamp and approached by a causeway.

BASSENTHWAITE A parish between Skiddaw and the lake of Bassenthwaite. The
old church of St Bega is between Mirehouse and Bowness Farm; the new church
of St John is 1¾ m. to the N. on the Chapel Beck. On the Dash Beck is the
village of Hawes or Hause, 2 m. N.E. of which is Overwater (*which see*). N. of
the lake, where the road to Bewaldeth and Caermote (*which see*) is crossed by
that from Uldale to Armathwaite Hall, is the Castle Inn. The river Derwent
flows from the lake at the N.W. beneath Ouse bridge (Norse, *oss*, 'outlet').
Between the Pheasant Inn on the N.W. side, and the lake is an ancient fort,
Castle How, on a wooded rocky hill with triple ramparts. The W. side of the
lake is steep and rocky with fine views of Skiddaw from Wythop Fell and Barf
(1,536 ft.). Good road all round the lake from Keswick, about 18 m. The lake
is 3¾ m. long, ¾ m. broad, 223 ft. above sea, and 70 ft. deep half-way along its
length, near the W. shore. It inspired Tennyson to write his description of the
passing of Arthur in *Idylls of the King*. *See* Mirehouse.

BEACONS Many beacon hills exist in the Lake Counties for ancient signalling
purposes. In the former county of Cumberland were Aspatria (*which see*),
Barrock Fell, Bewcastle (N. of the church), and Gillilees Beacon (S. of the
church), Black Combe (which seems to have been the Beacon of Bootle), Bothel
(i.e. the earthwork above Caermote), Brampton Mote-hill, Carlisle Castle,

Hardknott, Haresceugh (Daffenside Beacon), Ivegill or Raughton Beacon hill, Kirkoswald (Beacon hill above Parks), Lingy Close, Moota, Ravenglass or Muncaster (Newton Knott), St Bees Head, Sandale top, Skiddaw (probably not much used), and Workington (St Michael's Mount). In the former county of Westmorland there were beacons at Barbon, Farleton, Helton, Orton Scar, Stainmoor and Whinfell. In Furness and Cartmel beacons were found at Coniston Old Man, High Haume (above Ireleth), near to Furness Abbey, Gleaston, Lowick, Piel Castle, Rampside, Walney Island, Blawith and Cartmel (1 m. E. of the priory). Various 'watch hills,' not included here, were look-out stations rather than signals.

BEAUMONT A parish on the Eden (pronounced Beemunt) $1\frac{1}{2}$ m. E. of Burgh. The church is on an early medieval burg, which was built out of a mile-castle on the Roman Wall. Here was a ford often used by Scots raiders to avoid Carlisle. A great hoard of English, Scottish and foreign coins (Henry III to Edward III) was found here in 1884.

BECKERMET A village 2 m. S. of Egremont. St John's church has many interesting pre-Norman stones. St Bridget's church ($\frac{1}{2}$ m to the S.W.) is largely thirteenth century. In the churchyard are two pre-Norman crosses, one with an unusual inscription which appears to be in eleventh-century Gaelic (*see* p. 67). Carnarvon Castle or Coneygarth Cop, a mote-hill of the Flemings in the twelfth century, is 1 m. N.N.E. of St John's. In the late nineteenth century, during draining of the small Ehenside Tarn for agricultural purposes, several prehistoric implements were unearthed, including several partly finished stone axes and a splendid and rare example of a polished axe still in its haft. This is now in the British Museum. Recent radio-carbon dating suggests that the site was occupied around 3000 B C.

BEETHAM A village on the Beetha or Bela, 1 m. S. of Milnthorpe. Late twelfth-century church and Beetham Hall, in part of a mid-fourteenth-century fortified manor house. Nearby is the restored Heron Corn Mill, open to the public.

BELLE ISLE Windermere's largest island. Originally called Long Holm, the present name is derived from Isabella Curwen, the eighteenth-century owner and heiress. In 1774 the owner, Mr English, commissioned the architect John Plaw, to build a circular house. This was later sold to Isabella Curwen and her husband, John Christian Curwen. Wordsworth disapproved of the design and dubbed it 'a pepper pot.' The building is currently (1987) being converted into a small conference centre.

BERRIER A village in Greystoke parish, E. of Southerfell. On Berrier Hill, $1\frac{1}{4}$ m. E.N.E. are remains of a 'camp.'

BEWCASTLE A scattered parish, possibly taking its name from the ruined castle founded by Bueth, a twelfth-century lord, near the Roman camp on which is the church of St Cuthbert (Early English, restored), with the famous cross of Alcfrith (p. 106), and armorial headstones with quaint epitaphs. At Peelo-hill is a pele and a tumulus; at Border-riggs, Low-grains, and elsewhere are ancient houses. On Barnspike, 2 m. E. of the church, is a tumulus and a runic inscription, probably spurious. At Hazel Gill, $\frac{1}{2}$ m. N. of Barnspike, is another runic inscription, also believed to be forged as a practical joke on a former rector, the Rev. J. Maughan, a student of runes, who first gave a good reading of the cross.

BEWLEY CASTLE *See* Bolton.

BIRDOSWALD A farm on the site of Ambloganna or Cambloganna, a large 5-acre fort on Hadrian's Wall. Fine E. gateway with double guard chambers and the W. postern gate with a threshold marked by wheel-ruts. The Turf Wall ran through the site of the fort; the Vallum avoided it to the south and the Wall ran along its N. side, coinciding with the modern road. From the N. gate a Roman road (miscalled the Maiden Way) ran to Bewcastle and possibly beyond. Almost twenty altars dedicated to Jupiter Best and Greatest have been found buried around the perimeter of the parade ground of the fort.

BIRKBY A village near Crosscanonby; also a township S. of Muncaster, anciently Bretby or Brattaby, in which is Barnscar (*which see*).

BLACK COMBE The southernmost part of the mountains (1,969 ft.) of the Skiddaw slate, easily climbed from Bootle, Monk Foss, or Whicham in about one hour. Wordsworth was convinced that 'the summit commands a more extensive view than any other point in Britain.'

BLACKFORD A parish N. of Carlisle. N. of this in old times was the Border, from which the burghers of Carlisle were not allowed to take wives or apprentices.

BLACK SAIL The pass from Wasdale Head to Ennerdale (1,750 ft.) by an easy bridle-path. (Youth Hostel).

BLAKE FELL The highest summit (1,878 ft.) of the Skiddaw-slate hills between Ennerdale and Loweswater.

BLAWITH A parish in the Crake valley. Remains of sixteenth-century chapel near to nineteenth-century church. The Knott (812 ft.) is $1\frac{3}{4}$ m. E. of the church; to the N. of it is White Borran, a cairn; to the S. is the Giant's Grave, where an interment was found; and on the ridge between this and High Heathwaite, 1 m. S.S.W. are many cairns and enclosures, possibly medieval.

BLEA TARN A lakelet (i.e. Blue Tarn) on the moor between Borrowdale and

Wythburn (1,562 ft.). Also a place on the Roman Wall where ancient quarries form a pond near an artificial mound, not ancient. Also a lakelet between Dungeon Gill and Fell Foot, scene of Wordsworth's *Excursion* (*see* p.26).

BLEA WATER A tarn under the precipitous crags of High Street, at the head of Mardale.

BLELHAM TARN A small lake between Brathay and Hawkshead, with remains of a bloomery (iron smelting) on the N. side; the name anciently written Blaylolme. Now used for research purposes by the Freshwater Biological Association.

BLENCATHARA Ancient name for Saddleback.

BLENCOGO A village near Bromfield, written in the thirteenth century Blencoggen. The hall was seat of the Thomlinsons in the seventeenth and eighteenth centuries. The Rev. Jonathan Boucher, antiquary and author of a great part of Hutchinson's *Cumberland*, was born here 1737; died 1804.

BLENCOW The village of Great Blencow is in Dacre parish; Little Blencow in Greystoke. The hall consists of a pele, fifteenth century (the N. tower), and remains of a chapel about that date; to which Sir Henry Blencowe added, about 1590, two wings and the S. tower.

BLENNERHASSET A village near Aspatria with market cross.

BLINDCRAKE Properly Blencraik, a village near Isel.

BOARDALE A valley between Patterdale and Howtown on Ullswater, otherwise Boredale. From the Hause (1,260 ft.) there are fine views of the craggy side of the Helvellyn and Fairfield range.

BOLTON A parish between Torpenhow and Caldbeck (p. 87). Near Wearyhall, the seat of the Porters in the seventeenth century, is a moated enclosure, perhaps site of early hall.

BOLTON A village on the Eden, 4 m. N.W. of Appleby. Norman church with curious door and carvings at the back of the church of two knights tilting and an unreadable inscription; also fourteenth-century effigy. Bridge over the Eden built 1816. Bewley or Builly Castle, 1½ m. to S.S.W., is the ruin of one of the bishop's residences, later than the De Builli family, which died out in 1213.

BONGATE A suburb of Appleby, 'vetus Apelbi ubi Villani (Bondmen) manent.' *See* Appleby.

BOOT A village in Eskdale. From here a path runs up the Whillan Beck to the stone circles and cairns on Burnmoor, Scafell, the Screes, and Wasdale Head. Near the village is the terminus of the Ravenglass and Eskdale Railway; originally opened in 1875 as a 3-ft.-gauge line to convey iron ore from a mine at Nab Gill to the coast, it began to carry passengers in 1876. In 1915 the track was re-laid to a gauge of 15 inches. Today it is one of the best known of Lakeland's tourist attractions, known affectionately to thousands of visitors as 'La'al Ratty.' In the village, the corn mill, first documented in 1578 and still milling corn until the 1920s, has been restored and is open to the public. St Catherine's chapel on the bank of the Esk, has some interesting tombstones.

BOOTLE Former market town, charter 1347; $1\frac{1}{2}$ m. S.E. of Bootle railway station. In the church is an ancient font and the brass of Sir Hugh Askew, 1562. Up the road to the fell on the E. are many cairns and two ancient homesteads. At Seaton Hall, 1 m. N., are ruins (chiefly the traceried E. window) of Seaton or Lekely Nunnery, an early thirteenth-century Benedictine house. At Annaside, Gutterby, and Hall Foss were megalithic circles, now destroyed. The name Bothill possibly means beacon-hill, perhaps referring to Black Combe. *See* Beacons.

BORROWDALE The upper valley of the Derwent (pp. 119–20). At Grange was a farm of Furness Abbey, in the records of which the valley is named Borcheredale, i.e. valley of the fort, perhaps implying Castle Crag, on which remains of various ancient periods have been found; it was probably a stronghold from early times, used as a refuge down to the seventeenth century. S. of the slate quarries and above the road is the Bowder Stone, a poised block 36 ft. high by 62 ft. long, and reckoned to weigh 1,970 tons. It was probably left in this position by retreating ice 10,000 years ago. *See also* p. 119. Two m. above Grange is Rosthwaite, from which a path leads E. to Watendlath. At the church the valley forks, divided by Glaramara (2,560 ft.) and its buttresses; to the left is Stonethwaite hamlet, beyond which the valley of Greenupgill goes up under Ullscarth (2,370 ft.). One m. above Stonethwaite the path turns to right up Langstrath, a wild and lonely valley between Eagle Crag and Glaramara, with a bridle-path leading over the Stake Pass to Dungeon Gill, $3\frac{1}{2}$ hours from Rosthwaite. From the church to right the main road leads to Seatoller and Honister Hause for Buttermere ($7\frac{1}{2}$ m. from Rosthwaite). The main valley of the Derwent continues S.W. and across the bridge to Seathwaite ($1\frac{1}{4}$ m. from Seatoller). To reach the Borrowdale Yews and the former Plumbago Mine, keep straight on without crossing the bridge. One m. above Seathwaite is Stockley Bridge, crossing which, to the left, up Grains Gill, a track leads past Sprinkling Tarn to Esk Hause (2,490 ft.), the pass into Upper Eskdale; path from the summit of the pass to Scafell Pikes. From Stockley Bridge to right the bridle-path leads up past Taylor's Gill Force to Styhead Tarn and the Great Gable (2,949 ft.), or to Styhead Pass to Wasdale Head, an easy three hours from Seathwaite. Sourmilk Gill, and the wild dell of Gillercombe, between Baisbrown (2,120 ft.) and Brandreth (2,344 ft.), can be reached by crossing the valley from

Seathwaite, or by keeping the path past the Yews and Plumbago Mine. At the head of Gillercombe and over the Green Gable the Great Gable can easily be climbed, descending to Styhead.

BORROWDALE (formerly in Westmorland). A branch of the Lune Valley from the Roman camp at Low Borrowbridge. At High Borrowbridge the old turnpike from Kendal to Shap crosses the valley. (p. 11).

BOTHEL A village 3 m. S. W. of Aspatria; the name Bot-hill signifying the beacon on the hill 1 m. S.W. sometimes pronounced Bo'el.

BOUTH A small village in the Furness Fells once famous for its woodland industries. North of the village is the Hay Bridge Deer Museum and Reserve, established in 1971 as a memorial to Major Herbert Fooks. Visitors by appointment.

BOWERDALE A small, lonely valley running S. from the Upper Lune between Kelleth and Ravenstonedale up to Yorkside (2,097 ft.).

BOWFELL A mountain (2,960 ft.) in the volcanic ash formation, between Langdale and Upper Eskdale. From Dungeon Gill it is climbed by the band or the right edge of Hell Gill. From Little Langdale by the Three Shires Stone over the tops of Crinkle and Shelter Crags and past the Three Tarns. From Eskdale taking the valley to the E. of Esk Falls, and then up the middle one of the three gills that joins about half-way up. From Styhead, by Esk Hause, or from Angle Tarn. Pronounced Bō-fell.

BOWNESS-ON-SOLWAY A village on the bow-shaped promontory (ancient name Bogge-nes), W. of the last ford of Solway. Roman camp to N. of church, which is partly built of Roman stones, and contains an ancient font. A little W. of this the Roman Wall ran down to the water's edge and so terminated.

BOWNESS-ON-WINDERMERE The ancient village surrounding the parish church of Windermere, now a tourist resort. St Martin's church, rebuilt after a fire in 1480, has a fine old E. window brought from Cartmel Priory (not Furness) before 1523 (restored 1871) with the Crucifixion, the Blessed Virgin Mary, Saints John, George, Barbara, and Catherine, and fragments of archbishops in the lower lights; and above them the Resurrection, Virgin and Child, and entry into Jerusalem, with local heraldry, including the arms of John Washington, an ancestor of the first President of the United States. In the church are also sixteenth-century mural inscriptions discovered under whitewash in 1864, consisting of quotations from Coverdale's Bible (1535) and an early Catechism as well as Latin verses on the Gunpowder Plot. The churchyard contains the grave of Rasselas Belfield, an Abyssinian slave who died in 1822. Just outside the town is the Windermere Steamboat Museum with a unique collection of Victorian and Edwardian steamboats.

BOWSCALE TARN A lake 2 m. N. of Scales Tarn between Saddleback and Carrock Fell, which was said to contain two 'undying fish' (Wordsworth, *Song at the Feast of Brougham Castle*). Bishop Nicholson, however, wrote in 1703: 'So cold y^t nothing lives in it. Fish have been put in: But they presently dy.'

BRAITHWAITE A village formerly seat of woollen industry, etc., at the mouth of Coledale, a valley running up towards Eel Crag (2,649 ft.) and Grasmoor (2,791 ft.). From Braithwaite the Whinlatter Pass goes over to Lorton.

BRAMPTON A market town 1½ m. from Brampton station and three miles S. of Hadrian's Wall. Mote-hill about 150 ft. high at E. end of the town, probably seat of an early lord, afterwards used for a beacon; now bears a bronze statue of the seventh Earl of Carlisle, erected in 1870. The old church of St Martin, 1¼ m. W. of town was mentioned 1169; oldest part is of Roman stones, with a lancet window; tombs of various ages. The modern church of St Martin in the town has fine windows by Burne-Jones and Morris. In the market-place (charter about 1250) is the Octagonal Moot Hall, built 1817, and old stocks.

BRANDRETH A mountain (2,344 ft.) between Honister and the Gable, so called from having three spurs: a 'brandreth' in dialect (as in Anglo-Saxon and Icelandic) being a trivet on three legs to support the girdle, a plate on which cakes are baked; hence any stone at the meeting of three boundaries is called a brandreth stone.

BRANTHWAITE A village in the Marron Valley. The Hall has a remarkably well-preserved pele tower with a tunnel-vaulted basement. Calva Hall pack-horse bridge is one of the few in Cumbria bearing a date stone, 1697.

BRANTWOOD House overlooking the eastern shores of Coniston Lake, bought by John Ruskin in 1871 for £1,500. It remained his home until his death in 1900. Large collection of pictures and memorabilia. House, garden and woodland trail open to the public.

BRATHAY The river which, rising in Wrynose, passes through Elterwater and falls into Windermere, once formed the boundary between Westmorland and Lancashire; the Scandinavian *Breidh-á*, broadwater. Also name of parish with modern church. Brathay Bridge, Clappersgate, was built about 1681; since widened. Brathay Hall was built about 1890. It is now a centre for exploration and open-air activities.

BRAYTON A manor in the township of Aspatria. The hall was purchased early in the eighteenth century by the Lawsons of Isel and rebuilt. In the park fishpond a silver fibula with interlaced ornament was found some time before 1790.

BRETHERDALE A valley running W. from Tebay, with Castle How, site of an ancient fort, at its mouth.

BRIDEKIRK A village 2½ m. N. of Cockermouth, with ruins of old church of St
Bridget in the churchyard of the modern church; medieval and pre-Norman
grave-monuments. Norman tympanum, with rude figure of Christ in blessing,
over the S. door of new church, and inside is a celebrated twelfth-century font
with runic inscription (p.83).

BRIGHAM A village 3 m. W. of Cockermouth. Ancient church of St Bridget, with
pre-Norman and medieval monuments; old vicarage, with thirteenth-century
pointed-arch windows.

BRIGSTEER A village 3 m. S.W. of Kendal on the W. slope of the limestone scar.
Pretty cottages and woods. Church of St John, Helsington, built 1726.

BROCKHOLE A large house on the eastern shores of Windermere. Originally built
in 1899 by Henry Gaddum, a Manchester businessman, it was opened in 1969
as the Lake District National Parks Visitors' Centre. There is a permanent
exhibition explaining the development of the landscape, extensive grounds and
lake shore access, attractive gardens and refreshment facilities. In addition there
is a regular programme of lectures, slide shows and films and special facilities
for school parties.

BROMFIELD A scattered parish between Aspatria and Holm Cultram. Norman
church of St Mungo or Kentigern, containing pre-Norman and medieval monuments; in the churchyard is the base of a cross, from which in the eighteenth
century notices were cried. St Mungo's Well, a small, round building north of
the church in the adjoining field. The Gill, near High Scales, is said to have
been given by William the Lion of Scotland 1210, to the ancestor of the Rays
or Reays, a family which produced among other worthies John Ray the naturalist.

BROTHERS WATER A tarn in Patterdale, said to have got its name from the
drowning of two brothers. Anciently, however, it was called Broader or Broad
Water, possibly from a Norse word meaning the lake by the road, as an ancient
way led past it.

BROUGHAM A parish S. of Eamont Bridge, anciently Burgham, pronounced
Broom. The Roman fort, Brocavum, was located at the junction of the Roman
road over Stainmoor with the road from the south to Carlisle and that from the
S.W. from Ambleside and High Street. The ruins of the castle are located in
the N.W. corner of the Roman fort and close to the river; they are in an irregular
moated enceinte, and form a small court with late Norman keep, to which was
added a gatehouse on the N. with doorway inscribed 'Thys made Roger' (de
Clifford, late thirteenth century), who also raised the keep higher and built the
hall on the S.E. side. James I is said to have spent three days here in 1617; the

castle was restored by Lady Anne Clifford, Countess of Pembroke, in 1651. It is now in the care of English Heritage. St Ninian's or Ninekirks, 1½ miles N.E., was also rebuilt by Lady Anne and is furnished as it was in her time. S.W. of the castle is St Wilfred's thought by some to be fourteenth century but by others to be a rebuilding dating from 1658–9. The church contains some fourteenth-century glass.

BROUGHTON, GREAT and LITTLE Modern church at Great Broughton; site of medieval chapel of St Lawrence near the mill. Quakers' meeting-house built 1659; Baptist chapel 1672. The former colliery was developed in the eighteenth century by John Christian Curwen, M.P., who drove a level from Ewanrigg to the main seam at Broughton, which, with branches, was nearly 2 m. long, and made a wooden tramway to the harbour at Maryport.

BROUGHTON-IN-FURNESS An ancient market town though the Wednesday market has now lapsed. Eighteenth-century town hall. In the middle of the market place stands an obelisk erected in 1810 and the ancient fish-slabs and stocks. St Mary Magdalene's church was consecrated in 1547 but has a late Norman doorway. Broughton Tower, not open to the public, is a mansion built around a fourteenth-century pele tower, once the home of the ill-fated Sir Thomas Broughton (see p. 16). Pronounced Brawton but sometimes Browton.

BROUGH-UNDER-STAINMOOR Village S.W. of Appleby, formerly a market town (charter, 1330). Anciently Burg, pronounced Bruff. The Roman road from Stainmoor to Cumbria passed through, and ½ mile S. was the fort Verterae, where many coins, fibulae, and stones have been found, among them the inscription in Greek to Hermes of Commagene, discovered in 1879, and at first thought to be runic. The stone, now in the Fitzwilliam Museum, Cambridge, records the death of a sixteen-year-old Roman soldier from Syria. The Norman castle was built on the site of the fort, probably about 1095, and burnt by the Scots in 1174; accidentally destroyed by fire during the Christmas feast of 1521, and then restored between 1659–62 by Lady Anne Clifford, it was finally demolished by the Earl of Thanet in 1695. The ruins consist of late Norman keep and gatehouse near the centre of the S. side of the castle; Norman walls restored in Decorated style; hall with Tudor fireplace; Clifford's Tower, the round bastion at the S.E. corner, of Decorated and Tudor periods. The castle is now in the care of English Heritage. The church of St Michael to S. has an early Norman S. door and a sloping floor so that those at the back of the church could see the chancel. Hillbeck Hall was the seat of the Helbecks from Henry II to Edward II passing by marriage to the Blenkinsops, sequestrated under Cromwell. The present building is 'Georgian Gothic.' Augill Castle was built 1841–2.

BUCKBARROW A range of rocks above Bootle, of wild and curious forms. Also crags N. of the foot of Wastwater.

BURGH-BY-SANDS A village close to the Solway estuary. The Roman Wall ran just N. of the road, and the camp was on the site of the church, which was built partly of Roman stones in the twelfth century. The church tower was added in the fourteenth century as a defensive pele. There is no door to the outside and the ground floor is tunnel vaulted. Over the iron door between the church and the tower is an early tympanum or lintel, inner side grotesquely carved. Edward I lay in state here in 1307 having died on the nearby marshes *en route* to fight the Scots. John Stagg, the poet, was a native of Burgh (pronounced Bruff). No traces remain of the de Morvilles' castle at Handwalls. One and a half miles N. is a monument (erected 1685, rebuilt 1803, restored 1876) marking the spot where Edward I died in 1307. At Watch Hill was a small Roman fort.

BURNESIDE A village with paper mills; station on the railway line between Kendal and Windermere, anciently Bronolfs-head (pronounced Burnie-side). Ruins of the fifteenth-century hall of the Bellinghams, a pele, hall, and barnekin or outer wall and gatehouse, adjoining the farmhouse. Tolson Hall, built by Thomas Tolson, a tobacco merchant, in 1638. Godmond Hall, ancient farmhouse. Potter Fell, N. of the village (900 ft.), with tarn, fine panorama.

BURNMOOR The 'moor of the borrans' or stone heaps, between Boot and Wasdale Head; with several stone circles, tarn, and an ancient enclosure N. of the tarn.

BURTON-IN-KENDAL An old market town, Bortun in Domesday Book, 4 m. S.E. of Milnthorpe. Market cross; pre-Norman fragments in the church (p. 3). Near Dalton Hall are the remains of the deserted village of Dalton.

BUTTERMERE A lake $1\frac{1}{4}$ m. long, $\frac{1}{3}$ m. broad, 329 ft. above sea, 94 ft. deep, with char and trout. By road to Keswick via Newlands, 9 m; via Honister Hause to Seatoller, 6 m. By bridle-path via Scarth Gap and Black Sail to Wasdale Head, about $3\frac{1}{2}$ hours. The Buttermere green slate is quarried at Honister Crag at the head of the valley. Mary, the Beauty of Buttermere, was first brought into public notice by Budworth, author of *A Fortnight's Ramble to the Lakes* (1792), as the charming daughter of the Robinsons at the Fish Inn. John Hatfield, under the name of the Hon. Col. Hope, a bigamist and forger, married her; he was hanged at Carlisle, 3rd September 1803. Coleridge, Southey, and Wordsworth (*Prelude*, bk. vii) and the public in general took much interest in the case; chapbooks circulated the story, and it was put upon the stage. Mary afterwards married a farmer, and died many years after at Caldbeck. And public interest is still alive—see Melvyn Bragg's novel *The Maid of Buttermere*, 1987. The chapel at Buttermere used to be known as one of the smallest and poorest in the diocese.

CAERMOTE A Roman turf-built fort, possibly of Flavian date, on the left of the road from the Castle Inn, Bassenthwaite, to Torpenhow. Smaller turf-built fortlet in N. W. corner, probably second century. Above it is Bothel Beacon.

CAIRN A river running past Cumrew and Carlatton to join the Eden at Warwick.

CAISTON BECK A stream joining the Kirkstone Beck in Patterdale ½ m. S. of Brothers Water. Up the valley of the Caiston Beck and S. of the Little Hart Crag (2,091 ft.) is a pass into Scandale, and by Sweden Bridges to Ambleside.

CALDBECK A parish on the N. slope of the Skiddaw group of mountains. The village is 8 m. S.E. of Wigton; said to have grown up round a hospital or hospice built by Carlisle Priory for travellers through Inglewood. The rectory hall is said to be the hall of this hospice, which was dissolved under King John. The partly Norman church of St Mungo has a rude dial on the priest's doorway, and St Mungo's Well behind, on the bank of the Caldbeck. In the churchyard are buried John Peel and Mary of Buttermere. Half a mile W. of the church is a waterfall and cave called Fairykirk. In 1859 a large bobbin mill was built at the Howk, a picturesque gorge through which the Cald Beck flows. The overshot wheel, with a circumference of 132 ft. and a diameter of 42 ft., was thought to have been the largest in the country. In its heyday it employed some 60 men and boys; it ceased working in 1908 and was destroyed by fire in 1959. Caldbeck Fells were celebrated for lead and copper mining. The Brandygill, Roughtengill, and Silvergill mines were worked by Lord Wharton in the sixteenth century; Driggeth mine was opened 1790. At Whelpo the Quakers' meeting-house was built 1698, and one at Mosedale 1702. George Fox used to stay with the Bewleys of Caldbeck at Woodhall. Brownrigg was seat of the Vaux family.

CALDEW A river rising in Skiddaw, running round Carrock Fell, past Sebergham and Rose Castle, and joining the Eden at Carlisle.

CALGARTH HALL Near the mouth of the Troutbeck, Windermere, is Calgarth (anciently Calvgarth) Hall, the Elizabethan house of the Philipsons; bought by Dr Richard Watson, Bishop of Llandaff (*b.* Heversham 1737, *d.* here 1816) (*see* p. 18).

CAMBECK A stream rising near Gillilees Beacon, passing Kirkcambeck and Walton House (Castlesteads) to join the Irthing at Irthington Mill.

CAMERTON A parish on the Derwent. Ancient church, restored, with effigy of Black Tom Curwen, 1510.

CAM SPOUT A waterfall E. of Mickledore on Scafell.

CARDEW A manor between Dalston and Thursby. The hall was seat of the Dentons, of whom John Denton (*d.* 1617) is the father of Cumberland antiquaries; his *Accompt of the most considerable Estates and Families in the County* was written in prison in the Tower of London, 1610.

CARDUNNETH A hill above Cumrew, with tumulus and habitation sites.

CARDURNOCK A village N. of Moricambe, called Caerdurnock by John Denton, which he explains as 'town of thorns,' from an ancient thorn wood there.

CARGO A village on the Eden below Carlisle; anciently Carghow.

CARK-IN-CARTMEL Village 2 m. S.W. of Cartmel. In the early seventeenth century there was a paper mill here, and later, in the eighteenth century, a large cotton mill was built. This used a steam engine to pump water from the tail race back to the mill dam, thus ensuring a continuous supply. The Engine Inn takes its name from this machine. Holker Hall, N. of the village, was the favourite home of the seventh Duke of Devonshire and it remains in the hands of the Cavendish family. The nucleus of the house is an early seventeenth-century farm but the west wing, open to the public, is Victorian, being a rebuilding after a fire in 1871. Cark Hall, a late sixteenth-century house, was the home of Christopher Rawlinson, a prominent Anglo-Saxon scholar (*d.* 1733).

CARLETON Several places of this name: one near Carlisle; one near Penrith, seat of the Carletons from the twelfth century to 1707; another near Drigg.

CARLISLE Cathedral city, and principal administrative town of Cumbria. For early history *see* pp. 93–5. The castle is said to have been founded by William Rufus, 1092. On the W. of the entrance, in the spur of wall formerly connecting the castle with the W. walls of the city, is the Tile tower, on a Norman base, said to have been completed by Richard III, when as Duke of Gloucester he was governor of Carlisle. There is a small tower of original Norman work farther N. on the same side. Crossing the moat by a bridge, which replaces the drawbridge, you enter by William de Ireby's tower to the castle green, now gravelled and nearly surrounded with barrack buildings. To the right is the Inner Ward with the ancient gatehouse; the buttresses of the gatehouse may be Norman, but under Henry VIII the place was remodelled to carry cannon. Passing through the archway, with portcullis and holes in the roof by which an enemy could be assailed in the act of entering, you find to right the keep, Norman, though externally altered with Edwardian portcullised entrance, vaulted chambers on the ground floor with stone seats, and corkscrew stairs. By an external stair the higher floor is reached, where there is the prison of Major Macdonald (the real Fergus MacIvor of *Waverley*), with carvings by prisoners. Mary Queen of Scots was lodged in a tower at the other corner of the Inner Ward which, with the old hall, was pulled down 1824–35. The well in N. side of keep is said to be Roman, 78 ft. deep. The external staircase gives access to the ramparts with view of the Eden and Stanwix. The cathedral is a fragment of the Priory church, founded about 1123. Near the S. door to left, behind glass, is the runic stone (p. 98). The Norman church was gradually enlarged; as at Furness Abbey the building was divided by a screen, and the public admitted only to the W. end, which became the parish church, while the choir was the canons' church and cathedral. This division lasted until modern times; Sir Walter Scott was married in the nave part, while it was still a parish church, 1797. In 1292 a fire destroyed the choir, which was gradually rebuilt on a grand scale, with fine E. window, of which the upper part, representing Christ in judgment, is original glass. The capitals of the arches dividing aisles from choir have carvings, time of Edward III, representing the months. Another fire in 1372 made it necessary to rebuild the N. transept, and the sinking of masonry supporting the tower, about 1400, has left marks, though the tower was renewed. The stalls are fifteenth-century, with forty-six grotesque subjects beneath the seats. Prior Thomas Gondibour (1484) put in the wooden screen enclosing St Catherine's Chapel (S. of choir), and the curious old paintings at the back of the choir-stalls, which represent scenes in the life of St Augustine, St Anthony, St Cuthbert, and the twelve Apostles. In the N. aisle is the effigy of Bishop Irton (1292), in the S. aisle effigy of Bishop Barrow (1429), and in the floor a brass to Bishop Bell (1496). St Cuthbert's church was built in 1778 on an old site. When, under Elizabeth, the tower was rebuilt, a hoard of Northumbrian stycas (pre-Norman farthings) was found there. Tullie House (entrance to left of Castle Street between cathedral and castle) was built 1689 by one of the Tullies (p. 115); it is now the Carlisle Museum and Art Gallery.

The town hall was built 1717; the market cross, 1682; Edwardian Guildhall in the Green Market, and another Edwardian house in King's Arms Lane. The round courthouses (near the station) were built by Sir Robert Smirke, R.A., early nineteenth century, on the site of the ancient citadels. The statue of William, Earl of Lonsdale (*d.* 1842), is by Musgrave Watson. Robert Smirke also designed the Eden Bridges, completed 1815, leading to Stanwix, where the churchyard is on the site of a Roman camp.

CARNARVON CASTLE *See* Beckermet.

CARROCK FELL A mountain (2,174 ft.) forming the N.E. buttress of the Skiddaw range. Remains of the ramparts of an Iron Age hill fort on the top. Nearby are traces of medieval shielings.

CARRS The crest of Coniston fells running towards Wrynose, with crags at the head of Greenburn dale.

CARTMEL A parish and old market town 2 m. from Cark and 2½ m. from Grange-over-Sands. For history and description of Priory and old halls *see* pp. 39–40.

CARTMEL FELL A chapelry in the northern and hilly part of the district of Cartmel between Windermere and the Winster, bounded to N. by the Black Beck of Storrs. Highest point is Gummer's How (1,054 ft.), easily accessible from the Newby Bridge–Kendal road, the former Turnpike. The church of St Anthony, Cartmel Fell, has fifteenth-century glass, plate, and wood-work; picturesque site. Hodge Hill is an old house, with outside gallery and interior kept up in the old style. Quakers' meeting-house at The Height, dated on porch 1677.

CASCADALE A branch of the Newlands valley leading over Buttermere Hause to Buttermere; *alias* Keskadale, corrupted from Gatesgarthdale. Famous Keskadale oaks, a remnant of the original oak forest.

CASTERTON A parish E. of Lune. Charlotte Brontë's school was at Cowan Bridge, where the A65 road crosses the Leck. At Overburrow, 2 m. S. of Kirkby Lonsdale Bridge, was a great Roman camp on the Maiden Way.

CASTLE CARROCK A parish 4 m. S. of Brampton in Geltsdale. Near the church were two entrenchments, now disappeared.

CASTLE CRAG *See* Borrowdale, Shoulthwaite, Mardale.

CASTLE EWAIN N.E. of Tarn Wadling (drained) is the site of an early fortress connected in romances and ballads with King Arthur, who there fought a giant and was overcome.

CASTLE HEAD A hill (529 ft.) of basalt—neck of ancient volcano—formerly fortified; $\frac{1}{2}$ m. S. of Keswick; panorama. *See also* Grange-over-Sands.

CASTLE HOW The ancient hill fort at Peel Wyke, near Ouse Bridge, Bassenthwaite Lake. Another near Castle Sowerby was a palisaded retreat from raiders. *See also* Tebay.

CASTLE ROCK In St John's Vale. *See* p. 121.

CASTLE SOWERBY A parish in Inglewood, with church of St Kentigern. Ancient forts at How Hill $\frac{3}{4}$ m. E. of the church, at Castle How and Knights' Hill, Southernby.

CASTLE STEADS Roman camp near Walton on the Wall. Also a circular enclosure near Eaglesfield and an ancient fort $1\frac{1}{2}$ m. S.E. of Watercrook Roman camp, Kendal.

CATBELLS A range of hills (1,482 ft.) W. of Derwentwater.

CATSTYCAM (or Catchidecam). A spur of Helvellyn, N. of Red Tarn, called by Camden, Casticand.

CATTERLEN A village 1 m. N. of Newton Reigny, anciently Kaderlenge. The hall was seat of the Vaux family from about 1160; their pele was enlarged (1577) by Rowland Vaux into a mansion, which came by marriage to the Richmonds, who made additions dated 1657.

CAUDALE A little valley running E. from Patterdale up to Caudale Moor (2,214 ft.). The name a corruption from Calf-dale.

CAUSEY PIKE A mountain (2,000 ft.) E. of Newlands, ascended from Stair; fine views.

CHAPEL ISLAND An island formerly called Harlesyde, in the estuary of the Leven, with ruins of a 'chapel' (p. 38), i.e. a folly.

CLAIFE A township W. of Windermere in which are the Claife Heights (750 ft.) above Longholme (Belle Isle). The name from Norse *klief*, cliff. The legend of the Crier of Claife is to the effect that in the Reformation period the ferryman at Ferry Nab heard a cry on a stormy night and set out, but returned dumb with fear, and soon after died.

Terrible cries were heard on the lake until a monk from Lady Holme laid the ghost at a quarry in Heald Wood near Belle Grange.

CLAPPERSGATE A hamlet on the Brathay under Loughrigg, 1 m. S.W. of Ambleside.

CLEATOR A former iron mining district on the limestone between the Whitehaven coal-measures and the Skiddaw slate of the fells (*see* p. 73).

CLIBURN A village 5 m. S.E. of Penrith. Church of St Cuthbert with Norman door and rude dial; Roman stones in porch, one with inscription about rebuilding a bath; churchyard cross, restored. Old hall, built by Richard Cleburn, 1577.

CLIFTON The church is between Great and Little Clifton, 3 m. E. of Workington. In the church is a fine pre-Norman interlaced monument discovered 1900.

CLIFTON A village near Lowther. Norman church of St Cuthbert, partly rebuilt in 1846. The Hall is a small late fifteenth-century pele with sixteenth-century chimneys and battlements; built by the Wyberghs, who held the place from Edward III till the nineteenth century.

On Clifton Moor was fought the last battle in England, on 18th December 1745, in which the Duke of Cumberland, with Lord Cobham's, Lord Mark Kerr's, and General Bland's dragoons, overtook the Highlanders under Lord George Murray and drove them off the ground, but night coming on they failed to follow up the success. At Clifton Dykes is the Wetheriggs Pottery, a restored nineteenth-century industrial site, making slipware in the traditional manner.

COCKERMOUTH A market town from 1226; parliamentary borough in 1295, regular representation from 1640. The Castle and Barony are described, pp. 79–82. All Saints' Church, built 1852.

W. Wordsworth was born 1770 at a house in Main Street, N. side of lower end, now N.T. At Fitz Wood is an ancient fort, with oval rampart and ditch.

COCKLEY BECK A farm at the bend of the Duddon where the road over the Hardknott to Eskdale leaves the road from Wrynose down the river.

CODALE A moorland valley above Easedale, $1\frac{1}{2}$–2 miles from Grasmere, with tarn 1,523 ft. above sea; hence 1 m. W.N.W. High White Stones, summit of moor (2,500 ft.), from which an extensive panorama of mountain-tops.

COLEDALE A valley S.W. from Braithwaite.

COLTON A parish, with church, $2\frac{1}{2}$ m. from Greenodd. Colton Old Hall is $\frac{1}{2}$ m. S.E. of church, near the village of Bouth; it was seat of the Sandys family in the seventeenth century. One m. S. of Colton church is the old Baptist chapel of Tottlebank, founded 1669. Near Oxenpark is a cockpit.

COLWITH A hamlet in Little Langdale, with waterfall on the Brathay, 45 ft. high.

CONEYBEDS Ancient fort on Hay Fell, 2 m. E. of Kendal.

CONEYGARTH COP Another name for Carnarvon Castle, Beckermet, twelfth-century mote-hill of the Flemings.

CONISHEAD PRIORY An early nineteenth-century mansion 2 m. S.E. of Ulverston built by Col. R. G. Braddyll on the site of a twelfth-century priory of Augustinian canons, previously a leper hospital. It is now the Manjushri Institute of Tibetan Studies. House and grounds open to the public.

CONISTON A village at the head of Coniston Lake. The church, built 1586, now restored, contains a brass of the Flemings; John Ruskin's grave in the churchyard. Behind the Institute is the Ruskin Museum, with pictures, relics, etc. Brantwood, (*which see*) home of John Ruskin from 1871 to 1900, is 3 m. by road from the village. Tent Lodge, on the E. shore of the lake was inhabited by Tennyson in 1848. Coniston Hall, 1 m. S.S.E. of the church, opposite Brantwood, fifteenth-century seat of the Flemings, now a N.T. farmhouse. The lake is $5\frac{1}{4}$ m. long, $\frac{1}{2}$ m. broad, 143 ft. above sea; the northern basin is 150 ft. deep a little S. of Brantwood; the southern basin is 184 ft. deep between Fir Island and Oxenhouse at the mouth of Torver Beck. Opposite the latter is Peel Island (p. 45). Coniston Old Man (2,635 ft.) is the highest point of the Coniston Fells, easily climbed in 2 hours. One of the recent attractions on the lake is the steam yacht *Gondola* first launched by the Coniston Railway Company in 1859 and now restored by the National Trust.

COOME CRAGS Rocks on N. bank of Irthing, ancient quarries, with Roman inscriptions, SECVRVS, IVSTVS, MATHRIANVS, and at the foot of the cliff, FAVST, ET RVF. COS. Faustinus and Rufus were consuls in A.D. 210.

COPELAND The ancient name of the district between Ennerdale and Eskdale.

CORBY CASTLE A mansion across the Eden from Wetherall S.E. of Carlisle. The house was rebuilt c. 1812, around a thirteenth- or fourteenth-century pele; contains fine portraits and relics. Grounds open to the public on certain days.

CORNEY A parish on the S. coast, between Bootle and Eskmeals.

CRACKENTHORPE A village 2 m. N.W. of Appleby. The Roman road from York to Carlisle ran east of the village; at Redlands, opposite Powis House, $1\frac{1}{2}$ m. N.W. of the village, is a camp, Maiden Hold. At Chapel Hill, E. of village, ruins of a chapel of St Giles. Crackenthorpe Hall was the seat of the Machells, descended from Maelchael in the eleventh century; Henry VI is said to have taken refuge there after the battle of Hexham.

CRINKLE CRAGS The southern continuation of Bowfell, rising to 2,816 ft., with great cliffs over Oxendale. Old Norse: *Kringla* = a circle; crags which encircle the head of Great Langdale.

CROGLIN A parish on the side of the Pennines in the valley of the Croglin. The church of St John the Baptist has some interesting medieval tombstones. The Rectory, opposite, was fortified with a pele tower.

CROOK A small village 4 m. N.W. of Kendal. Of the seventeenth-century church of St Catherine, 1 m. W., the tower alone is left. The hall near it, formerly called Thwatterden Hall, was the seat of the Philipsons in the seventeenth century.

CROSBY GARRETT (i.e. Crosby of Gerard, an early owner). A village between Warcop and Kirkby Stephen. Old parish church with Anglian and fourteenth-century work. Nearby, several prehistoric burial cairns.

CROSBY-ON-EDEN A parish with church at the village of Low Crosby, 5 m. N.E. of Carlisle; High Crosby is $\frac{1}{2}$ m. farther. The Roman Wall and Vallum pass $\frac{3}{4}$ m. N. The Baron's Dyke, an ancient boundary, crosses the wall $\frac{1}{2}$ m. W. of Blea Tarn (*which see*).

CROSBY RAVENSWORTH A village 4 m. E. of Shap and 5 m. S.W. of Appleby. The church of St Lawrence, described by Pevsner as one 'of great architectural interest,' contains the tomb of Sir Lancelot Threlkeld (*d.* before 1492) who saved the young Cliffords in the Wars of the Roses (*See* Wordsworth's *Song of the Feast of Brougham Castle*). S.W. of the village are the remains of a large late Iron Age settlement at Ewe Close, one of the finest in the north of England. It takes the form of a complicated series of enclosure walls and hut circles, the largest of these huts being more than 50 ft. in diameter. It is almost certain that the settlement was occupied during the early Roman period. The gate leading on to Crosby Ravensworth Fell contains (1987) the following request in dialect to close the gate:

> Gedthren thi yows up, er laiten beeass in,
> Whaerivva thoo's gaan, whaerivva thoo's bin,
> Whee-ivva thoo is, oudther thin er else fat—
> Thoo mau't gang awae till thoo's shutten this yat!

CROSSCANONBY A village 3 m. N.E. of Maryport, with a Norman church finely overlooking the Solway. In the porch and against the S. wall are several curious pre-Norman sculptures. The church was built about 1100, partly of Roman stones; the aisle added thirteenth century; restored 1880. Crosby and Kirkby are villages in the parish, which was given by Alan, second Lord of Allerdale, to Carlisle Priory, and served by the canons, whence the name Crosscanonby.

CROSSCRAKE A parish in the Kent valley, including Sedgwick and Stainton. By the latter flows St Sunday Beck, up which is Bleaze Hall, a sixteenth-century house, with great oak table dated 1631, and the 'Dobbie' or flaying-stone—a prehistoric stone axe hung by a chain from a rafter—an ancient charm against evil spirits. The house has one of the finest decorated plaster ceilings in Cumbria.

CROSS FELL The highest point (2,930 ft.) in the Pennine Chain, from which the Helm Wind blows, i.e. a local easterly wind, raw and violent, accompanied with a peculiar cloud-cap on the mountain.

CROSTHWAITE *See* Keswick.

CROSTHWAITE A village on the Gilpin, 6 m. W. of Kendal. An ancient chapelry with modern church; several old houses near (*see* p. 6).

CRUMMOCK BECK A stream rising near Mealsgate, and joining the Waver near Abbey Town.

CRUMMOCK WATER Anciently Cromack Water; fed from Buttermere and Loweswater, and drained by the Cocker. The lake, owned by the N.T., is 2½ m. long, ½ m. broad, 321 ft. above sea, and 144 ft. deep. On its S.W. side is Scale Force (*which see*); at Peel, N.W. end, is an ancient moat, perhaps site of the Lindsays' twelfth-century manor house.

CUMDIVOCK A village on the Shawk Beck; at Cunningarth is said to be an ancient earthwork.

CUMREW A village on the side of the Pennines, E. of Eden. Site of Dunwalloght Castle is ½ m. E.S.E., and on Cardunneth Pike above is a tumulus in which an interment was found; also prehistoric settlements.

CUMWHITTON 3 m. S.E. of Wetheral. Old church and ancient cross-head. Ancient fort 1 m. S.W. on the Eden. On King Harry Moor, 3 m. S.E., is site of great megalithic circle called Grey Yauds, now destroyed; one single outlier remains.

CUNSEY A hamlet on Cunsey Beck, which drains Esthwaite Water into Windermere. Ancient ironworks, c. 1711.

CUNSWICK Anciently Conneyswick; the hall was seat of the Layburnes from the fourteenth century until the Jacobite rising in 1715; 3 m. W. of Kendal.

DACRE A village in the valley of the Eamont, 5 m. W.S.W. of Penrith; anciently Dacor. The castle (p. 129) was the seat of the Dacres, who took their name from the place, until 1715, when it became the property of the Hasells, who had bought Dalemain (*which see*) in 1665. In the churchyard are the Dacre bears (p. 129) and inside the church is a pre-Norman cross-shaft with figures of Adam and Eve, etc. Recent excavation in the churchyard has uncovered what is probably the site of an Anglian monastery mentioned by Bede in the eighth century. A splendid Viking 'thistle' brooch was found on nearby Fluskew Pike in the eighteenth century. It is now in the British Museum.

DALEGARTH A farm in Eskdale, old manor-house of the Stanleys; near Beckfoot station (Ravenglass and Eskdale Railway). On the hill above it is Dalegarth Force, or Stanley Gill Fall (60 ft.).

DALEHEAD On Thirlmere; the hall formerly seat of the Leathes family, whence the old name Leatheswater for the lake (p 121).

DALEMAIN A mansion east of Dacre (*which see*). A pele tower and medieval hall surrounded by a splendid Georgian façade. The ancestral home of the Hasell family since 1665. Cumberland and Westmorland Yeomanry Museum; house and grounds open to the public.

DALEPARK A valley between Rusland and Esthwaite; made into a deer-park by Abbot Bankes of Furness, 1516.

DALSTON A village 4½ m. S.W. of Carlisle. The hall built round a pele was seat of the Dalstons; now enlarged into a mansion. To N. and W. of it is an ancient rampart and ditch known as the Bishop's Dyke.

DALTON-IN-FURNESS Daltune in Domesday Book; an ancient market town, once the capital of Furness. Following an outbreak of plague in 1631, Dalton declined and Ulverston (*which see*) took its place as the most important market town in Furness. The castle is a fourteenth-century pele tower built by the Abbot of Furness. It is now owned by the N.T. George Romney was born in Dalton in 1734 and is buried in the churchyard.

DEAN A village 1 m. E. of the river Marron at Branthwaite. On Dean Moor, at Studfoldgate, are remains of a megalithic circle. Branthwaite Hall is an exceptionally well-preserved pele tower.

DEARHAM A former coal-mining village near Maryport. St Mungo's church with Norman door and rude dials; fortified tower of about 1300; fine pre-Norman cross now placed inside the church. The so-called 'Kenneth' cross-shaft and head, from the figure supposed to represent St Kenneth as a baby carried off by a bird, and as a monk with a bell; the 'Adam' grave-slab with runes indecipherable. Dearham Hall, E. of the church, ancient seat of the Dearhams. Ewanrigg or Unerigg, in the Middle Ages a castle, was from 1838 the seat of the Christians, connected with the Isle of Man.

DEEPDALE A wild valley under St Sunday Crag, Patterdale.

DENT Village near Sedbergh, transferred to Cumbria from Yorkshire in 1974. Picturesque stone cottages and cobbled streets. Much famed for its knitting, hence Southey's 'terrible knitters of Dent.' Birthplace of Adam Sedgwick, the nineteenth-century pioneer geologist and former Professor of Geology at Cambridge. A Shap granite memorial to him stands near to the church. Dent is in the Yorkshire Dales National Park.

DENTON Over Denton, 1½ m. W.S.W. of Gilsland has an ancient church built of Roman stones from the Wall; chancel measuring 11 by 12 ft.; twelfth-century chancel arch; tomb of Margaret Teasdale of Mumps Hall, 1777 (the inn where Captain Brown met Dandie Dinmont in *Guy Mannering*). Nearby is a ruined barn, probably the pele tower of the vicar. N. of the church is a mote-hill. Denton Hall was seat of the Dentons until Henry VII. Near it is another moated mound.

DERWENTWATER Formed by the river Derwent which rises in Sprinkling Tarn, flows through Borrowdale, Derwentwater and Bassenthwaite, past Isel and Cockermouth and enters the sea at Workington after a course of about 30 miles. The lake is 3 m. long, 1¼ m. broad, 244 ft. above sea level; greatest depth is 72 feet. It lies in two main basins, one off Brandelhow, and the other between Barrow and Rampsholme. The whole area of the lake is crossed by the remains of two parallel N. and S. ridges; the eastern ridge rising to its greatest height in Lord's Island (remains of the Ratcliffes' house), and in Rampsholme; the western ridge forms the Derwent and St Herbert's Islands. On the latter, the hermit Herbert is said to have died, 19th–20th March 687, on the same day as his friend St Cuthbert. His cult was revived in 1374; the ruins of a cell then erected may be traced. Derwent Island was the site of the German miners' houses in the sixteenth century (p. 115), and here in the eighteenth century Joseph Pocklington, a wealthy eccentric, built a number of follies including a fort, a battery, a Druids' circle and a chapel. From here he organized the celebrated Keswick Regatta and installed himself as Governor of the Island, repulsing the 'attacks' of a massed fleet of ships.

On the west shore of the lake, the overgrown spoil tips of the former copper mine at Brandelhow can still be distinguished. The estate of Brandelhow was bought in 1901 for the National Trust with subscriptions collected by Canon Rawnsley, Vicar of Crosthwaite and one of the founders of the Trust. It was the first property to be acquired by the Trust in the Lake District and the first sizeable property in the whole country; today the N.T. owns a considerable part of the lake shore. Above Brandelhow is the Catbells range (1,482 ft.) with the old road running along its flank. At Brackenburn, Hugh Walpole wrote his Herries novels in the 1930s; he died here in 1941 and is buried at St John's church in Keswick. Under Swinside (803 ft.) is Fawe Park, N. of which are the Nichol End boat landings. Hence Finkle Street leads to Portinscale, past Mossriggs, where the hoard of Neolithic stone axes (p. 108) was found in 1901. On the eastern shore is Friar's Crag and the memorial to John Ruskin who recalled a visit here as his first childhood memory. Rising behind is Castlehead or Castlet (529 ft.) a good view point. Thought to be the eroded neck or stump of a former volcano, it is one of the most famous geological sites in the Lake District. Behind Castlehead, the hill of Castlerigg gradually rises and approaches the lake southward until at Wallacrag it reaches 1,234 ft. wooded beneath and craggy above, with a narrow gully called the Lady's Rake (p. 115). S. of Catgill is Falcon Crag (1,050 ft.), beyond which Barrow Beck descends from High Seat (1,996 ft.) past that most photographed of all Lakeland bridges, Ashness Bridge, making waterfalls in the grounds of Barrow House Youth Hostel. S. of Ashness Fell, Watendlath Beck, between Gowdar and Shepherd's Crags, forms the falls of Lodore. In the bay off Lodore, the water plants in the shallow lake have sometimes accumulated into a thick peaty carpet which is occasionally lifted by gases formed by decomposition; under such circumstances, the famous 'Floating Island' can be seen. *See also* Borrowdale and Keswick.

DEVOKE WATER A large tarn $\frac{3}{4}$ m. long, $\frac{1}{4}$ m. broad, 766 ft. above sea, on Birker Moor; 2 m. S.S.W. of Dalegarth Force, Eskdale. Prehistoric settlements on its N. side.

DISTINGTON A village $4\frac{1}{2}$ m. N.N.W. of Whitehaven. The church (rebuilt) has some pre-Norman cross-heads and two medieval bells. Near Castle Mill, foundations and moat of Hayes Castle.

DOLLYWAGGON PIKE A summit (2,810 ft.) of the Helvellyn range (p. 127).

DOVE COTTAGE Wordsworth's house from 1799 to 1808. Formerly the 'Dove
and Olive Branch,' an ale house on the turnpike road. House and nearby
museum open to the public. *See* Grasmere.

DOVEDALE A rocky dell running W. from Brothers Water Inn, up to Dove Crag
(2,600 ft.) and Hart Crag (2,698 ft.).

DOVENBY A village about 2 m. N.W. of Cockermouth, anciently Dolfinby, from
the owner under Henry I. Hall built round a pele, seat of the Lamplughs, from
Henry IV to Elizabeth. The old Thorn Cross stands in front of the house.

DOW CRAGS A precipice above Goat's Water, W. of Coniston Old Man (p. 48).

DRIGG A village on the coast with station. Nearby bird sanctuary may be visited
with permit.

DRUMBURGH (pronounced Drumbruff) A hamlet on the Solway coast. Small
Roman camp on the hill N.W. of houses (p. 91). The castle built sixteenth
century by Lord Dacre with stones from the Roman Wall, which ran between
it and Solway.

DUDDON A river rising near the Three Shires Stone, flowing W. 2 m. through a
desolate valley. At Cockley Beck a road goes W. over Hardknott Pass to Eskdale;
the river turns S. between Harter Fell (2,140 ft.) and Greyfriar (2,537 ft.) to
Birks Bridge ($1\frac{1}{2}$ m.) and Stepping Stones ($1\frac{1}{2}$ m.), by which Grassguards and
pass to Eskdale can be reached. The river then runs through a ravine for 1 m.
to an open valley, at the head of which is Seathwaite (*which see*), where the
Walna Scar road from Coniston comes down into the valley. One mile below is
Hall Dunnerdale and bridge. The Kirk of Ulpha (Wordsworth's Duddon
Sonnets) was originally a Chapel-of-Ease of Millom Church, and below it is a
bridge leading to (1 m.) ancient homesteads, cairn and bloomery of Stonestar
on the left. Below the church, 1 m. on the W. bank, is Holehouse Gill; $\frac{1}{2}$ m. up
the road is Ulpha Old Hall, ruin of sixteenth-century pele. At 1 m. lower down
the valley is Duddon Hall, where Logan Beck meets the river; pretty ravine and
road over moors to Bootle. Another m. to Duddon Bridge leading to Broughton;
W. of the bridge is site of the eighteenth-century Duddon iron furnace and old
wharves are $\frac{1}{4}$ m. down E. bank. Hence the river widens into a sandy estuary,
which between Walney and Haverigg Point meets the sea.

DUFTON Two m. E. of Long Marton. The parish extends 9 m. eastward over the
fells, past Rundale and Seamore tarns to Caldron Snout, a great waterfall, in a

deep gulley of the Upper Tees.

DUNGEON GILL (or Ghyll) A waterfall (60 ft.) $\frac{1}{2}$ m. above Dungeon Gill New Hotel, and a little more above the Old Hotel (to the W.).

DUNMAIL RAISE Former boundary of Cumberland and Westmorland. A tumulus on the pass between Grasmere and Thirlmere, 783 ft. (*see* p. 124).

DUNMALLET A wooded hill W. of Pooley Bridge, Ullswater, with double ramparts near the top; not Roman but probably a Romano-British fort.

DUNNERDALE The valley of Duddon, Duddenerdale.

EAGLESFIELD A village about 2 m. S.W. of Cockermouth. At Castlesteads is a prehistoric ring-embankment. Roman road and remains have been found near. Robert de Eaglesfield, born at Allerby, founder of Queen's College, Oxford, was of the family anciently owning the place. Dr John Dalton, the scientist and father of the atomic theory (*see* Sellafield) was a native. Fletcher Christian, the *Bounty* mutineer, was born and lived at Moorland Close.

EAMONT BRIDGE A village 1 m. S. of Penrith. Arthur's Round Table and Mayburgh (*which see*). Several old houses, one with inscription OMNE SOLUM FORTI PATRIA EST. H.P.1671.

EASEDALE A pretty valley with Sourmilk Gill waterfall and tarn 1 hour N.W. of Grasmere by Goody Bridge.

EDENHALL A village 4 m. N.E. of Penrith. The hall, seat of the Musgraves, was built 1820 and demolished 1934. The 'Luck of Edenhall' is an ancient glass beaker in a fifteenth-century leather case, said to have been a fairy gift, celebrated in ballads by Philip, Duke of Wharton, and by Uhland, translated by Longfellow. It is now in the Victoria and Albert Museum. The old church of St Cuthbert has late seventeenth-century heraldic glass and two medieval bells; brass of W. Stapleton, died 1458, and his wife, also marble monuments of the Musgraves, to whom the hall came by marriage of Sir Thomas (*d.* 1469) with Jane, the heiress of the Stapletons, who had held it since 1327.

EEL CRAGS Rocks (2,749 ft.) at head of Coldale, S.W. of Braithwaite. Also rock (2,143 ft.) between the head of Newlands and Borrowdale.

EGREMONT A market town (charter 1267) with wide main street to accommodate stalls. The church, about 1220, restored, contains some early sculptures. The twelfth-century castle is an interesting ruin (p. 67). Crab (apple) Fair held on the third Saturday in September when the World Gurning Championship is held.

EHEN A river flowing from Ennerdale Water past Egremont (Egener-mont, from Egen, the ancient form of Ehen) to the sea at Sellafield.

ELLENBOROUGH A village S.E. of Maryport, now a suburb, anciently Alneburgh, the burg on the Ellen.

ELTERWATER A village in Langdale near the lake of that name, $\frac{1}{4}$ m. long, $\frac{1}{4}$ m. broad. Name derived from the Old Norse *elptarvatn*—swan's lake. Occasionally the lake is visited in winter by whooper swans from Scandinavia.

EMBLETON A scattered parish E. of Cockermouth. The Embleton sword (late first or early second century A.D.) in the British Museum was found near Wythop Mill, a recently-restored watermill.

ENNERDALE The upper valley of Ehen (Egener-dale), with a lake $2\frac{1}{2}$ m. long, $\frac{1}{2}$ m. broad, widening to $\frac{3}{4}$ m. at foot; 368 ft. above sea level; 148 ft. deep (*see* p. 74). Ennerdale Bridge is a hamlet with a nineteenth-century church (chapel originally founded in 1543), the scene of Wordsworth's 'The Brothers,' $1\frac{1}{2}$ m. W. of Waterfoot. Planting of the upper part of the valley by the Forestry Commission in the 1930s aroused much criticism. There is now a 9-mile marked trail through cleared woodlands giving splendid views.

ESK The Scottish river Esk enters Cumbria at Scots Dyke, passes Longtown, and flows into Solway S. of Gretna.

ESKDALE Valley of the Cumbrian Esk which rises between Scafell Pikes and Bowfell, forms the Esk Falls at Throstlegarth, turns W. at Brotherilkeld below Hardknott Castle, and flows between Muncaster Fell and Birkby Fell to Ravenglass. From Ravenglass a narrow-gauge railway runs up the valley to Dalegarth (station for Boot), 7 m., first going up the Mite valley to Irton Road where it crosses a low depression to Eskdale Green station, and through pretty woods and rocks to Beckfoot station from which Dalegarth Force (Stanley Gill) is 1 m. S. From Boot a path goes over Burnmoor (*which see*). From Boot, 1 m. up the valley, is the Woolpack Inn, centre for Upper Eskdale. In 1242 Furness Abbey acquired 14,000 acres of land in Upper Eskdale and created a huge sheep run. At Brotherilkeld farm, $1\frac{1}{2}$ m., a road goes up to E. past Hardknott Castle, Roman fort (pp. 57–9), over a pass to Cockley Beck. From the bend of Eskdale at Brotherilkeld, paths go up both sides of the valley to Esk Falls (2 m.). Hence the valley to right leads straight forward to the Ore Gap, the old route from the iron mines in Eskdale to smelting works in Langstrath. Half-way up this little valley a gill to right leads up to the Three Tarns and Bowfell. From Esk Falls to left follow the stream to Cam Spout Fall under Mickledore and Esk Hause for Styhead or Scafell Pike, which can also be climbed via Mickeldore by the Cam Spout Gill. By bearing to left when half-way up, Scafell can be climbed more easily than from Mickledore Ridge (p. 62).

ESTHWAITE WATER The lake of Hawkshead, a little over 1½ m. long, ¾ m. broad, 217 ft. above sea, and 80 ft. deep. It lies among glacial moraine-mounds, three of which form peninsulas. To N. is a pool called Priest-Pot, no doubt because used as a fishpond to the monks' house of Hawkshead Hall; because of the nutrient rich water, this area supports a wide range of flora and fauna. Esthwaite Hall, now a farm, was birthplace of Archbishop Sandys. *See* Hawkshead.

FAIRFIELD A mountain (2,863 ft.) between Rydal and Grisedale Tarn; supposed to mean sheep-pasture (Icelandic, *Faerifold*).

FAWCETT FOREST The wild district between Long Sleddale and Tebay, traversed by the old turnpike road.

FELL FOOT A farm in Little Langdale. Possible Norse 'thingmount' terraced mound behind the farm (p. 27).

FIELD BROUGHTON A village 2 m. N. of Cartmel.

FINSTHWAITE A village W. of the foot of Windermere. In the churchyard is buried the mysterious Clementina Johannes Sobiesky Douglas, died 1771, perhaps a daughter of Charles Edward Stuart.

FIRBANK A chapelry W. of Sedburgh; a church rebuilt 1742. In 1652 George Fox addressed a crowd of over 1,000 people at Firbank Fell.

FLEETWITH A mountain mass at the head of Buttermere, rising to Fleetwith Pike (2,126 ft.), with its N. side formed by Honister Crag.

FLIMBY A village (twelfth century, Flemingby) on the coast, 2 m. S. of Maryport.

FLOOKBURGH A village, once market town with charters from Edward I and Charles II (pronounced Flookboro). Famous for its shrimps from Morecambe Bay.

FLOUTERN A tarn (pronounced Flootern) on the moor, 1,250 ft. above sea, between Ennerdale and Crummock; 1½ m. W. of Scale Force.

FROSWICK A summit (2,359 ft.) in the Ill Bell range, between Kentmere and Troutbeck. The Scots' Rake, a Roman road, goes up its W. side.

FURNESS The district between Duddon and Leven, written in the twelfth century Fourneis and Furthernessa; perhaps meaning the Further Ness, as seen from Lancaster (*see* p. 29). For Furness Abbey *see* pp. 41–3. *See also* Barrow, Ulverston, Hawkshead, Gleaston, Dalton, Bardsea.

FUSEDALE A mountain valley running S. from Howtown, Ullswater.

GABLE, GREAT A mountain (2,949 ft.) of volcanic ash with precipitous rocks, the
Napes, to S., one of which is the Needle, (first climbed by Walter Parry Haskett-
Smith in 1886), standing isolated 100 ft. high. Easy ascent to the summit of the
Gable, under 1 hour, from Styhead; or in 3 hours from Honister Hause by
Brandreth and Green Gable, a lower summit to N. Very fine mountain panorama
of Scafell and Pikes, Wastwater, and Isle of Man, back of the Pillar Mountain,
Crummock, Skiddaw, Saddleback, Helvellyn, and Windermere. On the summit
is a bronze-tablet war memorial.

GAMBLESBY A village in the Eden valley under Fiends, Fins, or Finch Fell
(2,082 ft.), a summit of the Pennines. Anciently Gamelesbi. Fine village green
and ancient stocks.

GARBURN PASS Bridle-path (1,450 ft.) from Kentmere Hall to Troutbeck, 3 m.

GARRIGILL *See* Alston.

GATESGARTH A house at the head of Buttermere. Gatesgarthdale in old books
means Buttermere valley.

GATESGARTH The Pass (1,950 ft.) from Sadgill in Long Sleddale to Mardale,
about 5 m., rough on top; fine scenery on N. side.

GELT A river rising in the Pennine Moors, S. of Coldfell (2,039 ft.), and running
through Geltsdale Forest, receiving Howgill on the E., on both sides of which
are ancient cultivation terraces; then past Castle Carrock, receiving the Hell
Beck from Talkin Tarn. N. of the confluence is the Written Rock, and $\frac{1}{2}$ m.
higher up on the opposite side is the Pigeon Rock, both with Roman inscriptions
(p. 101). Near this the battle was fought between Leonard Dacre and Lord
Hunsdon (p. 100). The Gelt joins the Irthing near Edmond Castle. The valley
is best explored from Brampton (*which see*).

GIANT'S GRAVE *See* Penrith.

GILCRUX A former colliery village (pronounced Gilcruse) 4 m. N.W. of Maryport.
In the church is a pre-Norman cross-head.

GILLERCOMBE A wild valley W. of Seathwaite in Borrowdale, from which Sourmilk Gill, with falls, comes down past the former Plumbago (black lead,
graphite) mine.

GILPIN A river rising 2 m. E. of Bowness-on-Windermere, running past Crosthwaite and the Lyth, and joining the Kent near Heversham.

GILSLAND Properly the name of the district, from the twelfth-century owner, Gillēs; then applied to the celebrated spring sulphur Spa. The Roman Wall and Vallum can be seen near the railway. For Mumps Ha' and Sir Walter Scott, *see* p. 104. Gilsland village is in Northumberland.

GLARAMARA A mountain (2,560 ft.) between Seathwaite-in-Borrowdale and Langstrath. Many secluded 'coves' or combes in this fine rugged *massif*; easily climbed from Rosthwaite by Combegill, or by the ridge to W.

GLASSON A village 1½ m. S.E. of Port Carlisle. The Roman Wall passed to N.E. In cutting the canal (later a railway and now abandoned) fallen trees were found under the Wall.

GLASSONBY A village 2 m. S.E. of Kirkoswald. On the left of the road, after crossing Dale Raven, is a burial circle of the Bronze Age in which were found the urn and bead now in Tullie House Museum, Carlisle. White House Farm is a late pele or bastle with date 1598 over the door. Addingham church is S. of the village, and Long Meg stone circle 1 m. S. of the church, passing Maughanby (*which see*).

GLEASTON A village in Furness (Glassertun in Domesday), with ruins of the castle of the Harringtons, fourteenth century. St Michael's Well perhaps is named after Sir Michael le Fleming, of the family preceding the Harringtons.

GLENCOIN OR GLENCOYNE A dale W. of Ullswater; the beck, rising in Hartside (2,481 ft.), once divided Cumberland from Westmorland.

GLENDERAMACKIN The valley of a river rising N. of Saddleback in Scales Tarn, passing Mungrisdale and Threlkeld.

GLENDERATERRA The valley of a stream rising in Roughten Gill, head to head with the source of Glenderamackin, and flowing into the Greta at Brundholme.

GLENRIDDING A valley W. of Ullswater. The village was formerly a centre for lead mining but is now concerned almost entirely with tourism.

GOAT'S WATER (formerly Gaits-water) A deep tarn, 1,646 ft. above sea level, under Dow Crags (2,555 ft.) and Coniston Old Man (2,635 ft.).

GOSFORTH A village 3 m. N.E. of Seascale. Norman church, restored, with twelfth-century capitals to chancel arch; two pre-Norman hogbacks placed near the organ, beside which the 'Fishing Stone' (pp. 64–5) is built into the wall, with other fragments of early sculpture; above are two wheel-cross heads. In the porch is a late cross-head and some medieval grave-slabs. In the churchyard is the famous cross, 14 ft. high, a slender monolith of red sandstone, with wheel-cross head, and interlaced dragons; crucifix with Longinus and Mary Magdalen; Loki (the Norse Satan) chained under the serpent, with his wife, Sigun, catching the serpent's poison in a cup, as told in the Edda; Vidar rending the Wolf's jaw, Heimdal and his horn, also from Norse mythology; dating about A.D. 1000. For further description see W. G. Collingwood, *Northumbrian Crosses of the Pre-Norman Age*, Faber and Gwyn, 1927; R. N. Bailey, *Viking Age Sculpture*, Collins, 1980; K. Berg, 'The Gosforth Cross,' *Journal of the Warburgh and Courtauld Institute*, XXI.

Gosforth Hall, seventeenth-century seat of the Copleys and now an hotel, is near the church; and in the field above is a holy well with foundations of medieval chapel which enclosed it. Remains of an early homestead called Dane's Camp are in a long, narrow field ½ m. N.N.E. of the Hall, but not Danish.

GOWBARROW A fell (1,579 ft.) and park on the N.W. side of Ullswater, on the W. of which are Lyulph's Tower and Aira Force, *which see* (*also* p. 128).

GOWDER CRAG A rocky precipice above Lodore.

GRAINS GILL The dell running S. from Stockley Bridge up to Sprinkling Tarn. 'Grain' (Icelandic, *grein*, a branch) is often used for a dell branching from the main valley.

GRANGE-IN-BORROWDALE A hamlet on the site of a 'grange' of Furness Abbey in the Jaws of Borrowdale. Picturesque bridges; remarkable glaciated rock on the W. side. Hence a road going N. on the W. side of Derwentwater, and a footpath over Catbells to Newlands, give good views. Also a pretty footpath S. from Grange, behind Castle Crag, leads to the Hause Gill, half-way between Seatoller and the top of Honister Pass.

GRANGE-OVER-SANDS A nineteenth-century resort on the rocky, wooded shore of Morecambe Bay; sunny and sheltered. Castle Head (1 m. N.N.E.) is a high and isolated hill rising from the flats of the Winster estuary, tidal before the railway embankment was made; was site of Atterpile Castle, a Romano-British fort, occupied until Norman times. The present mansion was built by John Wilkinson, the ironmaster and inventor of iron ships etc., who died here 1808. His iron monument is near the roadside at Lindale. The house is now a field studies centre. For the caves, Humphrey Head, Wraysholme Tower, etc., *see* p. 40.

GRASMERE A village 4 m. N.W. of Ambleside, past the lake, 1 m. long, ⅜ m. broad, 206 ft. above sea, with a small island; boats for hire. The church of St Oswald has a picturesque rustic interior with mural decoration of 1687 and brass of the le Flemings; in the S. corner of the churchyard are the graves of the Wordsworths and Hartley Coleridge. Dove Cottage (in Wordsworth's time Town End) was Wordsworth's home, 1799–1808, and afterwards De Quincey's for twenty years; in 1890 the house was bought by Rev. Stopford Brooke, Professor Knight, and committee, and is now a showplace with relics of the distinguished occupants; nearby is the Grasmere and Wordsworth Museum and Library. The site of the Wishing Gate (*see* Wordsworth's poem) is E. of the lake on the middle one of the three roads crossing the hill between Rydal and Grasmere. Greenhead Gill (E. from the Swan Hotel) is the scene of Wordsworth's *Michael*, and leads up to Fairfield (2,863 ft.). Three-quarters of a m. N. of the 'Swan,' a bridle-path to right leads up to Grisedale Tarn (whence Helvellyn can be easily ascended) and over into Patterdale; $\frac{1}{2}$ m. from the main road up this path is a bridge leading to right up Tongue Gill to Grisedale Tarn; below the bridge is Tongue Gill waterfall. The main road runs N. to (2$\frac{1}{4}$ m. from the 'Swan') Dunmail Raise (800 ft.), the pass to Thirlmere and Keswick. From Grasmere village N.W. road over Goody Bridge and footbridge to Sourmilk Gill waterfall and Easedale Tarn (915 ft.), and Codale Tarn on the moorland above (1,523 ft.), whence High White Stones (2,374 ft.) can be reached in a mile of easy climbing, or Stickle Tarn and Dungeon Gill by a somewhat rough descent. From the N. side of Easedale (without crossing the footbridge) Helm Crag (1,299 ft.) can be climbed to the rocks at the S. end of the ridge which from below form 'The Lion and the Lamb,' and those on the N. end forming 'The Old Woman'; a descent can be made to N. into Greenburn and back by the old road W. of the Rothay. Allan Bank, Wordsworth's house, 1808–11, is to N.W. of the village. The road S. from the village leads over the Hause between Silver How and Loughrigg to Langdale (bearing to right from the top), to Loughrigg Tarn and Skelwith (bearing to left), or leaving the main road halfway up turn to left for Loughrigg Terrace, a path giving views over the lake towards Helvellyn, and leading down to a footbridge across Rothay between the two lakes, or along the S. side of Rydal Water to Pelter Bridge whence the return may be made by the main road to Grasmere passing Nab Cottage (*see* Rydal). The Grasmere sports are held on the third Thursday in August; wrestling, hound trail, and fell racing. The Grasmere Rush Bearing ceremony takes place on the Saturday nearest St Oswald's Day, 5th August.

GRASMOOR A mountain (2,791 ft.) E. of the foot of Crummock Water.

GRAYRIGG A scattered township, including Docker, Lambrigg, and other hamlets, in undulating ground beneath Whinfell Beacon (1,544 ft.).

GRAYTHWAITE On the S.W. side of Windermere; the Rawlinsons' old Low Hall, beside the road, with clipped yews and ancient interior, is of the sixteenth or seventeenth century; the High Hall (behind high walls) is the ancient (restored) seat of the Sandys family.

GREAT END A mountain (2,984 ft.) forming the northernmost buttress of the Scafell group; ascended from Esk Hause. In its W. side are the chasms of Greta Gill and Piers Gill.

GREAT GABLE *See* Gable.

GREAT ORTON Village 5 m. W.S.W. of Carlisle. Around the village was a rampart and ditch, and at Barras Gate there was a chain across the road, fastened every night for defence against the Scots. Fine cruck barn.

GREENBURN A deep valley going up from Fell Foot under Wetherlam to the Carrs, with a tarn formed by a dam, for old copper mines.

GREENBURN A valley N. of Helm Crag. *See* Grasmere.

GREENHEAD GILL *See* Grasmere.

GREENODD A village at the junction of the Crake with the Leven. Formerly port for Coniston slate, etc. Penny Bridge ¾ m. N.W., and Spark Bridge, 1 m. further up the valley, had flourishing iron-works in the eighteenth century.

GREENTHWAITE HALL Near Greystoke; built about 1650; seat of the Haltons from Richard II; heraldic and inscribed door, picturesque façade.

GREENUP GILL A lonely valley running from Stonethwaite in Borrowdale with Ullscarth (2,370 ft.) on the E. and Eagle Crag on the W., up to Greenup Hause (2,000 ft.), leading by a mountain track to Easedale or Wythburn.

GRETA The river from Thirlmere through St John's Vale (here sometimes called St John's Beck), joining the Glenderamackin at Threlkeld; it turns W. to meet the Derwent between Keswick and Portinscale. The name is Old Norse interpreted to mean the 'rocky river.'

GRETA FORCE A cascade in the gill from Great End, meeting Piers Gill ¼ m. below the fall, which is one of the wildest.

GREYSTOKE The seat of ancient barony which included all Cumberland between Inglewood, Penrith, and Castlerigg (Keswick). Lyulf (whence the name of Lyulph's Tower, Ullswater) is said to have received it from Ranulf Meschines before 1120. In 1506 Elizabeth, the heiress of Greystoke, married Thomas, Lord Dacre of Gilsland, and thence until 1569 the Dacres were lords of Greystoke. Their heiress married Philip Howard, Earl of Arundel, since when Greystoke Castle has been the seat of the Howards of Greystoke. The castle incorporates a nineteenth-century façade by Salvin, masking a medieval pele tower. The church of St Andrew (restored) has ancient bells, glass, and carved seats; a brass of Richard Newport (1451) and many other monuments. One m. W. of the castle is the site of a 'camp' on Berrier Hill, and ¼ m. N. of the castle is an earthwork. Greystoke Mid Farm (cottages) was built 1649.

GRINSDALE A village on the Eden, $2\frac{1}{2}$ m. N.W. of Carlisle, with church of St Kentigern. At the S.W. end of the village the Roman Wall may be traced close to the river.

GRISEDALE A little valley above Braithwaite under Grisedale Pike (2,593 ft.).

GRISEDALE A valley S.W. of Patterdale, running up between the crags of Dollywaggon Pike and those of the Fairfield group, to Grisedale Tarn.

GRIZEDALE 'The valley of the pigs,' between Satterthwaite and Hawkshead. Now at the centre of the huge Grizedale Forest. Wildlife and deer museum run by the Forestry Commission. Long-distance footpaths, nature trails, hides and observation points in the forest. The remarkable Theatre in the Forest, housed in out-buildings of the demolished Grizedale Hall, presents a programme of music and entertainment by national and international artists.

GUMMER'S HOW A mountain (1,054 ft.) forming the highest point of Cartmel Fell, S.E. of Windermere; climbed from the pass (700 ft.) on the road, the former Turnpike, between Newby Bridge Hotel and Strawberry Bank Inn. Fine views of Windermere.

GUNNERKELD A hamlet 2 m. N. of Shap near which are two concentric stone circles, the larger 100 ft. diameter; many cairns in the neighbourhood. Traffic on the south bound M6 speeds by within yards of the circles.

GUTTERBY On the coast near Bootle; once famous for a spa, and for a megalithic circle, now destroyed.

HACKTHORPE A village near Lowther; Jacobean hall of the Stricklands. Bronze Age circle and barrow, opened 1866; ancient homesteads to N. of it.

HAILE A village 2 m. N.W. of Beckermet; picturesque church with ancient monuments (one built into the S. wall, another in the vestry, others in the churchyard).

HALLIN FELL An isolated mountain (1,271 ft.) between Howtown and Sandwick, on Ullswater.

HARDKNOTT A mountain (1,803 ft.) E. of Upper Eskdale, to the S. of which is the pass (1,250 ft.) by a steep road from Eskdale to Cockley Beck (*which see*). On the Eskdale side, N. of the road, is the Roman camp, bath-house and parade ground (pp. 57–9).

HARRINGTON A former seaport and industrial village between Whitehaven and Workington (p. 74). The ancient Haverington, now High Harrington, 1 m. inland, was the seat of an old family of that name, and a baronage which died out in the person of the Duke of Suffolk (father of Lady Jane Grey), beheaded by Queen Mary Tudor.

HARRISON STICKLE The higher of the Langdale Pikes (2,401 ft.) (*which see*).

HARROP TARN A tarn from which flows Dob Gill, entering Thirlmere opposite Wythburn.

HARTER FELL A rocky mountain (2,140 ft.) S. of Hardknott Pass, easily ascended from the moor N.W. of Grassguards, above the stepping-stones on the Duddon, or from Hardknott Pass. Remarkable blocks of volcanic ash and lava; fine view of the Scafell group and the Hardknott Roman fort.

HARTLEY A village ½ m. S.S.E. of Kirkby Stephen; site of Hartley Castle, once seat of the Musgraves, and earlier of Sir Andrew de Harcla (Hartley), Earl of Carlisle, who defended Carlisle against the Scots, but was hanged, drawn, and quartered by Edward II in 1323 on a charge of high treason.

HARTSOP A manor S.W. of Brothers Water in Patterdale. The Hall, fifteenth century, was the manor-house of the Lancasters, at the mouth of Dovedale. Some fine seventeenth-century farm houses and a splendid half-cruck corn drying kiln.

HAVERTHWAITE A village on the Leven; Backbarrow (*which see*) is half a mile up the river. Bigland Hall is the ancient seat of the Biglands. The site of the former Low-wood gunpowder works is now occupied by craft workshops. *See also* Newby Bridge.

HAWESWATER A small but deep tarn near Silverdale.

HAWESWATER The reservoir which resulted from the damming of the former lake and the raising of the water level by 95 feet. Manchester began the construction of the dam in 1929 but water was not tapped off until 1941. The creation of the reservoir meant the destruction of the hamlet of Mardale with its seventeenth-century church and the Dun Bull Inn (*see* p. 135). Today the reservoir is fed not only by the surrounding streams from the fells but also by an underground pipeline from Ullswater. The North West Water Authority, the successor to the Manchester Corporation Waterworks Committee, has outlined plans to raise the height of the dam and so increase the capacity of the reservoir.

HAWKSHEAD A small town with market charter, 1608; then and until the nineteenth century a centre of the rural woollen industry. The church, on a hill above the town, has great nave-columns and round arches, but is not earlier than the fifteenth century; it contains Elizabethan effigies of William Sandys of

Graythwaite and his wife. The Grammar School below the church was founded by Archbishop Sandys, 1585; tablet to him, sun-dial. Wordsworth's name cut by him as a schoolboy there (1778–83) in the schoolroom. For many years it was thought that Wordsworth lodged with Ann Tyson in the village, but it is now argued that for most of his school years he stayed with Ann at Green End Cottage, Colthouse. Flag Street, formerly with an open beck running through it, is now covered in. Hawkshead Hall, ½ m. N.W., was the medieval manor-house of Furness Abbey; a fifteenth-century traceried window is to be seen in what was the gatehouse. At Colthouse is an old Quakers' meeting and graveyard, dating from about 1698. At Hawkshead Hill, 1½ m. W.N.W. on the road to Coniston, is a Baptist chapel built 1678, restored. Hence the road to right leads to Tarn Hows; to left over High Cross to Coniston. *See also* Esthwaite.

HAYESWATER A tarn (1,383 ft. above sea) in a deep cove under High Street, at the head of a valley running E. from Brothers Water.

HAYTON A village 2½ m. S.W. of Brampton. The castle hill is an ancient fort of doubtful date. Edmond Castle was built by Smirke in 1829. Also a village 2 m. W. of Aspatria; the castle is said to have withstood a siege by Parliamentarians in the Civil Wars, and was rebuilt after the Restoration by the Musgraves. Now a farm. Pevsner calls it 'a mystery house.'

HELL GILL *See* p. 26.

HELM CRAG *See* Grasmere.

HELVELLYN *See* pp. 125–6.

HERDHOUSE Corruptly Herdus, the rocky end of Great Borne (2,019 ft.) on the N. side of Ennerdale Water.

HESKET-IN-THE-FOREST i.e. in Inglewood. A parish between Carlisle and Penrith. Between High and Low Hesket, in a tumulus opened 1822, was found the interesting hoard of Viking arms with interlaced ornament, now in Tullie House. The site of Tarn Wadling and Castle Ewain (*which see*) is 1 m. E. of High Hesket.

HESKET NEWMARKET A small, decayed market town, 1½ m. S.E. of Caldbeck. Hesket Hall, with circular roof and twelve angles serving as a sun-dial, was built by Sir Wilfrid Lawson, some time after 1630. Bishop Nicholson in 1685 mentions 'Sir W.L.'s *whim* at Heskett.'

HESK FELL Or Hest (i.e. Old Norse = Horse) Fell (1,566 ft.), rises between Ulpha and Devoke Water.

HEVERSHAM A village near Milnthorpe. Much-restored medieval church with ninth-century Anglian cross-shaft in porch. Old Hall—some fourteenth-century work but additions in the sixteenth century. Original Grammar School founded in 1613. In a field next to the 'Old School' is the village cock-pit, still discernible. In the north of England, 'cocking' was regarded as a morale-building 'sport,' similar to 'the playing fields of Eton,' and often cock-pits were found close to the local schools.

HIGHHEAD A castle on the ravine of the Ive (Ivegill), seat of the Richmonds, sixteenth and seventeenth centuries. Gutted by fire in 1956. Now, 1987, being restored.

HIGH STILE A summit (2,643 ft.) in the craggy ridge S. of Buttermere.

HIGH STREET The Roman road from Brougham to Troutbeck, and especially the highest point in its course (2,633 ft.) between Blea Water and Haweswater, from which the road descends along the breast of Froswick by the Scots' Rake.

HINCASTER A hamlet 5 m. S. of Kendal; in Domesday, Hennecastre, and supposed to signify 'old camp.' The mounds, however, are natural.

HINDSCARTH The part of Buttermere Fell opposite Honister Crag.

HOFF A village 2½ m. S.W. of Appleby. There was anciently a chapel at Hoff. Barwise Hall was held till about 1350 by the Barwises, later by the Roos family. Present building largely sixteenth century. At Douglas Ing near Hoff Bridge was a battle with the Scots in the time of Richard II. Hoff Lund is supposed to mean 'temple grove,' but no remains of a Scandinavian temple have been found.

HOLKER HALL Former home of the Dukes of Devonshire near Cark-in-Cartmel. The oldest part dates from the early seventeenth century; the west wing is a rebuilding after a fire in 1871. Fine library of 3,500 volumes. House, gardens and motor museum open to the public.

HOLM The name, meaning 'island,' is given to the N.W. part of Cumbria between Allonby Bay and Moricambe Bay and the sea. The Holm is now divided into Holm Cultram, Holm St Cuthbert's, and Holm St Paul's. For Holm Cultram, see pp. 87–8, and Abbey Town. Holm St Cuthbert's is a parish W. of Holm Cultram, including Old Mawbray (anciently Mawbergh), 2 m. N. of Allonby, with Roman camp (inscribed stones found) and road; stone implements have also been discovered here: New Mawbray, Edderside, Cowper, Pelutho (formerly Pallat-how) near a tarn; and Beckfoot (remains of Roman fort), near which is the site of Wolsty Castle (*which see*).
Holm St Paul's or Holm Low includes Silloth and Skinburness (*which see*);

also Calvo, Seaville, and Blitterlees. The sea dyke, 1¼ m. long, was made under Elizabeth to protect the land from high tides.

HONISTER CRAG *See* Buttermere.

HORNBY HALL An Elizabethan manor-house at the ford over Eamont, ½ m. W. of Ninekirks. Turret gateway, heraldic carvings in stone and oak of the Birkbecks, sixteenth century, and Dalstons, seventeenth century. Fine hall, and drawing-room with heraldic glass, moulded ceiling, and great fireplace. Chapel at the top of the tower.

HOUGHTON A parish near Carlisle. *See* Linstock Castle.

HOWGILL CASTLE Half a mile E. of Milburn, has two towers with walls 10 ft. thick, perhaps late fourteenth century, built by the Lancasters who then held it. The buildings between are the seventeenth-century house of the Sandfords.

HOWTOWN A village at the mouth of Fusedale, between Hallin Fell and Swarth Fell on Ullswater. Served by the steamer service.

HUGILL A parish between Windermere and Kentmere, also called Ings. The High House is a fine old yeoman's residence with walls 9 ft. thick in some places, round chimneys, and stained glass dated 1562; said to have been the home of Richard Braithwaite, second son of Sir Thomas of Burneside, an Elizabethan writer, author of *Drunken Barnabee's Journal*, etc. From this ½ m. N.N.W. is a ring embankment containing hut-circles, N. of Borrans Farm. Probably Native Iron Age in date.

HUTHWAITE (or Hewthwaite) HALL Near Cockermouth, home of the Swin-burnes, 1581, has a remarkable carved and dated lintel stone—one of the finest in N.W. England.

HUTTON-IN-THE-FOREST A manor in Inglewood, where the family of Hutton were foresters until the time of James I, when they sold their estate to Sir Richard Fletcher, whose great-grandson, Sir Henry, became a monk at Douai, and the Hall went to his relatives the Vanes, who still hold it. The house is built around a fourteenth-century pele tower, with seventeenth- and eighteenth-century additions. Open to the public. The church, built 1714 on the site of an early chapel, contains monuments of the local families, and in the wall an interlaced pre-Norman fragment. One m. N.N.W. is the site of Collinson Castle, a square rampart of about 100 yards.

HUTTON JOHN A manor held from the fourteenth century by the Huttons, passing in the time of Queen Elizabeth by marriage to the Hudlestons, one of whom, John, was the Roman Catholic priest who followed Charles II after the battle of Worcester, and became the king's private confessor. Another, Andrew, together with Sir James Lowther, in October 1688 began hostilities against James II by capturing a royal ship at Workington, and handing it over to the Prince of Orange. The manor was bought, 1787, by the Duke of Norfolk. The hall has been built at various periods round a pele tower.

HUTTON ROOF A parish 2½ m. W. of Kirkby Lonsdale, Hotune in Domesday; Roof for Ralph, an early owner. *See* Kirkby Lonsdale.

HUTTON Huton in Domesday, is a scattered district E. of Kendal, in hilly country, including the chapelry of Old Hutton, the parish of New Hutton, and Hutton-in-the-Hay (*haie*, enclosure or deer-park).

ILEKIRK HALL 2½ m. S. of Wigton. Incorrectly written Islekirk, originally Hildekirk, a hermitage of St Hilda in Westward (*see* Inglewood), tenanted by Roger the hermit; granted by King John to Holm Cultram Abbey. Abbot Adam of Kendal went into retreat there in 1223 with a monk Radulfus, and after unsuccessfully trying to win the bishopric of Carlisle saw a strange dream of heaven and hell in the likeness of an abbey and a prison, and thereafter went mad. In that condition he was kept at Holm Cultram until his death.

ILL BELL A summit (2,476 ft.) between Troutbeck and the Kentmere reservoir (p. 19).

ILLGILL HEAD Highest point of the Wastwater Screes (1,978 ft.).

INGLEWOOD The district between the Eden and Shawkbeck, Greystoke, and Eamont. Inglewood proper does not include Westward, the forest land to W. of it, said by Nicolson and Burn, the county historians, to have been incorporated with it under Henry II. The name is supposed to be derived from settlements of Angles, but by the time of William Rufus it was uncultivated and thenceforward was a royal forest, 'full of wood, red deer and fallow, wild swine, and all manner of wild beasts.' Edward I slaughtered 400 harts and hinds in one day in 1279. It was twice or thrice granted to feudal holders but went back to the Crown and was used as part of the dower of the queens of England. William III granted it to Bentinck, Earl of Portland, and in the eighteenth century it was part of the subject of a long legal struggle between the Duke of Portland and the Lowthers.

In 1787 the manorial rights were sold to the Duke of Devonshire. While it was a royal forest it was the resort of outlaws (p. 99), and the scene of frequent Scottish raids upon the villages within it; forts and earthworks like those at Castlehill (Castle Sowerby) and Knights' Hill (Southernby) are said to have been retreats during invasion.

INGS A hamlet 2 m. E. of Windermere station. The church, with marble floor, was the gift, about 1740, of Richard Bateman, the Dick Whittington of Ings, who made a fortune in London with foreign trade.

IREBY A former market town 7 m. S. of Wigton. It had a market in 1237, and was an important corn-market in the seventeenth century. Market cross (restored). Old church, late Norman, 1 m. W. with medieval monuments. High Ireby and Ruthwaite are villages in the parish. Old writers mention a Roman camp here, probably meaning Old Carlisle.

IRELETH A village ½ m. E. of Askam-in-Furness, anciently Yerlythe—'lyth' meaning the long fellside reaching to Kirkby-in-Ireleth.

IRTHING A river rising in the moors N.E. of Bewcastle; running through a beautiful valley, past Gilsland and Lanercost, and joining the Eden at Warwick.

IRTHINGTON A parish on the Irthing, W. of Brampton. Norman church of St Kentigern, to S.E. of which is a mote-hill; another at Irthington Mill, ¾ m. N.E.

IRTON A parish on the Irt, a river flowing from Wastwater to Ravenglass. In the churchyard is a fine Anglian cross 10 ft. high, probably of the eighth or ninth century. The Hall is a mansion built round a pele, now a special school.

ISEL A parish on the Derwent, with church (3½ m. m. N.E. of Cockermouth) which has Norman door with rude dial; three others on the S. window of the chancel. The famous 'triskele' stone, dating from pre-Norman times, was stolen in 1986. Isel Hall and Hewthwaite Hall (see pp. 83–4).

IVEGILL A parish E. of Rose Castle (see Highhead).

JOHNBY A village 1½ m. N.N.W. of Greystoke. The Hall was built by William Musgrave about 1584, a late pele; S.W. wing added 1637; outbuildings later. Quaint inscription over the doorway.

KABER A village 3 m. N.E. of Kirkby Stephen, anciently Kabergh, sometimes Caber. For the Kaber Rigg or Kipper Rigg Plot see p. 142.

KENDAL A market town on the river Kent; Cherchebi in Domesday Book and later, Kirkby-in-Kendale. With a population of 22,000 it was the largest town, though not the county town, of the former county of Westmorland. Market charter granted in 1189; incorporated in 1575, represented in Parliament in 1832. From the thirteenth to the sixteenth centuries, Kendal was an important woollen town, manufacturing the famous 'Kendal Green' cloth; the town's motto is still 'Pannus mihi Panis'—'Wool is my Bread.' The old parish church, rebuilt in the thirteenth century, and remodelled in the sixteenth, contains a number of interesting memorials. The first castle was a motte-and-bailey

construction on the west side of the river Kent, still clearly visible; the second
was stone-built in the thirteenth century, and was the birthplace of Catherine
Parr, the most successful wife of Henry VIII (*see* p. 8). Watercrook, 1 m. S.,
was the site of the Roman fort, Alauna, occupied from the time of Agricola
until the late fourth century. The Kendal Museum in Station Road contains
local exhibits and natural history displays. The Abbot Hall Art Gallery and the
Museum of Lakeland Life and Industry are housed in one of the most splendid
of Kendal's buildings, a mansion built in 1759 by John Carr for Col. George
Wilson of Dallam Tower near Milnthorpe. The Brewery Arts Centre, located in
the former brewery, offers a programme of theatre, cinema, and art exhibitions.

KENTMERE A valley running N. from Staveley formerly containing a lake, now
drained. At Bryant's Gill the remains of an eighth-century rectangular building
have recently been excavated. The old church, 4 m. from Staveley, finely placed
on a hill, and surrounded by mountains, contains a memorial to Bernard Gilpin,
the Apostle of the North, born 1517 at the Hall close by, which has a ruined
pele of the fifteenth century. Thence a path goes over Garburn (*which see*) to
Troutbeck. Three m. up the valley, under Ill Bell (2,476 ft.), is Kentmere
reservoir, an artificial lake finely surrounded with crags, from which a steep
path leads over Nan Bield Pass (2,100 ft.) to Mardale. The river Kent, rising in
the head of this valley, passes Staveley, receives the Sprint from Long Sleddale
at Burneside, and the Mint at Kendal, then turns S., and after a rapid and fall
in Levens Park, passing under Levens Bridge, widens into a sandy estuary,
which meets Morecambe Bay at Arnside.

KEPPEL COVE A combe, N. of Catstycam with a tarn.

KESKADALE, C. *See* Cascadale.

KESWICK An ancient market town and former centre of the woollen and mining
industries; now a great tourist resort. For history of the neighbourhood *see*
pp. 108–10 and for description, *see* Bassenthwaite, Derwentwater, Skiddaw etc.
Moot Hall, 1813, on the site of an earlier building. Museum and Art Gallery,
Fitz Park, has manuscripts by Wordsworth, Southey, Coleridge, Ruskin and
Hugh Walpole. Some items once owned by that remarkable eccentric, Peter
Crosthwaite (*see* p. 116). Half a m. from the town centre is Crosthwaite (the old
parish) church, supposed to be on the spot where St Kentigern (*d.* about
603) set up a preaching cross; the twelfth-century church was replaced by a
fourteenth-century building, enlarged about 1554, restored 1845. The E.
window is relatively modern, 'consecration crosses' on the left hand of several
windows, outside and inside; some ancient glass, probably from about 1523,
with figure of St Anthony. Font, late fourteenth century with inscriptions
interpreted by Sir A. W. Franks as referring to the shields (*scuta*) with emblems
of the Trinity, the Mother of God, the King of England, and the Lord Christ;

also 'Pray for the soul of Sir Thomas d'Eskhede, late vicar of this church' (*d.* 1390).

Brass of Sir John Ratcliffe and his wife, Alice Sutton of Dudley, 1527. The lady lived 27 years after this date, and left money for the enlargement of the church. In the S.E. corner of the church are effigies of a fifteenth-century civilian and lady, unknown, each holding a heart. Southey's monument, with inscription by Wordsworth. In the churchyard, N.W. of the tower, is Southey's grave; also the graves of Jonathan Otley, the geologist and guide-book writer and Peter Crosthwaite, 'guide, geographer and hydrographer to the nobility and gentry.' Sadly, his tomb was destroyed recently by a falling tree. The modern church gates incorporate symbols associated with St Kentigern (or Mungo)—a tree, a fish, a bird and a bell—all of which are found on the arms of the City of Glasgow. Kentigern is the city's patron saint.

N. of Keswick, under Skiddaw, are Ormathwaite, once the home of Dr Brownrigg, F.R.S., the chemist (p. 116), Applethwaite (*which see*), and Millbeck Hall, a fifteenth-century pele with sixteenth-century additions. A mile and a half E. of Keswick is the Castelrigg Stone Circle, a ring of 38 stones, the largest over 7 ft. high, with an enclosure on the E. side. The circle, sometimes called the Carles, is the second largest in Cumbria after Long Meg. Greta Hall, the home of the Coleridge and Southey families, is now part of Keswick School. It is not open to the public.

KIDSTY PIKE A summit (2,560 ft.) N. of High Street (p. 20).

KIRKANDREWS-ON-EDEN A village near the mouth of the Eden, of which the parish church was ruined before 1703; the churchyard is on the site of a Roman mile-castle on the Wall. At Kirksteads (1 m. S.) Roman remains have been found.

KIRKANDREWS-ON-ESK A border parish on the Esk and Liddel. The church was rebuilt 1776. Kirkandrews Tower is a pele built by the Graham family in the first half of the sixteenth century.

KIRKBAMPTON A village 2 m. S.W. of Burgh. Norman church with rude tympanum with carving of an abbot, or bishop, over the door, and capitals to chancel-arch: Roman inscribed stone built into S. side of chancel; cross-broaching on stones in the wall. Medieval grave-slab in the churchyard. Oughterby and Little Bampton are villages in the parish.

KIRKBRIDE A village at the mouth of the Wampool. British, Roman, and Anglo-Saxon remains have been found on the site of the church of St Bridget, whence the name 'Kirk-brydoch,' i.e. the Irish for 'little, dear Bridget.'

KIRKBY-IN-FURNESS A scattered village; church, with Norman door, ancient font, and curious effigy. The Kirk, 1 m. up Brooms Gill, is a ring embankment

at which games used to be held at Easter (compare Arthur's Round Table), and
$\frac{1}{4}$ m. N. is a tumulus in which an interment was found.

Cross House, or Kirkby Hall, is the early sixteenth-century manor-house of
the Kirkbys, with wall paintings in the loft, formerly a chapel. Great slate
quarries in the hillside above.

KIRKBY LONSDALE 'Church-farm or town in the dale of Lune' (pronounced
Kirby). Received a charter for market and fair in 1227. A bridge across the
Lune existed before 1275, but the date of the famous Devil's Bridge, now closed
to traffic, is unknown though it is probably late fifteenth or early sixteenth
century. Near the vicarage is a motte and bailey. St Mary's church (restored)
has three Norman arches in the nave, with pillars inspired by Durham Cathedral;
the rest of the nave and chancel is early thirteenth century. There is some
evidence to indicate that the church was one of those destroyed by Scottish
raiders after their victory at Bannockburn in 1314. The Middleton Chantry at
the north-east corner of the church was founded in 1486 but destroyed at the
Reformation; all that remains is a stone tomb carrying a mutilated alabaster
figure and heraldic shields along its side. The church was restored in 1619;
tower rebuilt, 1704; new roof 1806; restored again in 1866. Abbot's Hall and
Deans Biggin are said to have belonged to St Mary's, York, who held the
patronage until the Dissolution. Grammar School originally founded in 1591.
One and three-quarter miles W. of the Kirkby Lonsdale church, at Hutton
Roof, is a small oval embanked prehistoric settlement.

KIRKBY STEPHEN The pre-Norman church-town or farm of some owner
Stephen; received a market charter 1351-2, formerly the centre of the knitted
stocking industry. The church of St Stephen was built 1220-30 on the site of
a Norman church, and this on the site of a previous church, as shown by the
'Bound Devil,' a tenth- or eleventh-century Jellinge-style fragment of a grave-
cross, and other early fragments in the Musgrave chapel. Most of the church
was rebuilt, fourteenth to sixteenth century, and greatly restored in the nineteenth. The Musgrave chapel S. of the choir contains (besides early fragments)
the tomb of Sir Richard Musgrave and family, about 1470, and effigy perhaps
of an earlier namesake about 1420-30, who is said to have killed the last wild
boar (p. 143). In the Wharton chapel on the other side of the choir are effigies
of Lord Wharton (d. 1568) and his wives. Modern engraved glass by John
Hutton.

KIRKBY THORE A village 4 m. N.W. of Appleby. The church, restored 1851,
has some Norman work; medieval bell, thought by some to have come from
Shap Abbey. The Rev. Thomas Machell, antiquary and chaplain to Charles II,
was rector here between 1677 and 1698. South of the church, at Burwens, the
Roman fort of Bravoniacum has yielded many remains; it probably served as a
checkpoint and depot for the lead coming from the mines at Alston. Kirkby
Thore Hall, a house formerly belonging to the Wharton family, has some

fourteenth-century work, but mostly dates from the sixteenth century.

KIRKCAMBECK A decayed market town, charter 1251, of which the church was ruined by the Scots in the time of Edward II, now restored: 6 m. N. of Brampton.

KIRK FELL The W. buttress of Great Gable, overlooking Wasdale Head and Black Sail.

KIRKLAND A village on the W. slope of Cross Fell, past which the Maiden Way runs over the Pennines to Alston. Church of St Lawrence rebuilt 1768 (Pevsner suggests 1880); thirteenth-century effigy, said to be of a le Fleming; piscina and churchyard cross; medieval bell. The so-called 'Hanging Walls of Mark (or St) Anthony,' otherwise Barons or Borrans Hill, $\frac{1}{4}$ m. S.E. of the church; a series of cultivation terraces, the name of St Anthony suggesting a hermitage.

KIRKLINTON A parish 4 m. S.E. of Longtown, anciently the kirk of the barony of Levington. Ruins of a castle of the Boyvills. Church, built 1845, contains ancient piscina, Roman stones, and a rebuilt Norman chancel arch.

KIRKOSWALD A decayed market town in the Eden valley, charter 1201. Church of St Oswald with Norman nave; effigy of a lady, fourteenth century; alabaster tablet of the Bertram family with figures and inscription early seventeenth century, and other monuments. Medieval grave-slabs in the churchyard, and early cross-head, etc., built into the wall behind the W. end of the church. The bell tower on the hill above was built time of Henry VIII, rebuilt in the late nineteenth century; one of the bells dates 1619, the other two 1729. The 'College,' to the left of the road opposite church gate, was, before the dissolution, the residence of a collegiate body attached to the church; subsequently the seat of the Dacres and since of the Featherstonehaughs. Ruins of the castle are S.E. of the town, on a site occupied by the Engaynes and de Morvilles in the twelfth and thirteenth centuries; but the earliest part of the existing buildings is the work of the Multons under Edward II, enlarged and moated by Thomas, Lord Dacre, in 1500 (see p. 103). The castle was dismantled 1604–24 and soon became a ruin. Two towers on the S. and the staircase tower on the N. remain, with foundations of the great hall which Sandford described as 100 ft. long, with portraits of all the kings of England. Many of the contents were taken to Naworth, where they perished in the fire of 1844; some of the glass went to Corby Castle and to Wetheral church; some furniture went to Lowther. At Old Parks ($1\frac{1}{2}$ m. S.E.) a Bronze Age tumulus was found in 1892–4 to contain an urn, two incense cups (one with cannel beads), thirty-two interments, and flagstones with incised spirals and other patterns. The Beacon hill above was site of a beacon.

KIRKSANTON A village near Millom in the township of Chapel Sucken. The name is popularly connected with a belief that a church is 'sunken' in a little peaty tarn, now drained; similar beliefs exist about Old Brampton, Urswick,

Semerwater (Yorks), etc. It is probably derived from the Old Norse *sókn* meaning a district. The name in Domesday Book appears to have been San-tacherche; perhaps Kirk of St Sanctan, as in the Isle of Man. At the farm of Standing Stones are the remains of a megalithic monument, two stones, 15 ft. apart, 8 and 10 ft. high, with a cup-marking on the larger. *See also* Lacra.

KIRKSTONE PASS The road from Ambleside, joining that from Windermere by Troutbeck, rising to 1,476 ft. above sea at the Travellers' Rest Inn, third highest inn in England (3 m. from Ambleside, 7 from Windermere), and to 1,481 ft. at the summit of the pass; beyond which is the rock called the Kirkstone, appearing more like a church from the N. side. Two m. down the pass is Brothers Water Hotel, with Hartsop Hall and Dovedale to W. The tarn of Brothers Water lies beyond the inn; the valley to E. leads to Hayeswater, to W. is Deepdale. Patterdale village is 2 m. farther.

KNOCK Anciently Knock Salcock; a village 2 m. N.N.E. of Long Marton, under Knock Pike.

KNOCKMURTON A hill (1,476 ft.) S.E. of Murton in Lamplugh, N. of Ennerdale water-foot.

KNOCK'S CROSS An ancient cross ('As old as Knock's cross,' proverb), now gone, on a mound between Glasson and Bowness-on-Solway.

LACRA A farm on the hill between Millom and Silecroft, sometimes written Lowcrow, with prehistoric remains—the Old Kirk, a heap of ruins from which the megaliths are gone, an ancient dyke and terraces, and two stone circles. *See* Kirksanton.

LAMMERSIDE CASTLE A ruin 1 m. S. of Wharton Hall (*which see*) about which almost nothing is known; it is supposed to have been a castle of the Whartons. On the hill near are cultivation terraces.

LAMPLUGH A village 2 m. E. of the southern end of the Marron Valley. Gateway S.E. of church, arms, and date, 1595; the pele of the Lamplughs is destroyed, as is the ancient cross. Kirkland, Murton, Winder, and Rowrah are villages in the Lamplugh parish.

LANERCOST A parish with church N.E. of Brampton (for the Priory church, *see* pp. 101–3).

LANGDALE A little valley, tributary to the upper Lune, E. of Tebay.

LANGDALES The valleys of the Brathay and its tributary, Langdale Beck; the upper reach of the Brathay forms Little Langdale, the Langdale Beck runs through Great Langdale. In the lower reach of the river are Clappersgate, Brathay, and Skelwith (*which see*). Elterwater is at the junction of the two upper valleys.

In Great Langdale, above Elterwater (*which see*) and the village of the same name is Chapel Stile, at the narrow gate of the valley, where the mountain sides begin to rise high on either hand above the flat valley floor.

Paths lead up the hill to Dungeon Gill Force, a fall of 60 ft. in a chasm on the side of the Langdale Pikes. Hence a track leads up to Stickle Tarn (1,540 ft.) under the precipice of Pavey Ark, to S. of which are Harrison Stickle (2,401 ft.) and Pike of Stickle (2,323 ft.) with bold rocky fronts overlooking the valley. Opposite and across the valley is Lingmoor, a large mountain mass (p. 26), with the sharp spur of Side Pike (1,187 ft.) to W. of which a road crosses from the Old Hotel to Blea Tarn and Little Langdale.

The main valley splits into Mickleden (Icelandic *Mikill* = large) and Oxendale, the former leading N. past remains of primitive dwellings or possible shielings and an ancient bloomery (iron-smelting place). A path to N. zigzags up to the Stake Pass (1,576 ft.) and over into Langstrath and Borrowdale; to the W. a path goes up Rossett Gill to Angle Tarn (1,553 ft.) under Hanging Knott, the N. end of Bowfell (*which see*), and by Esk Hause to Scafell Pikes and Styhead (*which see*). Oxendale is a deep valley under Bowfell and the Crinkle Crags with Hell Gill (waterfall) to right, Crinkle Gill in front, and Brownie Gill to left, leading up to Red Tarn between Pike of Blisco (2,304 ft.) and Cold Pike (2,250 ft.) over Wrynose. In 1947 a Neolithic stone axe factory was identified on the slopes of Pike of Stickle. Using the fine-grained volcanic rock, axes were roughed out here and then transported to the coast for finishing and polishing. The factory seems to have been at its most productive during the period 2730 to 2500 B.C. Since the original discovery, other sites on mountains such as Glaramara, Harrison Stickle and near the summit of Scafell Pike have been identified. Axes from these sites have found their way to the Isle of Man, S.W. Scotland, the Lothians, Yorkshire, and the chalklands of S. England. Many of the farms in Great Langdale were donated to the National Trust by the late historian Dr G. M. Trevelyan.

Little Langdale begins at Colwith, 4 m. from Ambleside; waterfall (60 ft.); to left at the foot of the tarn is Slater's Bridge, a fine example of the ancient bridges of the pack-horse roads. Hence a cart-road leads by the S. side of the tarn (340 ft. above sea, about $\frac{1}{4}$ m. long) to rejoin the main road N. of the valley at Fell Foot and the terraced 'thingmount' (p. 27). Here three roads meet: to N. by Blea Tarn Pass to Dungeon Gill; to S. by Tilberthwaite a rough cart-road leads to Coniston; and to W. the ascent commences towards Wrynose Pass, where formerly the three Lake counties met at the Three Shires Stone (1,270 ft.) and to Cockley Beck, $4\frac{1}{2}$ m. by a steep road from Fell Foot. Traces of the Roman road which ran from Galava, the fort at the head of Windermere, to Hardknott and Ravenglass, may be traced on the fellside above the modern road. S. from the top of Wrynose Pass an easy though rugged climb can be taken up Wetside

Edge to the grassy ridge of the Carrs (2,525 ft.) and Coniston Old Man; N. from Wrynose, by the Red Tarn is the Pike of Blisco (2,304 ft.), a good point for view of Crinkle Crags, Bowfell, and the Pikes, and keeping up the ridge to left the Crinkle Crags and Bowfell can be ascended.

LANGSTRATH The wild valley entered 1 m. S.E. of Stonethwaite-in-Borrowdale, and going up between Glaramara and the *massif* of Langdale Pikes to Angle Tarn. Bridle-paths on both sides, and foot-bridges for about half the distance, where the path to the Stake Pass branches off to S. The long-distance footpath, the Cumbria Way, follows the valley. No house between Stonethwaite and Dungeon Gill, 7 m., or about 3 hours.

LANGWATHBY A village 5 m. N.E. of Penrith, anciently Lang-Waltheof's-by, often called Lananby. The church, rebuilt 1718 and since restored, has some earlier work in the tower, old muniment chests, and early sixteenth-century bell. The fine old seventeenth-century bridge over the Eden was destroyed in a flood in 1968.

LATRIGG The southern buttress of the Skiddaw group; from its summit (1,203 ft.) is a fine view of Derwentwater.

LAUNCHY GILL On Deergarth Gill, a rocky gully between Bull Crag and Fisher Crag, S.W. side of Thirlmere, with fine waterfalls. The Cop Stone is on the S. side, about half-way up (*see* p. 122). Nature Trail.

LAZONBY A village on the Eden, church of St Nicholas, restored; many carvings by Canon Wilson, a former vicar; churchyard cross. On the fell, 3 m. N.W. at Castlerigg, is the site of a moated ruin, 1 m. S. of which are two earthworks. Leysing, who gave the name to the place, lived about 1116.

LEGBERTHWAITE A scattered village in the valley of Helvellyn Gill, N. E. of Thirlmere.

LEITH A river flowing N. from Shap, turning E. at Melkinthorpe, and joining the Eden at Temple Sowerby.

LEVEN The river draining Windermere (p. 16). Beck Leven is the name of a stream S. of Brantwood, running into Coniston Lake.

LEVENS HALL One of the finest Elizabethan houses in Cumbria. Built around a pele tower. Remarkable plaster work and splendid topiary gardens (*see* p. 8). Open to the public. Nether Levens, W. of the Hall, is largely early sixteenth century with a N. wing added in 1594. Solidly-built cylindrical chimney stacks.

LEVERS WATER A tarn (1,350 ft. above sea) under rugged crags in the Coniston fells above the copper-mines. High up, under Great How Crags, is a fine example of a Goose Bield fox trap, a bell-shaped corbelled dry-stone wall structure which was baited with a dead goose.

LIDDEL STRENGTH Or the Moat; earthworks of a Norman castle (p. 106) near Kirkandrews-on-Esk.

LINGMELL A mountain (2,649 ft.) forming the N.W. buttress of the Scafell group with Lingmell Gill to the S., Piers Gill to the E., and Lingmell Beck to the N. Good point of view for the cliffs of Scafell.

LINGMOOR A mountain (1,500 ft.) between Great and Little Langdale (p. 23).

LINDALE In Cartmel, a village 2 m. N. of Grange-over-Sands; Castlehead (p. 40) is $\frac{1}{2}$ m. S.E. At Buck Crag, Edmund Law, Bishop of Carlisle, was born 1703. Monument to John Wilkinson, Ironmaster (p. 40).

LINDAL-IN-FURNESS A former mining village between Ulverston and Dalton, built around a green which was formerly a tarn.

LINE A river rising N. of Bewcastle and passing Kirklinton to join the Esk near its mouth.

LINSTOCK A village $2\frac{1}{2}$ m. N.E. of Carlisle. The castle, of which tower and moat remain, was an ancient seat of the bishops of Carlisle; Edward I stayed here in 1307. Drawdykes Castle, on the Roman Vallum, was rebuilt around a pele tower by the Aglionbys in 1676.

LIZA A river running from the Great Gable into Ennerdale Water (pronounced Leesa) with remarkable glacial moraines in the upper part of its valley, where it is crossed by Black Sail and Scarth Gap path.

LODORE FALL A waterfall S.E. of Derwentwater, formed by the beck from Watendlath Tarn, falling beneath Gowder and Shepherd's Crags in broken cascades for about 100 ft. The name was formerly Lowdore or Low-door, 'door' meaning a gap or cleft; but seems to be fixed as Lodore by Southey's celebrated poem.

LONG MARTON A village 2 m. N. of Appleby. Norman church with curious tympana (p. 138).

LONG MEG AND HER DAUGHTERS The greatest standing stone and circle in the Lake counties, 1 m. N.E. of Little Salkeld. The sixty-five 'daughters' are set in an ellipse formed of two semicircles with 300 ft. span, having their centres 60 ft. apart on a common axis 360 ft. in length, E. and W. Long Meg stands apart to the S.W., 12 ft. high; on the side towards the circle are concentric circles and other figures rudely incised. *See also* Maughanby.

LONG SLEDDALE The valley of the Sprint which joins the Kent at Burneside, from which Garnett Bridge, at the gate of the valley, is 3 m. N. and 3½ m. beyond is the church, built 1712. Skeggles Water is a tarn on the moor 1¼ m. W.N.W. of the church. From the church 2 m. N. is Sadgill, the highest farm; hence a track leads in 2½ m. W. to Kentmere, and a rough path in 2 m. N. to Gatesgarth (1,950 ft.), the pass into Mardale and Haweswater (about 2 hours from Sadgill). Fine crag scenery on the N. side of the pass. Under Whiteside Pike, about ½ m. N. of Murthwaite (1¼ m. above Garnett Bridge) there is a prehistoric settlement. Yewbarrow Hall is a small pele tower with tunnel-vaulted ground floor.

LONGTOWN A market town, the last in England on the A7 road, which sprang up in the eighteenth century. Good centre for visiting Arthuret, Liddel Strength, etc., and Sollom or Solway Moss, where the Scots were defeated 1543.

LORTON A chapelry in the valley of the Cocker; church of St Cuthbert, 4 m. S.E. of Cockermouth: famous old yew mentioned by Wordsworth in his poem *Yew Trees*. Hence the fine pass of Whinlatter leads to Keswick, 9 m., and road S. to Scale Hill, 3 m., Loweswater and Crummock. Lorton Hall, pele tower with seventeenth-century neo-classical façade.

LOUGHRIGG A mountain (1,101 ft.) between Ambleside and Grasmere, 'the ridge of the lough' or tarn on the Skelwith side (*see* Ambleside).

LOWESWATER A lake 1 m. long, ¼ m. broad, 429 ft. above sea, and 60 ft. deep, with trout, pike, and perch. Owned by N.T. The village of the same name is on the Park Beck which drains the lake into Crummock Water.

LOWTHER The castle, former seat of the Earl of Lonsdale, was designed by Sir Robert Smirke on the site of a thirteenth-century hall which was destroyed by fire in 1720. It was completed about 1811. Most of the castle is now merely a shell, the interior having been demolished in 1957. The church of St Michael, restored 1856–7, contains monuments to the Lowther family—Sir James was created Earl of Lonsdale in 1784—and their mausoleum, built in 1857. The church also contains three Anglo-Scandinavian hogback tombstones. Lowther New Town was built by Sir John Lowther c. 1683 to replace an earlier estate village. Lowther Village, c. 1765–1773 was planned by James Adam and his brother, Robert.

Lowther Adventure Park—130 acres of parkland and adventure playground—open to the public.

LOW WATER A tarn, 1,786 ft. above sea, under the crags of Coniston Old Man. Hence a tall waterfall descends to Pudding Stone Cove (p. 48).

LUNE A river rising in St Helen's Well, Newbiggin, Ravenstonedale (so it is locally said), and flowing W. to Tebay; thence S. through a deep valley past the Roman camp at Borrowbridge to Lowgill, below which is the Crook of Lune; thence through a more open valley by Sedbergh to Kirkby Lonsdale; ¼ m. below the Devil's Bridge it passes into Lancashire; thence through undulating country to Lancaster and the sea. The chief tributaries of the upper reach are the Bowderdale and Langdale Becks to S.; the Raisbeck and Birkbeck (from Wasdale to the N.; the Borrow Beck enters at Low Borrowbridge, the Rawthey and Dee (united) at Sedbergh.

LUPTON Lupetun in Domesday, a village 3 m. N.W. of Kirkby Lonsdale.

LYTH VALLEY Old Norse *hlidh* = slope. A valley in the S.E. Lake District between the limestone scars of Whitbarrow and Underbarrow, famous for its damsons and in spring, its blossom.

LYULPH'S TOWER *See* Aira Force, Greystoke.

MAIDEN CASTLE The name of several ancient forts; one on Burnmoor, one on Stainmoor, one (Caerthanoc) on Soulby Fell, N.W. of Pooley Bridge.

MAIDEN HOLD A name of the Roman camp at Redlands, near Kirkby Thore.

MAIDEN MOOR The name of a ridge of hills (1,887 ft.) between Borrowdale and Newlands.

MAIDEN WAY The Roman road from Carvoran on the Wall past Whitley Castle (camp) near Alston, over the Pennines (2,000 ft. at the pass) to Kirkland and Kirkby Thore, where it crosses the Carlisle–Stainmoor Roman road. Thence past Crosby Ravensworth (*which see*) into the Lune Valley at Tebay, with Borrowbridge camp and crossing the river continuing down the E. bank to Overburrow (*see* Casterton). The meaning of the name 'Maiden' is not agreed upon.

MALLERSTANG The highest part of the valley of the Eden, running S. from Kirkby Stephen. *See* Pendragon (pp. 144–6). The ancient church was repaired (1663) by the Countess of Pembroke, Lady Anne Clifford.

MANSERGH Manzserge in Domesday; 2 m. N. of Kirkby Lonsdale.

MARDALE The valley at the head of Haweswater Reservoir, running up to Blea Water (1,584 ft. above sea) under High Street (2,663 ft.) and to Small Water (1,484 ft.) on the Nan Bield Pass. The hamlet of Mardale was destroyed when the reservoir was created. *See* p. 135.

MARTINDALE A parish on the east side of Ullswater, said to be the smallest independent parish in the Church of England. Contains two churches, St Peter's, at the top of the pass between Howtown and Martindale, was built in 1880; St Martin's in Howe Grain (Icelandic, *grein* = branch) was built in 1633 on ancient foundations. Higher up, this valley forks into Bannerdale and Rampsgill, divided by the Nab (1,887 ft.); lower down it joins Boardale to form Sandwich Beck which flows into Ullswater; to the W. is the little valley of Scalehow Beck and to the E., on the far side of Hallin Fell (1,271 ft.), is Fusedale. Martindale Common has a protected herd of red deer.

MARYPORT A small industrial town on the W. coast; the original name was Ellenfoot but it was renamed after the wife of Humphrey Senhouse who developed the town in 1749. During the eighteenth and nineteenth centuries, prosperity was built on coal mining and ship building but the 1930s depression was severe. The harbour was closed to shipping in 1961 but the maritime tradition survives in the recently developed Maritime Museum. The Roman fort, Alauna, north of the Ellen, was first excavated in 1766 and more recently in the 1960s by the Cumberland and Westmorland Antiquarian and Archaeological Society. The fort seems to have been occupied in the fifth century and it has yielded a Chi-Rho inscription, indicating the presence of Christians. At nearby Netherhall there is a very fine collection of altars from the fort; it is hoped that these will soon be displayed in a new museum. At the S. end of the town rises a conspicuous motte, the eleventh- or twelfth-century castle, of which there is no known history, but it is probably the original Alneburg or fortress on the river Ellen. The railway to Carlisle was completed in 1845; in 1846 a cast-iron lighthouse was built; in 1853 and onwards the new docks were constructed. The church of St Mary, a chapel of ease under Crosscanonby, was built in 1760.

MATTERDALE The valley of the Troutbeck with Mell Fell (1,760 ft.) on the E., and Flaska Moor rising to 1,216 ft. on the W. The church was licensed in 1573, rebuilt 1685 and restored about 1846. Troutbeck, Wallthwaite, Matterdale End, Dockray (inn), and Dowthwaite are villages in this parish. *See also* Lyulph's Tower.

MAUGHANBY A hamlet (pronounced Maffanby) $\frac{1}{2}$ m. N. of Long Meg, and between Glassonby and Little Salkeld. Small circle of great stones one of which has concentric and spiral markings. An interment was found in the circle.

MAYBURGH A great circular rampart of stones $\frac{1}{2}$ m. S.W. of Eamont Bridge. It is 383 ft. diameter from crest to crest, with opening to E., and a standing stone, 9 ft. 2 in. high, nearly in the centre. The ruins of wall on the crest are modern. A bronze celt and a stone celt have been found, but no interment (*see* p. 129).

MEABURN Mauld's Meaburn, 1 m. N. of Crosby Ravensworth, is named from Matilda de Morville, the heiress of the manor, who married William de Veteripont. Elizabethan hall, S. wing dated 1610. King's Meaburn, 2 m. S.W. of Morland, was the other half of the manor taken by the king when Sir Hugh de Morville's estates were confiscated.

MEASAND Beck (with waterfall) on the N. side of Haweswater.

MELLBREAK The mountain (1,668 ft.) W. of Crummock.

MELL FELL The isolated mountain (1,760 ft.) of red conglomerate—the lowest beds of the Carboniferous formation—rising E. of Matterdale. Little Mell Fell, rising 1½ m. E.S.E., has a ring embankment on the top.

MELMERBY A village 4 m. N.E. of Langwathby. Old church of St John Baptist, with three-decker pulpit and gallery, medieval cross-slab and piscina but restored and altered in the nineteenth century. The name is said to be from 'Melmor, a Dane,' i.e. Maelmor, a Viking-Irish name. Many of the trees in the village have been planted as windbreaks against the fierce Helm Wind.

MICKLEDEN *See* Langdale.

MICKLEDORE *See* p. 62.

MIDDLETON A chapelry in the Lune valley. The Hall is a fifteenth-century manor-house, fortified, but with no pele tower, and containing Elizabethan woodwork. Near it is a Roman milestone found on the Maiden Way, and re-erected 1836.

MILBURN A village set around a rectangular green, 3 m. N.E. of Temple Sowerby (see p. 138). The church has a late Norman doorway with two rude dials; brass of Anne Sandford, 1605; effigy unknown; on the green is a maypole set in the base of an ancient cross. *See also* Howgill Castle.

MILLOM A nineteenth-century iron town on the shores of the Duddon estuary. The Earl of Lonsdale began limited iron mining operations at Hodbarrow about 1845 and by 1856 the first major deposit of haematite ore was being exploited; twelve years later it became apparent that there was a large body of ore under the Duddon estuary and two sea walls, the Inner Barrier (1888–90) and the Outer Barrier (1900–05) were built to exclude the sea and allow the extraction of the largest haematite deposit in England. Meanwhile, the furnaces of the Millom Ironworks Company had been 'blown in' in 1867; prosperity seemed assured but the dream turned sour. The output of ore declined and in the late 1960s both the mines and the furnaces were closed. (*See* p. 50.) The Millom Folk Museum has a full-scale reconstruction of a drift mine at Hodbarrow. The thirteenth-century castle north of the town was mostly rebuilt after the Scottish invasion of 1322; licence to 'crenellate' was given to Sir John Hudleston in

1335. The tower is late sixteenth century. In 1644 it withstood a siege by
Parliamentarians and afterwards gradually became ruinous. Adjacent Holy
Trinity church is late Norman with additions in the thirteenth and fourteenth
centuries. Alabaster effigies of Sir John Hudleston (*d.* 1494) and his wife. Near
the castle and the church is Gallows Hill where the Lords of Millom dispensed
justice.

MILNTHORPE A market town from the thirteenth century. Close to the Kent
estuary, it was once Westmorland's only port. In the eighteenth century it
imported sulphur and saltpetre for the gunpowder works of S. Lake District
and exported the powder to Liverpool. Eighteenth-century market cross. Nearby
Dallam Tower, built 1720–1722, is not open to the public but can be seen from
the road to Arnside. Herd of fallow deer in the park. The Heron Corn Mill is
a restored watermill demonstrating the technique of flour milling.

MIREHOUSE Late Georgian house on the E. side of Bassenthwaite Lake. The
home of the Spedding family. While staying here, Tennyson drew much of his
inspiration for 'Morte D'Arthur' from the surrounding countryside. House,
grounds, nature trail and woodland walks open to the public.

MITERDALE Valley of the Mite, which rises in Burnmoor, and runs between the
Wastwater Screes and Eskdale, falling into the sea at Ravenglass.

MOCKERKIN A village and tarn about 6 m. S.W. of Cockermouth.

MORESBY (pronounced Morrisby) Originally Maurice-by from a twelfth-century
owner. St Bridget's church, 1822–3, is built on the site of an earlier church in
the corner of the Hadrianic Roman fort, Tunnocelum. Moresby Hall, the seat
of the Fletchers, is a pele tower heavily disguised by a splendid rusticated
façade, 1690–1700. The Sir Nicholas Sekers Theatre at Rosehill, built in 1959,
attracts national and international artists and musicians.

MORLAND A parish 5 m. W. of Appleby. St Laurence's church, though altered,
has the only Anglo-Saxon tower in Cumbria; the two lower storeys date from
the eleventh century, the upper from the sixteenth and seventeenth centuries.

MOSEDALE A village running S. from Loweswater village to Floutern. Also a
little valley between Hardknott and Crinkle Crags, running down to Cockley
Beck, and a valley running N.W. from Wasdale Head.

MOSSER A village in the chapelry of Lorton, anciently Mosergh, i.e., the shieling
or dairy farm on the moss. Before the dissolution there was a chantry here.

MUNCASTER Formerly Mulcastre, i.e. the castle on the Meols or Sandhills,
perhaps meaning the Roman fort at Ravenglass (p. 55). In the churchyard is an

Anglo-Norse cross; picturesque site. The castle was the seat of the Penningtons from the thirteenth century. The building is chiefly nineteenth century with a fourteenth-century pele tower; it contains many old pictures and relics, among which is 'The Luck of Muncaster' (p. 55). House and gardens open to the public.

MUNGRISDALE A village E. of Saddleback, formerly Mungo-Grisdale, i.e. Swine-dale of St Mungo's church.

MUSGRAVE Great Musgrave, 2 m. S.W. of Brough, is a village with nineteenth-century church of St Theobald's. Little Musgrave is a village in Crosby Garrett parish. *See* Brough, Kaber.

NADDALE The valley of Naddale Beck, which rises near Shoulthwaite Castle (*which see*) between the Benn and High Seat (1,996 ft.), and falls into the Greta near Castlerigg Circle (*see* Keswick). Pronounced and often written Naddle.

NADDALE A little valley S. of Haweswater. Naddale Forest is between this valley and the lake.

NAN BIELD PASS *See* Kentmere.

NATEBY A hamlet in a deep valley, 1 m. S.E. of Kirkby Stephen, near Stenkrith Bridge. Hence a steep road goes over the fell E. past the Nine Standards to Swaledale in Yorkshire.

NATLAND A chapelry S. of Kendal, in which is the Roman camp of Watercrook, and Helmfell with a small oval hill fort.

NAWORTH CASTLE The seat of the Earl of Carlisle. (*see* p. 103). Partly open to visitors.The oldest part of the castle is the early fourteenth-century Dacre Tower, the pele tower. A fire in 1844 destroyed part of the castle but it was faithfully restored by Salvin.

NENTHEAD *See* Alston.

NETHER WASDALE A chapelry at the foot of Wastwater with old church (4 m. E. of Gosforth), containing oak carving from York Minster at the E. end. Wasdale Hall, an early nineteenth-century mansion finely situated on the lake facing the Screes, now a Youth Hostel.

NETHERBY The seat of Sir Fergus Graham, on the E. bank of Esk, built round a pele, on the site of a Roman camp (p. 107).

NEWBIGGIN A village in the parish of Dacre with limestone quarries. In Silver

Field, S.W. of the village, the famous Fluskew (or Flusco) penannular 'thistle' brooch was found. *See* Dacre.

NEWBIGGIN-ON-LUNE Near Ravenstonedale. Site of priory of the Sempringham order of monks; foundations of a chapel at St Helen's Well. At Capelrigg are cultivation terraces, 'crosswise ploughing.' On the fell are ancient enclosures and foundations known as Severals.

NEWBY BRIDGE The bridge at the foot of Windermere. From here the Leven flows in rocky rapids through Backbarrow (*which see*) and a wooded valley 2 m. to Haverthwaite. One m. N. is the Stott Park Bobbin Mill, a museum of woodland industries. The Lakeside and Haverthwaite Railway operates steam trains in summer from Haverthwaite to connect with the passenger ships of the Windermere Iron Steam Boat Company. *See also* Haverthwaite, Finsthwaite.

NEWLANDS A township in the valley W. of Derwentwater, running S. from Braithwaite. The church, rebuilt 1843, is at the point where the valley forks, half-way along its length; the S. branch going up to Dalehead Fell (2,473 ft). In this branch is the Goldscope lead mine, worked with great profit in the earlier part of the nineteenth century; in the time of Elizabeth the German Company of the Mines Royal (pp. 114–15) exploited the Newlands workings. From the church Keskadale runs S.W. to Buttermere Hause. At Stair were woollen mills.

NEWTON ARLOSH A village between Abbey Town and Kirkbride. The settlement was founded in 1305 by Holm Cultram Abbey after Skinburness, a market town, had been destroyed by the sea in 1301. It is said on doubtful authority that St Ninian built a church here about A.D. 400. The existing church was built by Holm Cultram Abbey in or soon after 1305, with pele tower to serve as a refuge. In 1580 it was decayed, and so remained until it was restored in 1844.

NEWTON-IN-CARTMEL A village in pretty scenery between Cartmel and Cartmel Fell.

NEWTON REIGNY A village 1½ m. N.E. of Blencow. Old church of the twelfth and thirteenth centuries, restored, with vault of the Vaux family of Catterlen, tombs of the Richmonds; rhymed epitaph of James Pearson, 1676. East of the church is a large oval 'camp'; ½ m. S. near Sewborrens are tumuli in which burial urns have been found. *See also* Catterlen. Nearby is Newton Rigg, Cumbria's College of Agriculture and Forestry.

NIBTHWAITE A hamlet on the E. side of Coniston Waterfoot. At Low Nibthwaite is the site of a great eighteenth-century bloomery or charcoal furnace for iron.

NICHOL FOREST A chapelry, including Kingfield, Catlowdy, and Scuggate on the Liddel; formerly a wild district named from its owner, Nicholas de Stuteville, in the reign of King John.

NUNNERY Site of a convent, founded at Armathwaite before 1200 and removed to Staffield on the ravine of the Croglin near its junction with the Eden. The nunnery was suppressed 1536, and the house rebuilt by the Aglionbys in 1715, now a guesthouse. Nunnery Walks, two miles of wooded paths through the sandstone gorge of the Croglin.

OLD CARLISLE A farm 1½ m. S. of Wigton, near which was great Roman fort in a loop of the Wiza Beck; many altars, inscriptions, etc., have been found here. A civil settlement lay to the N.E. and S.E.

ORMSIDE (or Ormshed) A village 2 miles S.E. of Appleby. The church has an early Norman arch in the N. wall of the chancel; late Norman chancel arches; the rest was rebuilt seventeenth century, and restored 1885–6; two ancient bells, several medieval grave-slabs; three Hilton brasses of the seventeenth century. In the churchyard was found in 1689 a hoard of brass and pewter vessels; the famous Ormside Cup (in the Yorkshire Museum), an Anglian work of gold and enamel, was found here in 1823, described by Pevsner as 'the richest and most Carolingian piece of Anglo-Saxon metalwork.' It dates from the ninth century. Why is it in York? A sword and other relics of the Viking age were found in 1899, now in Tullie House Museum, Carlisle. The old hall was the seat of the Hiltons in the seventeenth century.

ORREST HEAD *See* p. 14.

ORTON A market town in the time of Edward I. All Saints' Church has medieval remains. The old hall (Petty Hall) is much as it was in 1604, the date over the door. Orton Hall was built by Richard Burn, LL.D. (1709–85), author of *The Justice of the Peace* and part author of Nicolson and Burn's *History of Cumberland and Westmorland* (1777). George Whitehead, one of the founders of the Society of Friends, was born in the village. For prehistoric remains near Orton, *see* Crosby Ravensworth, Raisbeck, Sunbiggin.

OUSBY A village 5 m. E. of Langwathby under Cross Fell, anciently Ulvesby (farm of Ulf). The church of St Luke has sedilia and piscina, with an effigy of a knight of the thirteenth or early fourteenth century, 7 ft. long. Unusually, it is carved in oak, one of less than a hundred such figures in England. The Maiden Way crosses Ardale Beck, 1½ m. E. of the church, running N. to Alston. Crewgarth is a five-sided 'camp,' 2 m. W.N.W. of the church, probably of post-Roman or early medieval origin, and used as a pele-garth for protecting cattle during raids.

OVERWATER A tarn 3 m. N.E. of the Castle Inn, Bassenthwaite, between Binsey

(1,466 ft.) and Great Scafell (2,329 ft.), the northern summit of the Skiddaw group. South of the tarn is a square 'camp,' probably the garth of an early medieval settler. Orthwaite (Allerthwaite) Hall has a seventeenth-century façade, and over a stage-door the arms of Richmond impaling Hudleston and 'C. R. 1675.'

OXENDALE *See* Langdale.

PAPCASTLE A village 1 m. N.W. of Cockermouth. Here was the Roman fort Derventio, now nearly obliterated by buildings and the road. Barrack blocks and commandant's bath-house excavated 1961–2. This large fort, $6\frac{3}{4}$ acres in area, seems to have housed a cavalry unit. The medieval owner, Pipard, probably gave his name to the place, but *see* p. 79*n* for an alternative derivation.

PARDSHAW A village 2 m. E.N.E. of Ullock. The White Causeway is a stony platform adjoining a raised ring of gravel and boulders, near the N. base of the Crag, where are rock terraces used by George Fox, the Quaker, as a pulpit and open-air meeting-place.

PARTON A village, anciently a port, $1\frac{1}{2}$ m. N. of Whitehaven. In 1705 Mr Fletcher, of Moresby, tried to establish a new pier, but was opposed by Sir John Lowther. In 1796 the harbour was destroyed by storm.

PATTERDALE A village in the main valley at the head of Ullswater, on the Goldrill Beck, which flows from Kirkstone through Brothers Water. At the Waterhead is the church of St Patrick, with St Patrick's Well. In the thirteenth century the name was Patricdale probably from Patric, the landowner, rather than the saint. Helvellyn can be climbed in $2\frac{1}{2}$ hours by the path up the N. slope of Grisedale, over the ridge, and thence by Striding or Swirrel Edge. Aira Force is 4 m. by road. Place Fell (2,154 ft.) may be climbed in about $1\frac{1}{2}$ hours, and St Sunday Crag (2,756 ft.) in about 2 hours. By Kirkstone to Windermere, 14 m., and to Ambleside, 10 m. by road; by Boardale Hause to Howtown is about 6 m., and by Grisedale to Grasmere, 9 m., mountain paths.

PAVEY ARK The great crag over Stickle Tarn; *see* Langdale. *Ark* is probably another form of *ergh*, i.e. shieling.

PEEL ISLAND, CONISTON WATER *See* p. 45.

PEEL WYKE The 'bay of the castle' near the foot of Bassenthwaite Lake, where are Castle How (p. 109), and Pheasant Inn.

PENDRAGON CASTLE At Castlethwaite, half-way up the valley of Mallerstang, on a hill in the middle of the valley, are the ruins of a Norman castle, burnt by the Scots, 1340, restored and then ruined in 1541, restored by the Countess of

Pembroke, 1660, and dismantled by the Earl of Thanet, 1685. Locally connected with Uther Pendragon, father of King Arthur (p. 144). In the reign of Henry II, the castle was the home of Hugh de Morville, one of the four knights who murdered Thomas Becket in 1170.

PENNINGTON A village, Pennigetun in Domesday, $1\frac{1}{2}$ m. W.S.W. of Ulverston. Close by is Ellabarrow, an artificial mound (p. 37) near which an ancient sword and stone implements were found. Prettily situated church at the west end of which is a re-set tympanum from the original church on this site. It dates from c. 1160 and bears a fragmentary runic inscription relating to Kamial or Gamel, Lord of Pennington in the twelfth century. Half m. farther up the hill behind Castle Hill farm is an ancient fort—earthen ramparts over a ravine—the early seat of the Pennington family.

PENRITH An ancient market town. Near the railway station are ruins of the castle (p. 131). Down the street from the station and to right is Dockwray with the Two Lions Inn, Gerard Lowther's house (p. 131), and the Gloucester Arms, said to be fifteenth century but the evidence suggests late sixteenth century. To the left through the market-place is the parish church of St Andrew, built 1720–22, with medieval tombs, and in the churchyard the Giant's Thumb (a pre-Norman wheel cross, upper part gone) and the Giant's Grave (a rearranged group of pre-Norman grave monuments, two crosses, and four hogbacks). Robert Bartram's house to W. of churchyard with bay window dated 1563. Christ Church was consecrated 1850. The Grammar School was refounded by Queen Elizabeth 1564, having been a medieval school attached to Bishop Strickland's chantry, 1395. Penrith Steam Musem, near the castle, consists of a collection of steam traction engines and ancient farm machinery. Penrith Beacon, above the town, once blazed out a warning of marauding Scots; it is now a local viewpoint.

PETTERILL A little river rising near Greystoke and flowing through Inglewood to join the Eden above Carlisle.

PIEL CASTLE The Pile of Foudrey at the entrance to Walney Channel. Ruins of a castle built in 1327 by Furness Abbey as a woollen warehouse and as a defence for the harbour. Lambert Simnel, the pretender to the throne, held court here in June 1487, before his defeat by Henry VII's troops at Stoke. Here, according to Gerarde's *Herball* (1597), the barnacle goose was bred from barnacles. Ferry in summer from Roa Island. The castle was given to the townspeople of Barrow by the Duke of Buccleuch as memorial to men killed in the First World War.

PIERS GILL A deep, zigzagged ravine on the N. side of Scafell Pikes (*which see*).

PIKE OF BLISCO A summit (2,304 ft.) 1 m. N. of the summit of Wrynose Pass. Good mountain panorama. Ascent by Oxendale and Browney Gill from

Dungeon Gill, or by Wrynose from Little Langdale or Cockley Beck.

PIKE OF STICKLE *See* Langdales.

PILLAR The isolated rock to N. of the Pillar Mountain, S. of Ennerdale. Scene of the death of one of 'the brothers' in Wordsworth's poem. Various routes of ascent, none easy for inexperienced climbers attempting it alone. First climbed in 1826 by John Atkinson, a local man.

PLACE FELL A mountain (2,154 ft.) E. of Patterdale, ascended via Boardale Hause.

PLUMBLAND An ancient parish with church ($1\frac{1}{2}$ m. S. of Aspatria). Norman chancel arch from 1130–40. Pre-Norman fragment on first floor of tower; Anglo-Norse hogback tombstone beneath yews in churchyard. For a story of the place, *see* p. 86.

PLUMPTON Village 5 m. N. of Penrith on the A6 road. One m. N. at Castlesteads the remains of the Roman fort Voreda can be seen on the west side of the road. Although it has yet to be fully excavated, many inscriptions have been found which indicate that the Second Cohort of Gauls was in garrison during the third century A.D.

POOLEY BRIDGE On the Eamont at foot of Ullswater. To N.W. is Dunmallet (*which see*). Near Trestermont (Crossdormont), on a green mound jutting from the S.E. shore of the lake, $1\frac{1}{4}$ m. S.W. of Pooley Bridge, traces of a motte-and-bailey; site mentioned about 1320. Moor-divock remains are mentioned on p. 129.

PORT CARLISLE In 1819–23 a canal was made from Carlisle to a harbour at Fisher's Cross, previously a hamlet with two houses and the Binnacle Inn; the canal was replaced by a railway, 1854–5, now removed. The Roman Wall from here to Bowness is about 100 yards S. of the road.

PORTINSCALE A village 1 m. W. of Keswick.

PRESTON PATRICK 4 m. S.E. of Kendal, Prestun in Domesday, afterwards owned by Patrick de Culwen, ancestor of the Curwens, who gave land here in 1119 for an abbey which was afterwards removed to Shap (*which see*). The church is rebuilt, but contains Norman or Early English grotesque fragments. Preston Old Hall is a fourteenth-century pele with upper part rebuilt and Jacobean wings added. The Gatebeck Gunpowder works, the last in Cumbria, were closed in 1937.

RAISBECK A village $1\frac{1}{2}$ m. S.E. of Orton (*which see*). At Gamelands is a circle 138 ft. in diameter, formerly having 40 stones, some now gone, others fallen; no interments found.

RAMPSIDE Village on the shores of Morecambe Bay, 3 m. S.E. of Barrow. Rampside Hall, late seventeenth-century home of the Knipe family, has twelve chimneys known locally as the Twelve Apostles. A Viking warrior complete with sword was uncovered in the graveyard of St Michael's church in 1909. Outside the village is the gas terminal for the Morecambe Bay gas field.

RANNERDALE A little valley running E. from Crummock Water, between Rannerdale Knotts (1,160 ft.) and Grasmoor (2,791 ft.). The setting for Nicholas Size's novel *The Secret Valley*.

RAUGHTON HEAD A chapelry near Rose Castle.

RAVEN CRAG Rocky heights at Thirlmere, Patterdale, and Yewdale (Coniston), S. of Red Screes, etc.

RAVENGLASS A decayed port and former market town. Junction for the Ravenglass and Eskdale Railway. The remains of the Roman fort, Glannaventa or Clannaventa, were destroyed in 1850 when the West Cumberland Railway line ran through the site. However, the bath-house, known as Walls Castle, remains (p. 54). Ravenglass Railway Museum records the history and development of the Ravenglass and Eskdale line. Across the estuary is a bird reserve with the largest colony of black headed gulls in England.

RAVENSTONEDALE A village 5 m. S.W. of Kirkby Stephen, formerly a market town, locally pronounced Russondal. Church of St Oswald rebuilt 1774, with three-decker pulpit with a seat for the parson's wife and box pewed like a college chapel; window to the memory of Elizabeth Gaunt, a native, burnt at Tyburn, 1685, for sheltering a fugitive from Monmouth's rebellion. She was the last woman in England to die for the Protestant faith. In the churchyard is a sundial on a cut-down cross-shaft. The parks were enclosed with a great wall by Lord Wharton, 1559; Gallows Hill and ancient dykes. N. of the parks, Giants' Graves, i.e. rectangular moated hillocks; not interments; possibly artificial rabbit warrens.

Farther N. on the fell at Severals and Old Biggin, are entrenchments and foundations of early dwellings. Tarn House, built 1664, 2 m. E. of the village, is the ancient seat of the Fothergills.

RED BANK The road S. of Grasmere with view over the lake, Helvellyn, etc. *See* Grasmere.

RED PIKE The summit (2,479 ft.) above Sourmilk Gill, Buttermere (p. 76). Also a summit (2,707 ft.) N.W. of Wasdale Head, under which is Scout Tarn.

RED SCREES A mountain (2,541 ft.) N.W. of Kirkstone Pass, easily ascended from the pass; good panorama of mountains and lakes.

RED TARN The tarn (2,356 ft.) between Striding Edge and Swirrel Edge under Helvellyn. Also a small pool (1,700 ft.) between Pike of Blisco and Crinkle Crags at the head of Browney Gill. Here Lanty Slee, the smuggler, had one of his many illicit whisky stills about 1860.

RENWICK A village on the slope of the Pennines, 3 m. N.E. of Kirkoswald, formerly Ravenwick. The church, rebuilt 1733 and 1845, has an ancient bell. One m. S.E. is Haresceugh Castle, held in the sixteenth century by the Dacres of Lanercost.

REVELIN A mountain S. of Ennerdale Water.

ROBINSON The highest summit (2,147 ft.) between Buttermere and Newlands.

ROCKCLIFFE (or Rocliff). Two villages at the mouth of the Eden. Rockcliffe Churchtown has a pre-Norman churchyard cross. Rockcliffe Castletown is at the site of a sixteenth-century castle of the Dacres, demolished after the rebellion of Leonard Dacre, 1569 (p. 100).

ROMAN WALL *See* pp. 90-3, 101, 105.

ROSE CASTLE The Bishop of Carlisle's residence, 7 m. S. Carlisle (p. 98).

ROSELEY A village 5 m. E.S.E. of Wigton, famous for its eighteenth- and nineteenth-century horse and cattle fairs.

ROSSETT GILL *See* Langdales.

ROSTHWAITE A village in Borrowdale, 2 m. S. of Grange, centre for excursions; *see* Borrowdale.

ROTHAY The river running from Dunmail Raise through Grasmere and Rydal Water to Windermere.

ROUDSEA WOOD A National Nature Reserve S.W. of Haverthwaite (*which see*). Animals include roe deer, red squirrel, stoat, and weasel. Access by permit only from Nature Conservancy Council in Windermere.

ROUGHTEN GILL Two valleys of this name, one between Skiddaw and Saddleback, and the other N. of the Skiddaw group; both former mining places.

RUCKCROFT A village in Ainstable parish, between the Croglin and the Eden.

RUSLAND Anciently Rolesland, a pretty dale between Windermere and Coniston lakes; two tarns on Rusland Heights to S.E., waterfalls at Force Forge (Old

Norse, *foss* = waterfall), where iron works established before 1680 once existed. Later the falls were used to operate bobbin mills. Rusland Hall, late seventeenth century, was the home of the Rawlinsons. At Black Beck near the village of Bouth, gunpowder works were established in 1862, closed 1928–9. Near the junction of the roads to Satterthwaite and Dalepark is Rook How or Abbot Oak, a Quaker meeting-house, founded 1725. Tottlebank Baptist chapel, 1669. Arthur Ransome, journalist and author, was buried at Rusland church in 1967.

RYDAL A village E. of Rydalwater, a lake $\frac{1}{2}$ m. long, $\frac{1}{4}$ m. broad, with small islets. The hall, seat of the le Fleming family since the fifteenth century and now a Church of England conference centre, is to right above church; in its grounds are the two waterfalls; the higher fall $\frac{1}{3}$ m. upstream is the greater (about 60 ft.). Rydal Mount, Wordsworth's home from 1813 to 1850, is open to the public. Nab Cottage, $\frac{1}{2}$ m. on the Grasmere road, with date 1702 over the door, was the home of Hartley Coleridge; Nab Scar is above, and Loughrigg opposite. Pelter Bridge, to right of the road from Rydal to Ambleside, leads to the Loughrigg Terrace, on the breast of the fell, with fine views over the lakes. Rydal Sheepdog trials held each August.

SADDLEBACK A mountain (2,847 ft.) anciently called Blencathara, rising with a series of bold ridges above the valley of Threlkeld; easily climbed from Threlkeld or Glenderaterra Bridge by the S.W. spur; or from Scales. Scales Tarn lies under crags, to the N. of the ridge by which the ascent is made. Scott in *The Bridal of Triermain* alludes to the story that this tarn lies in such a hollow that it reflects the stars at noon. Sharp Edge, the narrowest ridge in the Lake District, is that over Scales Tarn. *See also* Bowscale, Southerfell.

ST BEES A little seaside town 4 m. S. of Whitehaven. For some account of the Priory Church, Grammar School, etc., *see* p. 68. The Head, with red-sandstone cliffs rising over 300 ft., has a lighthouse erected 1867, showing a fixed white light. The St Bees Head Bird Reserve has several footpaths with observation points. It is a breeding ground for puffins, razorbills and fulmars.

ST BRIDGET'S, CALDERBRIDGE *See* Beckermet.

ST JOHN'S VALE The valley of the Upper Greta, or St John's Beck, between Legberthwaite and Threlkeld, between the Castle Rock (p. 121) and Wanthwaite Crags to the E., and Naddale Fell to the W. In a depression of the latter is St John's church, and farther N. Tewit Tarn. The valley is thought to have taken its name from the Knights Hospitallers of the Order of St John of Jerusalem who are believed to have had a church on the site of the present building as early as the thirteenth century.

SALKELD Great Salkeld, a village 2 m. S. of Lazonby. The fortified church of St Cuthbert (compare Newton Arlosh and Burgh-by-Sands) has an early Norman door with grotesque capitals and rude dial.

The western tower is a pele built about 1380 for defence against Scottish raids; chancel perpendicular. Effigy of Thomas de Caldbec, Archdeacon of Carlisle, died 1319; effigies of Anthony Hutton, died 1637, and his wife— removed from Penrith, perhaps in 1720 when the Penrith old church was rebuilt; and other tombs. Some armour of about 1600 is kept in the tower, the breastplate with a great cut on the left shoulder.

The church was assigned to the Archdeaconry of Carlisle from 1292 to 1855; Bishop Nicholson, when archdeacon, was rector, 1682–1702.

At Salkeld Dyke are old earthworks to defend the village. Little Salkeld is a village on the opposite bank of the Eden; nearest bridges at Lazonby and Langwathby. The watermill has been restored to working order.

SANTON BRIDGE Over the Irt, 3 m. from the foot of Wastwater, 2 m. from Irton Road station (Ravenglass and Eskdale railway).

SATTERTHWAITE A village between Grizedale and Force Forge in the Rusland Valley, Furness Fells. The name means, in Norse, 'the sæter (dairy farm) in the clearing,' appropriate since the village is in a clearing in Grizedale Forest.

SAWREY Hamlets between Esthwaite Water and Windermere. Near Sawrey, i.e. nearer to Hawkshead, and Far Sawrey, under the Claife Heights. Hill Top, at Near Sawrey, was the home of the children's writer Beatrix Potter. The National Trust has faithfully preserved the interior of the cottage which is open to the public.

SCAFELL Sometimes written Scaw-fell; a mountain (3,162 ft.) which, with the three Scafell Pikes (3,206 ft., highest point in England), Great End, and Lingmell, form a group dividing Wasdale Head from Upper Eskdale. They are of volcanic ash (Borrowdale series) formation, with a patch of granite at the foot of Lingmell. To the N., between Lingmell and Great End, is the chasm of Piers Gill, into which runs the gully of the Greta Fall; a track leads from Lingmell Beck (between the Pikes and Great Gable) by the E. bank of Piers Gill to the Pikes.

Another, marked by cairns at intervals, goes up from Esk Hause over Great End to the Pikes. From Wasdale Head there are bridges over Lingmell Beck, from which Lingmell may be climbed, and thence to the Pikes; or Lingmell Gill, S. of Lingmell, may be ascended to the Pikes. From Eskdale the Pikes may be reached by Cam Spout and Mickledore, which is the gap, bridged by a narrow roof-top between the Pikes and Scafell. From Mickledore up the crags of Scafell there are three difficult approaches; the least difficult is the Lord's Rake (gully to right, with pinnacle). The Chimney is a gully to left, and the Broad Stand is the crag in the middle. These are rock climbs and are not safe for inexperienced and unaccompanied climbers. Scafell can be climbed from Cam Spout, bearing to left half-way up to Mickledore, or from the Burnmoor side, without difficulty.

The view from the top of the Pikes is not better than from many lower points. At sunset the Mourne Mountains in Ireland, about 115 m. away, are sometimes seen, N. of the Isle of Man, and on a clear day with favourable conditions, Snowdon to S.S.W., about 105 m.; but these are seen from others of the Lake mountains.

SCALEBEY A village 6 m. N.N.E. of Carlisle. The castle, ½ m. S., was built by Robert de Tilliol, 1307; besieged by the Parliamentary army (1648) and burnt; great concentric moats remain.

SCALE FORCE The tallest waterfall in the district, 125 ft. high, in the dark chasm on the S.W. side of Crummock Water, reached by path 2 m. from Buttermere village.

SCALES TARN *See* Saddleback.

SCANDALE A valley N. of Ambleside, approached by Low Sweden Bridge, leading up to High Sweden Bridge, whence a path goes up the head of the valley to Little Hart Crag (2,091 ft.) and over to Caiston Beck and Brothers Water. From the top of the hause Red Screes can be easily climbed.

SCARTH GAP Sometimes written Scarf Gap; the pass from the head of Ennerdale to Buttermere by a bridle-path (1,400 ft.).

SCREES The Wastwater Screes (*skridha*, in Icelandic, is a landslip) are the steep slopes of broken rock from the range of crags S. of the lake.

SEASCALE A former nineteenth-century seaside resort, now a dormitory settlement for Sellafield (*which see*). The Hall, bearing a date 1606 (though Pevsner suggests approx. 1700), was the manor house of the Senhouse family. Near Seascale Howe Farm is Grey Croft Circle, restored in 1949 after many of the stones had been buried in the nineteenth century by a local farmer.

SEATALLAN A mountain (2,266 ft.) N.W. of Wastwater, on the side of which is Greendale Tarn.

SEATHWAITE At the head of Borrowdale. Notorious as the wettest place in England with an average annual rainfall of 131 inches.

SEATHWAITE A scattered village in the valley of the Seathwaite Beck, issuing from Seathwaite Tarn, W. of the Old Man, ½ m. long, 1,210 ft. above sea, near disused copper-mines. The church, 7½ m. from Broughton-in-Furness, or 6 m. (and 1,900-ft. climb) from Coniston by Walna Scar, has the grave of 'Wonderful Walker'—the Rev. Robert Walker, born here 1709, curate 1735 or 1736, died here 1802 (*see* p. 49). Church rebuilt in 1874. On either bank of Longhouse Gill, going up towards Dow Crags, are ruins of ancient dwellings.

SEATOLLER A hamlet in Borrowdale at the foot of Honister Hause; pretty bridge, wood and crag scenery.

SEATON Two places of this name; one is 1 m. N. of Bootle, with ruins of a Benedictine nunnery, thirteenth century, formerly called Lekely. The other Seaton is a village N. of Workington.

SEAT SANDAL The southernmost summit of the Helvellyn range (2,415 ft.), easily climbed from Dunmail Raise or Grisedale Tarn.

SEBERGHAM (Pronounced locally Sebberam) A parish in Inglewood on the Caldew, spelt Seburgham in the thirteenth century; said to have been first settled by the hermit William of Wastall (Wasdale) in the twelfth century. His cell is supposed to have been on the site of St Mary's church, which contains monuments to the Dentons and to Josiah Relph, the poet, born here 1712, and died here 1743. The Rev. Thomas Denton (1724–77) was also a poet, native of Sebergham. Warnell Hall, originally a pele, was acquired by the Dentons, 1496, and sold by them (1774) to the Lowthers.

SEDBERGH Formerly in Yorkshire but annexed by Cumbria in 1974. Sedbergh is closely connected with the Westmorland Lune Valley in which it lies, although it is situated within the Yorkshire Dales National Park. Castle How is an early burg. The Grammar School, founded under Henry VII in 1525, is now a modern public school. Ingmire Hall is an ancient mansion.
    North of Sedbergh are Arrant Haw (1,989 ft.), Great Dummocks (2,150 ft.), and the Calf (2,220 ft.); S.E. is the secluded valley of Dent (p. 9).

SELLAFIELD On the coast north of Seascale (*which see*). British Nuclear Fuel's reprocessing plant (formerly called Windscale) and nearby Calder Hall, the world's first industrial nuclear power station, opened in 1956. John Dalton, the pioneer of the atomic theory, was born just 20 miles away at Eaglesfield (*which see*).

SELSIDE A scattered township N. of Kendal. The Hail, ancient seat of the Thornburghs, thought to be fourteenth century but altered in the sixteenth century.

SERGEANT MAN A summit (2,414 ft.) on the moorland heights N. of Stickle Tarn.

SETMURTHY A chapelry N.E. of Cockermouth. S.W. of the church is Elva Hill; a stone circle on Elva Plain. Higham Hall, an early nineteenth-century 'Strawberry Hill Gothic' mansion, is Cumbria's Adult Education Residential College.

SHAP Former market town (charter 1687) with nearby granite quarries. The Market Hall is now the public library. Ancient name was Heppe. At Gunnerkeld Bottom, $1\frac{1}{4}$ m. N.N.E. of the church, are the remains of a large stone circle. Similarly, $1\frac{1}{4}$ m. S.S.E. of the church are the remains of another circle and an avenue of standing stones, now partly covered by the railway embankment. The Thunder Stone and the recently re-erected Goggleby Stone are remnants of the avenue.

Shap Abbey, St Mary Magdalene's, is 1 m. W. of the village, a house of the White Canons (Premonstratensian) removed here from Preston Patrick (*which see*) about 1199, suppressed in 1540. The ruins are those of a thirteenth-century church, with the western tower of approximately 1500. Adjoining the S. transept was the vestry; next to which and opening on to the cloister was the chapter house with dormitory over it and extending over the calefactory, where the canons could sit at fires in cold weather. The frater (dining hall) was S. of the cloisters, over cellars, and W. of the cloister were store-rooms with guest-chambers above. Off the S.E. corner of the group of buildings was the infirmary. A few grave-slabs still remain. At Keld, $\frac{1}{2}$ m. S., is a fifteenth- or sixteenth-century chapel owned by the N.T. At West Farm Prince Charlie stayed 17th December, 1745, just a few hours ahead of 'Butcher' Cumberland. Curious date stone on a house at the N. end of the village—'Tho. Cooper A.M. 5815'; assuming Bishop Ussher's date for the Creation to be 4004 B.C., this gives a date of 1811 for the house.

SHAWK BECK Sometimes written Shalk, Choke or Chalk, rises near Caldbeck, and joining the Wiza near Drumleaning forms the Wampool; anciently the W. boundary of Inglewood. The quarries of freestone were worked by the Romans; the Latin inscription is now gone.

SHOULTHWAITE CASTLE One and a quarter m. S. of Shoulthwaite Farm in Naddale, on an isolated rock in a deep valley between Thirlmere and High Seat. The neck of land joining the castle rock with the side of the hill has a triple rampart crossing it. A well and bits of freestone have been found here; tradition makes it a retreat in times of invasion.

SIDE PIKE The sharp peak (1,187 ft.) between Great Langdale Head and Blea Tarn. Excellent view of Langdale Pikes.

SILLOTH Quiet seaside resort on the Solway estuary. Originally planned as a port for Carlisle; railway, 1856, and dock 1859, but the town never fully met expectations. Near Wolsty Hall, S. of the town, some oval enclosures and hut circles have been identified from the air; probably pre-Roman.

SIZERGH The ancient hall of the Stricklands since 1239, 3 m. S.S.W. of Kendal. Nothing remains of the thirteenth-century building; the present castle is constructed round a pele tower of about 1360, with fifteenth-century and Elizabethan wings. One of the most impressive houses in Cumbria; 'No other house in England has such a wealth of Early Elizabethan woodwork of high quality' — Pevsner. N.T. open to the public.

SKELSMERGH Anciently Skelmerserge, 'the dairy of the shed by the mere.' A parish 2 m. N.N.E. of Kendal. Skelsmergh Hall was a fifteenth-century pele tower of the Leyburne family; sixteenth- and seventeenth-century additions.

SKELTON A parish 6 m. N.W. of Penrith. Hardrigg Hall, formerly seat of the Southaiks, was built round a pele, now in ruins.

SKELWITH A village on the Brathay, 3 m. W. of Ambleside; Force, $\frac{1}{4}$ m. above the bridge (path by the N. bank). Loughrigg Tarn and Elterwater are close by.

SKIDDAW A mountain (3,058 ft.) in the Skiddaw slate formation. Climbed from Keswick in about six hours, up and down, easy walking; an early morning start is best to avoid the sun on one's back during the ascent. View embraces Criffel and the Scottish hills and chief lake mountains. The forest of Skiddaw is the wild bare mountain land to N.E. (see p. 117 and Keswick).

SKINBURNESS A village near the Grune (Groyne) Point, at the N. of the Holme; anciently Skynburgh. Here Edward I collected a fleet for the invasion of Scotland, and granted a market-charter to the place; but the harbour and town were destroyed by sea 1301. See Newton Arlosh.

SKIRWITH A village 3 m. E.S.E. of Langwathby. Church built 1859 with a short spire to withstand the fierce Helm wind. 'The Abbey,' an early nineteenth-century house, is said to be on the site of a religious house, supposed to have been of the Templars.

SMALL WATER A tarn in a deep hollow (1,484 ft. above sea) on the N. side of Nan Bield Pass.

SNITTLEGARTH Between Uldale and Torpenhow, S. of which is an oblong moat enclosing a raised platform, site of the fourteenth-century manor house of the Tilliols.

SOCKBRIDGE A hamlet 2 m. S.W. of Eamont Bridge. Old hall, formerly seat of the Lancasters, has lost its pele (removed about 1825), but has late fifteenth-century hall, butteries, and kitchen with 'corbie-step' gable and octagonal chimney, and on the S. side Elizabethan building with wainscot and plaster-work ceiling.

SOULBY A village between Pooley Bridge and Dacre.

SOULBY Anciently Sulleby, a parish on the Eden between Great Musgrave and Crosby Garrett. Church built about 1665 by Sir Philip Musgrave.

SOUTHERFELL *See* p. 119.

SPRINKLING TARN The source of the Derwent (1,960 ft. above sea) under crags of Great End.

STAINMOOR The pass (1,436 ft.) over the Pennines—Roman road and ancient routeway. Maiden Castle was a Roman fort on the road built in the second century and occupied until the late fourth century. At the summit of the pass, $1\frac{1}{2}$ m. above Maiden Castle, are the remains of a Roman marching camp and to the right the Rey (Rere) Cross, in the eleventh century the boundary between Scotland and England, probably erected in the tenth century as a grave monument; re-erected in 1887. The area is currently (1987) under threat from road-widening schemes.

STAINTON A village in the parish of Dacre. At Kirkgarth there have been ancient buildings and burials.

STAINTON N. of Corney, has many cairns and ancient enclosures on the fell. S. of Barnscar.

STAINTON A hamlet in Low Furness with ancient hall and cockpit on the green to E.

STAKE PASS Bridle-path from Rosthwaite to Borrowdale through Langstrath over the ridge (1,581 ft.) of the depression between the mass of the Langdale Pikes and that of Bowfell; descending into Mickleden to Dungeon Gill.

STANLEY GILL *See* Dalegarth.

STANWIX A suburb of Carlisle, N. of the Eden. The churchyard and vicarage grounds on the site of a Roman camp, housing a cavalry unit of 1,000 men. (pp. 92–3).

STAVELEY-IN-CARTMEL A hamlet at the foot of Windermere near Newby Bridge.

STAVELEY-IN-KENDAL i.e. in Kent-dale: a village at the mouth of Kentmere valley, formerly an important centre for bobbin manufacture, market town in the time of Edward III. St James's Church has glass by Burne-Jones.

STEEPLE A mountain (2,769 ft.) with great crags, forming the W. part of the Pillar mountain; ascended from Windy Gap, between the Pillar and Steeple.

STICKS HAUSE A pass (2,450 ft.) from Legberthwaite to the former Greenside lead mines and Glenridding, over the N. part of the Helvellyn range.

STOCKDALEWATH A village on the Roebuck, S.E. of Rose Castle; the three ancient 'camps' have now disappeared.

STOCK GILL FORCE Waterfall at Ambleside in broken cascades for about 100 ft.

STOCKLEY BRIDGE A lonely bridge 1 m. S. of Seathwaite in Borrowdale, at the junction of Grains Gill (leading to Sprinkling Tarn) and Taylor's Gill (leading to Styhead).

STONETHWAITE A quaint hamlet in a branch valley of Borrowdale, 1 m. S. of Rosthwaite.

STRANDS *See* Nether Wasdale: a village between Gosforth and Wastwater. The Nether Wasdale Nature Trail, a $3\frac{1}{2}$ m. walk, begins near the village.

STRICKLAND Great and Little Strickland are villages between Clifton and Shap. The church of Little Strickland has a tablet with Latin verses on Fletcher of Strickland, 1695, also old oak seats.

STRIDING EDGE The arête or ridge running E. from Helvellyn, S. of Red Tarn (*see* p. 126).

STYHEAD The pass between Borrowdale and Wasdale Head; bridle-path from Seathwaite by Stockley Bridge, 1 m., then $1\frac{1}{2}$ m. steep climb past Taylor's Gill (waterfalls) to Styhead Tarn (1,430 ft. above sea), and $\frac{1}{2}$ m. further to the summit (1,600 ft.). Hence a rough path of $2\frac{1}{2}$ m. leads steeply down under the Great Gable, beside Lingmell Beck to Wasdale Head. This was once a much-used pack-horse track. A path from Styhead Tarn leads S.E. via Sprinkling Tarn (1,960 ft.) to Esk Hause, whence Scafell Pikes are ascended, or descent S. into Eskdale can be made, or continuing S.E. past Angle Tarn and down Rossett Gill into Mickleden, and Great Langdale.

SUNBIGGIN A village $1\frac{1}{4}$ m. N.E. of Raisbeck, with tarn to E. On the scar above are tumuli and Castle Fold, an enclosure and fort, said to be a pele-garth used for safeguard in border forays. Also written Sunbegin.

SUNBRICK A hamlet in Furness between Urswick and Bardsea. Double stone circle $\frac{1}{3}$ m. E. on the road to Bardsea. Appleby Slack, with ancient earthworks, is $\frac{2}{3}$ m. N. Foula, with ancient ramparts, is 1 m. W.S.W. From Birkrigg Common (400 ft.) good panorama of Furness. Near the hamlet is a Quaker burial ground where George Fox's widow, Margaret, is buried.

SUNKENKIRK A megalithic circle at Swinside on the fell between Duddon Bridge and Bootle. Also called the Swinside Stone Circle. The circle is the third largest (after Long Meg and Castlerigg), consisting of fifty-five stones (some gone), the largest 7 ft. high.

SWARTH FELL A summit (1,832 ft.) to S. of Moor Divock over which runs the Roman road known as High Street.

SWARTHMOOR The sixteenth-century hall is 1 m. S. of Ulverston; home of George Fox, the Quaker, who married Margaret, widow of Thomas Fell, the owner, and built a meeting-house near it, 1688. *See* Sunbrick. The Hall is administered by the Society of Friends and is open to the public. Troops under Martin Schwartz encamped on Swarthmoor, 1487, having landed at Piel to join Lambert Simnel's insurrection.

SWINDALE A valley between Haweswater and Shap. Old church, perhaps seventeenth century, and school adjoining, built 1703. John Hodgson, historian of Northumberland, was born here, 1780.

SWINSIDE The farm near which is Sunkenkirk (*which see*). Also a farm at Newlands (Keswick), and the hill between it and Portinscale. Also a place between Carrock Fell and Bowscale Tarn. Swindale and Swinside meant pastures for swine.

SWIRREL EDGE The ridge from Helvellyn between Red Tarn and Keppel Cove Tarn, by which (easy path) Helvellyn is ascended from Glenridding.

TALKIN A village and tarn, 1½ m. S. of Brampton. Talkin Tarn Country Park— 165 acres of woodland and pasture.

TARN HOWS A farm N.W. of Coniston but popularly the name of a tarn, one of the most visited and photographed sites in the Lake District. Visited by approximately ¾ million people each year, this must be one of the most frequented beauty spots in Britain. Owned by the N.T. and given as a memorial to Sir James and Lady Scott. Because of its altitude and shallowness, it often freezes over in winter and is popular with skaters.

TARN WADLING A tarn between Armathwaite and Hesket, drained about 1850, on the N. side of which is the site of Castle Ewain (*which see*).

TEBAY Former railway village and junction in the upper Lune valley. Nearby and close to the M6 motorway is Castle How, the remains of a motte-and-bailey.

TEMPLE SOWERBY A village between Penrith and Appleby. Church built in

1754, enlarged 1770; said to have belonged to the Order of the Knights Templar, hence the derivation of the name. The Order was suppressed in 1312. Acorn Bank is an early eighteenth-century manor house in the care of the National Trust; the house is let to the Sue Ryder Foundation, but the grounds and the herb garden, which contains the largest collection of culinary and medicinal plants in the north of England, are open to the public.

THIRLMERE A lake, formerly Leathes-water, from the family at Dalehead Hall, and earlier Brackmere. Since 1894 a reservoir, 3 m. long, $\frac{1}{4}$ m. broad, with nineteenth-century embattled buildings, and modern road all round, replacing the ancient road on the W., and the old road on the E. For some description of the surroundings *see* pp. 120–24.

THORNTHWAITE A village at the head of Bassenthwaite Lake, under the Crags of Barf (1,536 ft.) and Lord's Seat (1,811 ft.) and at the foot of the Whinlatter Pass to Lorton. The Forestry Commission's Whinlatter Visitor Centre is on Whinlatter Pass above the village.

THRELKELD A scattered village under Saddleback (*which see*) and until 1980, granite quarries, above which are ancient hut circles and cairns near an old pack-horse track leading to Wanthwaite. The church, rebuilt 1777, has two medieval bells. Annual sheepdog trials in August.

THUNACAR KNOTT A summit (2,351 ft.) on the moorland N. of Langdale Pikes.

THURSBY A village between Wigton and Carlisle. At Kirksteads, $\frac{1}{2}$ m. from the church, foundations were dug up in the eighteenth century, and it was argued that this had been a temple to Thor, whence the old name Thoresby; which, however (compare Kirkby Thore), may be for Thored's or Thorfins-by, as a howe near Crofton Hall bore the name of Torquin (i.e. a corruption of Thorfin), perhaps an early burg. The village was the birthplace of Thomas Bouch, the unfortunate engineer who built the ill-fated Tay Rail Bridge. Aerial photography has recently revealed settlements and rectangular field systems near the village.

TILBERTHWAITE A hamlet with quarries, some abandoned, 3 m. N. of Coniston. The path S. of the bridge, to left past quarries, leads to the Gill, a fine ravine.

TINDALE The E. part of Farlam parish; abandoned coal-pits and spelter works erected 1845. Tindale Tarn is a sheet of water $\frac{2}{3}$ m. long.

TIRRIL A village 2 m. S.E. of Eamont Bridge; Quaker's meeting, 1733, and graveyard where Charles Gough (p. 125) is buried.

TORPENHOW An ancient parish (pronounced Torpenno) S.W. of Aspatria; written in the twelfth century Thorpenhow, i.e. Thorfin's Howe: *see* Thursby.

Church, with Norman arches and capitals and early font. *See also* Caermote.

TORVER A scattered village $2\frac{1}{2}$ m. S.W. of Coniston. Church consecrated 1538, rebuilt 1884. On the moors to N.W., under Walna Scar and the Old Man, are ancient earthworks—the long dyke on Bleaberry Haws, ring embankment on Hare Crags, cairns, and circle.

TRIERMAIN A hamlet 3 m. W. of Gilsland, site of the castle of de Vaux of Triermain, licensed 1340. Mention is made of an eleventh-century church of wattles at 'Treverman.' Watch Hill, $\frac{1}{2}$ m. N., is a ring-fort.

TROUTBECK Scattered community near Matterdale. Close to the junction of A66 and A5091 are remains of a small Roman fort and two temporary camps, probably marching camps.

TROUTBECK A valley near Windermere between Wansfell and the Ill Bell range, with long, scattered village, old houses, church with window by Burne-Jones, William Morris and F. M. Brown. At the head of the valley is the Scots' Rake (*see* High Street), and in the valley bottom above the Tongue are remains of an ancient settlement. The village was grouped around a series of wells which still remain. Several seventeenth-century farm houses, including Town End, built in 1626 by George Browne, a yeoman farmer, and occupied by his family until 1944. Original furnishings. The house is owned by the N.T. and open to the public.

At the N. end of the village is 'The Mortal Man' Inn, so called from the sign, painted by Julius Caesar Ibbotson about 1800, with a lean and fat man, portraits of natives, and the rhyme:

> Thou mortal man, that lives by bread,
> How comes thy nose to be so red?
> Thou silly ass, that looks so pale,
> It is by drinking Sarah Birkett's ale.

Pevsner confuses this Troutbeck with the Troutbeck near Matterdale with erroneous results

ULDALE A village 1 m. N. of Overwater (*which see*), also Aughertree.

ULLOCK A village on the Marron. Crakeplace Hall, a sixteenth-century building, has a fine doorway, dated 1612.

ULLSCARTH A mountain (2,370 ft.) between Greenup Gill and Wythburn; sometimes written Ullscarf—*skarth* in Icelandic means mountain pass.

ULLSWATER One of the most beautiful and varied lakes in Cumbria. The 'three reaches' give it a serpentine shape, $7\frac{1}{2}$ m. long, greatest depth, 205 ft., greatest width, less than $\frac{3}{4}$ m., 476 ft. above sea level. The lake is legally a public highway and a 'steamer' service (i.e. diesel!) operates between Glenridding, Howtown and Pooley Bridge (*which see*). *See also* Gowbarrow, Aira Force, and Patterdale.

ULPHA A chapelry W. of Duddon. The Old Hall, $\frac{1}{2}$ m. up Holehouse Gill, is a ruined sixteenth-century pele. In the ravine is the Lady's Dub, where a lady of the hall is said to have been drowned while fleeing from a wolf. Seventeenth-century chapel; wall paintings discovered during restoration in 1934. Unusual dated and initialled gate stoup near the lych gate—'J.G. 1766,' almost certainly the initials of John Gunson, a local farmer.

ULVERSTON A market town in Furness, with a thirteenth-century charter. The Ulvrestun of Domesday Book. The parish church of St Mary was founded in 1111. After the dissolution of Furness Abbey in 1537 and the disruption of Dalton's market by the plague of 1631, Ulverston began to flourish. Capitalizing on its position at the northern end of the Morecambe Bay cross-sands route to Lancaster, the town became, in the words of one writer, 'a pocket edition of the metropolis, mimicking its dissipation and copying its manners.' John Rennie's canal connecting the town with the sea was opened in 1796 but is now disused. The Hoad monument, N.E. of the town, was built in memory of a local worthy, Sir John Barrow (1764–1848) who became Secretary to the Admiralty, encouraged Arctic exploration, and was a founder of the Royal Geographical Society. Appropriately, it takes the form of a lighthouse. The town was overshadowed in the nineteenth century by the rise of Barrow (*which see*). Local industries include Glaxo Laboratories, manufacturing antibiotic drugs, and Cumbria Crystal.

UNDERBARROW A village, 3 m. W. of Kendal, under a limestone scar; church built 1708. *See* Cunswick, Crook.

URSWICK Great and Little Urswick are two villages 3 m. S.S.W. of Ulverston, between which is the medieval church of St Mary and St Michael; largely thirteenth century but enlarged in fourteenth century. Fragment of an Anglian cross with runic inscription and also a part of an Anglo-Scandinavian cross. Some excellent early twentieth-century woodcarving. Fifteenth-century Mater Dolorosa, much weathered, on the outside of the W. tower. Annual rush-bearing ceremony in September. At Skelmore Heads, above Great Urswick, is a small hill fort. The 'Stone Walls' near Little Urswick are the remains of an Iron Age or Romano-British settlement.

WABERTHWAITE A hamlet $1\frac{1}{2}$ N.E. of Eskmeals on the Esk, at the ancient wath or ford to Muncaster, with old church; pre-Norman cross-shaft re-erected in the churchyard, Anglian fragment in the vestry. The finest Cumberland sausage is made here! Barnscar (*which see*) is 2 m. E. of the church, and Devoke Water $1\frac{1}{2}$ m. beyond. Pretty valley of the lower Esk from the church upward. In the sand dunes at Eskmeals, extensive traces of Neolithic and Bronze Age habitation have been found.

WAITBY A village $1\frac{1}{2}$ m. S.W. of Kirby Stephen, anciently Waltheof's-by, said to have been a market town, with chapel of which Early English ruins have been discovered. Complex dyke and lynchet system near village..

WALLA CRAG *See* Derwentwater.

WALNA SCAR The pass over the S. end of the Coniston Fells to Seathwaite in the Duddon Valley. *See* Coniston.

WALNEY ISLAND The long island off the S.W. coast of Furness; 8 m long and 1 m. broad. Biggar and North Scale are two villages originally established as granges or home farms of Furness Abbey. The monastery also built Biggar Dyke, a medieval attempt at land reclamation from the sea. Vickerstown is an early twentieth-century planned dormitory town for Barrow shipyard workers. Bird reserve at the S. end of the island, one of the rare English nesting grounds of the eider duck. Also lighthouse built in 1790 by the Port of Lancaster. Nature reserve at the N. end of the island; extensive evidence of Mesolithic and Neolithic man. The very rare Walney geranium, *Geranium lancastriense*, grows in the sand dunes. *See also* Barrow and Piel Castle.

WALTON A village, $3\frac{1}{2}$ m. N. of Brampton, on the Roman Wall. Castlesteads (in the garden of a mansion in S.S.W.) was a fort which has yielded many remains. East of Walton the road follows the Wall, off and on, by Banks, Wallbowers, and Birdoswald to Gilsland, 9 m.

WAMPOOL A river (anciently Wathenpool) formed by Shawk Beck and Wiza near Drumleaning, and falling into the Moricambe Bay near Kirkbride.

WANSFELL A mountain (1,581 ft.) with fine views of Windermere and mountains, easily climbed from Troutbeck, Low-wood, or Stock Gill.

WARCOP A village in the Eden Valley 2 m. W. of Brough, anciently Warthecop, i.e. Beacon Hill. The Roman road, from Carlisle and over Stainmoor, ran through the parish. Castlehill and Kirkstead, S.E. of the village, are said to be sites of a castle and chapel. Warcop Hall is Elizabethan with Georgian and Victorian additions. Brough Hill fair is held in this parish. Annual Rush Bearing ceremony at the church.

WARWICK A village on the Eden, $1\frac{1}{2}$ N. of Wetheral, anciently Warthewyk. The church of St Leonard is remarkable as a Norman building with an apse, noted by Pevsner as 'the most memorable Norman village church in Cumberland.' Aglionby, the seat of a Norman settler, Agullon, is $1\frac{1}{4}$ m. W.

WASDALE The valley of Wastwater, a lake nearly 3 m. long, $\frac{1}{2}$ m. broad, 200 ft. above sea, and 260 ft. deep. At the foot of the lake is Nether Wasdale (*which see*). The S.E. side of the lake is walled by the Screes (1,983 ft.), and on the N.W. are Middlefell (1,908 ft.), with Greendale Tarn, Seatallan (2,266 ft.), and Yewbarrow (2,058 ft.), behind which are Low Tarn and Scoat Tarn, under the Red Pike (2,707 ft.), and Steeple (2,687 ft.). From the head of the lake two great and two small valleys diverge; to N. runs Mosedale, with the Black Sail Pass, between Yewbarrow and Kirkfell (2,631 ft.); to N.E. runs the valley of Lingmell Beck up to Styhead Pass, between Great Gable (2,949 ft.) and Lingmell (2,649 ft.). Lingmell Gill runs E. from the Waterhead up to Mickledore, between Scafell and the Pikes; and S. a depression between the Screes and Scafell leads over to Burnmoor. In the middle of the flat valley bottom (Wasdale Head) is the little old church, and Wastwater Hotel. Will Ritson, a celebrated wrestler and wit, was landlord until 1879; died 1890, aged 83, at Strands. The crags of Scafell and Gable make Wasdale Head a favourite place with climbers. Undoubtedly the most Scandinavian of all the Lake District valleys.

WASDALE A small valley S.W. from Shap Wells.

WATENDLATH A tarn and hamlet on the fell between Borrowdale and Thirlmere, $1\frac{1}{2}$ m. N.E. of Rosthwaite by bridle-path; 3 m. S. of Barrow on Derwentwater by road. The tarn is 847 ft. above sea. Blea Tarn is $1\frac{1}{4}$ m. S.S.E. on the open moor, 1,562 ft. above sea, under crags rising to Ullscarth 2,370 ft. Hence Wythburn may be reached via Harrop Tarn and Dob Gill in about 2 m. The hamlet was used by Hugh Walpole as the setting for his novel *Judith Paris*. All the farms are owned by the N.T.

WATERCROOK On the Kent, 1 m. S. of Kendal; site of a Roman fort (p. 10), probably built just before A.D. 100.

WAVER A river rising near Caldbeck and running past Ilekirk and Waverton to Moricambe.

WESTWARD A parish which was formerly the hunting ground of the lords of Allerdale, W. of Inglewood. In it was the hermitage of St Hilda (*see* Ilekirk Hall). The present parish church is 3 m. S. of Wigton; monuments of the Barwis family, among them that of the 'Great Barwis,' died 1684, who could walk round his court at Ilekirk Hall carrying his wife at arm's length in one hand and a great stone in the other. The Roman road from Maryport to Carlisle passed through the parish, and at Old Carlisle (*which see*) was a great fort and civil settlement, known as Palmcastre in medieval times. Clea Hall, in the eighteenth century, was the seat of a family of Fletchers, previously of Cockermouth Castle.

WETHERAL A village 4 m. E. of Carlisle. Railway viaduct 100 ft. high, over the

Eden; this is the subject of Wordsworth's sonnet, 'Motions and Means,' etc. Another of the sonnets describes the monument of Mrs Howard by Nollekens, in Wetheral Church (p. 100), where are also effigies of Sir Richard Salkeld and his wife, about 1500. The Priory, founded about 1110 by Ranulf Meschines, was on the steep bank of Eden, opposite Corby; ruins of fifteenth-century gatehouse remain. Hence to S. by path along the bank to the caves of St Constantine (p. 100), possibly used as hiding places for the Priory's treasures during Scottish raids in the fourteenth century.

WET SLEDDALE Small valley running S.W. from Shap Reservoir constructed by Manchester Corporation.

WHARTON Ancient seat of the Whartons, 2 m. S. of Kirkby Stephen. The hall consists of a pele, about 1415–18, with hall and chambers attached (N.E. of the court); ruins of a banqueting-hall and kitchen, built by Sir Thomas (1493–1568), raised to the peerage for services at the battle of Sollom Moss, 1542; his effigy is in Kirkby Stephen church (p. 142). The gate-house is dated 1559; in the chamber on the left it is said that bloodhounds were kept, and the rooms to left of the gate-house were a priest's lodging, and on the N.W. side of the court adjoining them was the chapel. This and the gallery between it and the pele were Elizabethan, also the ruined tower at the N.W. angle outside.

WHICHAM A village under Black Combe (1,969 ft.) at the mouth of this pretty little valley of Whicham, running up to the Baystone Bank Reservoir; at the back of the hill which heads the valley is Sunkenkirk (*which see*).

WHINLATTER The pass (1,040 ft.) between Keswick and Lorton, between Grisedale Pike and Lord's Seat; *see also* Thornthwaite.

WHITBECK A hamlet between Whicham and Bootle on ancient road at the foot of Black Combe. At Monk Foss, 1 m. N. above, a low green hill, is the Cockpit (so called), which may have been originally fishponds of the Furness monks, who had a grange here.

WHITEHAVEN Port and industrial town on the W. coast. For early history *see* pp. 70–1. In 1725 Daniel Defoe described the town as 'grown up from a small place to be very considerable by the coal trade, which is increased so considerably of late, that it is now the most eminent port in England for the shipping of coals except Newcastle and Sunderland, and even beyond the last, for they wholly supply the city of Dublin, and all the towns of Ireland on that coast.' This neatly encompasses the reasons for Whitehaven's development—coal from the local seams and the ease with which Dublin and the east coast of Ireland could be supplied by water. By the middle of the eighteenth century, Whitehaven had emerged as a serious rival to both Bristol and Liverpool; shipbuilding and the ancillary trades such as rope and sail making grew rapidly and the warehouses of Whitehaven were stocked with rum from the West Indies and tobacco from Virginia. However, unlike Liverpool and Bristol, Whitehaven did not possess an economically productive hinterland and by the early decades of the nineteenth century, geographical factors asserted themselves and the economic decline began. Many of the graceful town houses reflect the prosperity of the town during its golden age; St James's church (1753) has a fine Georgian interior and an altarpiece given by the third Earl of Lonsdale and thought to have come from the Escorial. St Nicholas's church (1693) was sadly damaged by fire in 1971, and only the tower now remains. George Washington's grandmother is buried in the churchyard. And another hero of the United States, John Paul Jones, made a lightning raid on the port in 1778 and managed to spike 36 cannon at the fort and battery but the action was really no more than a skirmish. The raid and other aspects of Whitehaven's maritime past are recalled in the town's Museum. Although Whitehaven's fortunes were based on coal, the last mine in the area closed in March 1986 and employment is now largely based on the chemical industry, light industrial plants and the Sellafield complex, ten miles to the S.

WHITELESS PIKE A mountain (2,159 ft.) N. of Buttermere village, behind Rannerdale Knotts.

WHITESIDE PIKE A mountain (1,302 ft.) E. of Long Sleddale, on the W. side of which is a prehistoric settlement.

WIGTON A market town in 1262, and still a centre of trade in agricultural produce for mid-Cumberland. Church, said to have been built by Odard de Wigton, first baron, in the twelfth century, with materials from the Roman camp at Old Carlisle (*which see*), and rebuilt 1788, contains monuments of the seventeenth and eighteenth centuries. Distinguished natives of the parish were Ewan Clark, the Cumbrian poet (1734–1811), and R. Smirke, R.A., the artist (1752–1845), father of Sir R. Smirke, R.A., the architect of Lowther Castle, Eden Bridges, Carlisle court-houses, etc., and Melvyn Bragg, the novelist and writer.

WINDERMERE Resort town and England's largest lake. The town developed around the small hamlet of Birthwaite when the railway arrived from Kendal in 1847. Originally the intention had been for the line to carry on to Ambleside and Keswick but this plan was thwarted by the objections of what would now be known as the environmentalist lobby. Ruskin joined the crusade and, writing of the tourists who would surely come by excursion trains, declared 'I don't want to let them see Helvellyn when they are drunk.' The Windermere Hotel was opened in 1847 and this was followed by a rash of villas and mock-Gothic houses of the *nouveaux riches* who discovered that it was possible to commute to Manchester on the early train and be back in time to enjoy dinner overlooking the lake.

The lake is 130 ft. above sea level, 10 m. long and nearly 1 m. broad between

Miller Ground and Belle Grange. Glacial erosion, which formed the lake, has created two basins, the N. one 219 ft. deep and the S. one 134 ft. deep, separated by a shallow area and the central group of islands which include Belle Isle (*which see*), Thompson's Holme, The Lilies of the Valley, Lady Holme, on which there used to be a chapel of the Virgin Mary, and Crow Holme. S. of the islands is the ferry; here the lake is barely 560 yards wide and the main ferry service has operated here for centuries. In October 1635 some 48 or 49 wedding guests returning from a celebration in Hawkshead, were drowned when the ferry sank. Today the ferry operates as a foot and vehicle vessel. Windermere is the most popular of all the lakes; over 1,500 boats use it at the height of the season, from passenger 'steamers' and motor boats to yachts and sailboards. Speed restrictions are in operation in several areas. Passenger service in summer between Lakeside, Bowness, and Waterhead (Ambleside) by the ships of the Windermere Iron Steamboat Company. *See* Bowness-on-Windermere, Ambleside, Newby Bridge, Brockhole.

WINDSCALE *See* Sellafield.

WINDY GAP The high pass (2,500 ft.) between Wasdale Head and Ennerdale via Mosedale and between the Pillar and Steeple.

WINSTER A river rising near Bowness and flowing between Cartmel Fell and Witherslack into Morecambe Bay at Castlehead, Grange; it divides Lancashire from Westmorland. The village of Winster occupies the upper part of the valley (p. 15). Jonas Barber, the clockmaker, lived here in the seventeenth century; succeeded by Philipson of Winster. William Pearson (1780–1856), naturalist, poet, and friend of Wordsworth, lived at Borderside. The writer Arthur Ransome lived for some years at Low Ludderburn.

WINTON A village 1 m. N.N.E. of Kirkby Stephen, the birthplace of Dr John Langhorne, translator of Plutarch, and of Dr Richard Burn (*see* Orton).

WITHERSLACK A parish between the limestone scar of Whitbarrow and the river Winster. The prettily situated church was built about 1671 under the will of John Barwick, Dean of St Paul's and a native of the parish. The Hall was once a seat of the Earl of Derby; the manor was forfeited by the Harringtons after the battle of Bosworth, and given to Sir T. Broughton of Broughton Tower. He took part in Lambert Simnel's rebellion, 1487 (*see* Swarthmoor and Piel Castle), after which he is said to have lived in concealment in the woods at Witherslack. The manor was then given to the first Earl of Derby. The Witherslack Viking sword was found locally; it is now in the Kendal Museum.

WIZA A river rising near Rosley, flowing past Wigton, and joining the Shawk Beck to form the Wampool.

WOLSTY CASTLE The site, at which foundations only remain, is 2 m. S. of Silloth. The castle was built in the thirteenth century by Holm Cultram Abbey, as Piel Castle was by Furness, to protect their sea board. After the dissolution Wolsty Castle was held by a branch of the Chambers family of the Holme, and was ruined by T. Fitch, Cromwellian governor of Carlisle.

WORKINGTON An ancient port and industrial town on the coast at the mouth of the Derwent; for early history, *see* pp. 82–3. Workington began to export coal before 1650, but in 1676 the superficial deposits had been exhausted, and the place decayed. About 1770 the example of Whitehaven (*see* pp. 70–1) induced the Curwens to revive coal-mining at Clifton, with steam-pumps to enable them to get at the deeper seams. Sir James Lowther also opened a mine there, and laid down a tramway to the harbour; but the Lowther mines were suddenly closed in 1781 after yielding about two million tons. The Curwens continued mining, and about the year 1800 had nine pits at work, giving annually about 100,000 tons, 50,000 more being raised by others in the neighbourhood. In 1837 occurred the great flooding of three pits which had been carried out under the sea. Other industries have also been carried on at different times; despite considerable reductions, the steel-rail plant continues in production and the Thames Board Mill produces cardboard packaging based on thinnings from local forests. Sadly, Workington Hall, the seat of the Curwens, is now a ruin.
For the Roman camp, hall and church, *see* pp. 82–3.

WOTOBANK A hamlet on the Ehen, N. of Beckermet, near which is an artificial mound, perhaps an early fort. The story, as commonly told, is to the effect that a lady of Beckermet was here killed by a wolf (*see* Ulpha), and the lament, 'Woe to thee, Bank!' became the name of the place; but an early form of the name was Wodabank.

WRAY At Low Wray, between Claife Heights and Brathay, a turreted and battle-mented castle was built, 1840–7, by Dr James Dawson, a Liverpool surgeon. It cost £60,000. Now owned by N.T. Public access to grounds and lake shore.

WREAY A village S. of Carlisle. Church rebuilt 1842 in a remarkable and unusual form by Sarah Losh.

WRYNOSE The pass (1,270 ft.) anciently Wreneshals or Wrene-hause (the pass of the wild stallion), between Little Langdale and the Duddon Valley; a steep road, 4 m. from Fell Foot to Cockley Bridge. On the summit of the pass is the Three Shire Stone, or Brandreth, marking the point where the boundaries of Cumberland, Lancashire, and Westmorland formerly coincided. The Roman road from Ambleside to Hardknott and Ravenglass can be traced on the pass.

WYTHBURN All that now remains of the former hamlet at the head of Thirlmere is the small church built in 1640 and restored in 1872. A car park has been opened behind the church for the convenience of walkers wishing to ascend Helvellyn.

WYTHOP A township between Embleton and Bassenthwaite Lake. Splendid water-powered saw-mill and exhibition of wood-working machinery.

YANWATH That is, Eamont-wath (ford), a fourteenth-century pele with fifteenth-century additions forming Yanwath Hall. It was built about 1322 by John de Sutton; soon after 1500 it came by marriage to the Dudleys and in 1671 it passed into the hands of the Lowthers. It is one of the finest peles in England.

YEWBARROW The mountain (2,058 ft.) W. of Wasdale Head.

YEWDALE The valley N. of Coniston, under Lang Crags, the White Lady (waterfall seen only in wet weather, 500 ft. high down the crag), Yewdale Crag, and Raven Crag, the sharp rock rising above High Yewdale farm. At Yew Tree farm is one of the finest so-called 'spinning galleries' in the Lake District. Behind High Yewdale farm is a row of bee-boles (shelters for straw bee skips) forming part of a drystone wall.

SELECT BIBLIOGRAPHY

Since *The Lake Counties* was first printed in 1902, hundreds of books about the Lake District have been published. The list below includes some of the more recent additions to the literature.

ARMSTRONG, A. M., MAWER, A., STENTON, F. M. and DICKINS, B. *The Place Names of Cumberland*, (3 volumes), 1950, 1952

BAGLEY, J. J. *A History of Lancashire*, 1976

BALDWIN, J. R. and WHITE, I. D. (eds) *The Scandinavians in Cumbria*, 1985

BARNES, F. *Barrow and District*, 1968

BARRINGER, C. *The Lake District*, 1984

BLAKE, B. *The Solway Firth*, 1955

BOUCH C. M. L. and JONES, G. P. *The Lake Counties, 1500–1830*, 1961

BRADBURY, J. B. *A History of Cockermouth*, 1981

BRAGG, M. *Speak for England*, 1976, *Land of the Lakes*, 1983

BRUNSKILL, R. W. *Vernacular Architecture of the Lake Counties*, 1972

CLARE, T. *Archaeological Sites of the Lake District*, 1981

COLLINGWOOD, W. G. *Northumbrian Crosses of the Pre-Norman Age*, 1927, *Lake District History*, 1928

DAWSON, J. *Torver*, 1985

DICKINSON, J. C. *The Land of Cartmel*, 1980

EKWALL, E. *The Place Names of Lancashire*, 1922

FELL, C. *Early Settlement in the Lake Counties*, 1972

FFINCH, M. *Portrait of the Kent Valley*, 1983, *Portrait of the Howgills and the Upper Eden Valley*, 1982

GAMBLES, R. *Man in Lakeland*, 1975

GARLICK, T. *Romans in the Lake Counties*, 1970, *Hardknott Castle Roman Fort*, 1985

HARRIS, A. *Cumberland Iron*, 1970

HAY, D. *Whitehaven, An Illustrated History*, 1974

HIGHAM, N. *The Northern Counties to A.D. 1000*, 1986

HINDLE, B. P. *Roads and Trackways of the Lake District*, 1984

HOLMES, M. *Proud Northern Lady*, 1984

HUGILL, R. *Castles of Cumberland and Westmorland*, 1977

LEFEBURE, M. *Cumberland Heritage*, 1970

MARSHALL, J. D. *Portrait of Cumbria*, 1981, *Old Lakeland*, 1971

MARSHALL, J. D. and DAVIES-SHIEL, M. *The Industrial Archaeology of the Lake District*, 1969, *The Lake District at Work*, 1971

MARSHALL, J. D. and WALTON, J. K. *The Lake Counties from 1830 to the mid-nineteenth century,* 1981

MILLWARD, R. and ROBINSON, A. *The Lake District,* 1970 *Cumbria,* 1972

NICHOLSON, N. *The Lakers,* 1955, *Portrait of the Lakes,* 1963, *Greater Lakeland,* 1969

ORDNANCE SURVEY AND THE A.A. *The Lake District Leisure Guide,* 1984

PARKER, C. A. *The Gosforth District,* 1926

PARKER, J. *Cumbria, a Guide to the Lake District and its County,* 1977

PEARSALL, W. H. and PENNINGTON, W. *The Lake District: a Landscape History,* 1973

PEVSNER, N. *The Buildings of England series: Cumberland and Westmorland,* 1967, *North Lancashire,* 1969

POTTER, T. W. *Romans in North West England,* 1979

PROSSER, R. *Geology Explained in the Lake District,* 1977

ROLLINSON, W. *A History of Man in the Lake District,* 1975, *Life and Tradition in the Lake District,* 1987, *A History of Cumberland and Westmorland,* 1978, *Lakeland Walls,* 1978

ROWLING, M. *The Folk Lore of the Lake District,* 1976

ROYAL COMMISSION ON HISTORICAL MONUMENTS, ENGLAND. *Westmorland,* 1936

SANDS, R. *Portrait of the Wordsworth Country,* 1984

SHOTTER, D. C. A. *Roman North-West England,* 1984

SMITH, A. H. *The Place Names of Westmorland,* (2 volumes), 1967

TAYLOR, C. D. *Portrait of Windermere,* 1983

TAYLOR, S. *Cartmel People and Places,* 1955

THOMASON, D. and WOOF, R. *Derwentwater: The Vale of Elysium,* 1986

VICTORIA AND ALBERT MUSEUM. *The Discovery of the Lakes,* 1984

WALTON, J. E. *A History of Dalton in Furness,* 1984

WATERHOUSE, J. *The Stone Circles of Cumbria,* 1985

WYATT, J. *The Shining Levels,* 1973, *Reflections on the Lakes,* 1980, *The Lake District National Park,* 1987.

INDEX OF NAMES